Watsuji Tetsurō

Pilgrimages to the Ancient Temples in Nara

Koji Junrei

Watsuji Tetsurō

Pilgrimages to the Ancient Temples in NARA

Koji Junrei

Translated with an Introduction by
Hiroshi Nara

MERWIN ASIA

Portland, Maine

59 West St., Unit 3W,

Portland, ME 04102

USA

Distributed by the University of Hawai'i Press

Library of Congress Control Number: 2011939897

978-1-937385-10-1 (Paperback)

978-1-937385-11-8 (Hardcover)

Printed in the United States of America

The paper used in this publication meets the minimum requirements of the American National Standard for Information Services—Permanence of Paper for Printed Library Materials, ANSI/NISO Z39/48-1992

Contents

ACKNOWLEDGMENTS

During the preparation of my essay and translation, I have incurred many debts. I would like to express my appreciation to the Japan Iron and Steel Federation endowment at the University of Pittsburgh for allowing me to travel to Japan in the summer of 2010, to the Hewlett International Small Faculty Grant of the University Center for International Studies for helping me to defray the cost of images for this book, and to the Toshiba International Foundation for providing me a publication subsidy grant.

In Japan, I received a great deal of help from the Nara National Museum and the photographic studio Asukaen in Nara in obtaining suitable images for this translation. I am thankful to their assistance. I am grateful to Donald McCullum of UCLA for guiding me through the maze of securing permission from temples for publishing images. Hiroyuki Good, Japanese bibliographer of the East Asian Library of the University of Pittsburgh, was also very helpful. I would like to thank Brenda G. Jordan for going over the translation and to J. Thomas Rimer for giving me comments on the introductory essay and draft translation. Lastly, I would like to express deep gratitude to Doug Merwin of MerwinAsia for his willingness to work with this project and oversee all aspects of the production of this book.

INTRODUCTION TO THE TRANSLATION OF *KOJI JUNREI*

Hiroshi Nara

HISTORICAL BACKGROUND

Toward the end of Meiji and during the Taishō eras, approximately from 1890 to 1925, the seemingly wholesale, unbridled adoption of all things Western had ended and intellectuals were becoming increasingly more critical about the applicability of Western concepts and frameworks to Japan. There was a general yearning for a return to what were thought to be Japan's more traditional values, especially in the arts. Now the pendulum was swinging the other way. Even during this period of general leaning to more traditional values, however, intellectuals continued to study and absorb European ideas and test their applicability to Japan.

The Japanese public at the end of the nineteenth century and the beginning of the twentieth century, when Watsuji Testurō (1889–1960) was growing up, began to have a sense that Japan was finally and deservedly coming of age in the international political arena. By this time Japan has renegotiated unequal treaties with Western nations, and emerged victorious in two international conflicts, one against China's Qing dynasty (Sino-Japanese War, 1895–1896) and another against Russia (Russo-Japanese War, 1904–1905). By winning the war over China, the cause of which revolved around conflicting interests in the Korean peninsula, Japan gained control of Korea, the Liaodong peninsula, Taiwan, and some islands in the Taiwan Straight. Japan made clear that it was mightier than China militarily and that it was no longer under China's sole tutelage in international affairs and culture. Japan began to seek a role in the same geopolitical, colonial struggle in which Western nations were engaged.

The victory in the Russo-Japanese War had given Japan a firmer foothold on the continent because of its control of Korea. Japan's leaders, the young Watsuji included, thought that this conflict had been justified in order to put a stop to the West's aggression in colonizing Asia and that Japan was the only Asian nation that possessed not only military power but also Asia's mandate to push back against Western expansion. With a victory in the Russo-Japanese War, Japan's leaders felt that the country was rapidly becoming a first-class nation in the world. Many intellectuals and politicians held their heads high, swelling with pride, and they believed that Japan was making progress on the right path toward further expansion of Japanese influence abroad.

In broad terms, Watsuji's life and work may be said to embody this modern age's tension between West and East. Watsuji, like many others of the young elite who became the next generation of Japan's leaders, pondered the question of what it meant to be a human being in this difficult age, what it meant to be Japanese and Asian, how to live an authentic life, and what place an individual held in society. Watsuji also reflected and wrote prolifically on these and more wide-ranging questions about Japan's cultural and ethnic identity, its connection to China, to religious traditions, to the imperial system, to the relationship between people and their land, and to ethical attitudes, to name a few. When he passed away in 1960, he had authored more than thirty books and numerous articles on a broad range of subjects. Most of his writings have been collected in the twenty-seven volume *Watsuji Tetsurō Zenshū* (Tokyo: Iwanami Shoten, 1961–1963). By any yardstick, his contribution to the Japanese interwar intellectual scene was enormous.

Watsuji's legacy is mixed. He was one of the few philosophers of any importance in interwar Japan to conduct scholarly studies of Japan's cultural history from a highly critical point of view. At the same time, Watsuji was the only major philosopher who was never once apologetic about his views on the imperial system, and he steadfastly voiced support for it even after the war. The historian Robert Bellah describes Watsuji's inclination toward national particularism as "national narcissism."[1] Suspending judgment for the moment about whether particularism or narcissism, or both, characterizes Watsuji's legacy, it is nonetheless safe to say that Watsuji was one of main architects of prewar cultural nationalism. Such a label does not always carry a negative connotation. Cultural nationalism, so long as it did not become chauvinism, can be a healthy recognition of one's own country's culture and history. It is ironic that Japanese cultural nationalism probably would not have developed in the form that we understand it now had Watsuji not done so much spadework for it. Indeed, throughout his scholarly life, beginning from his earliest days in his philosophical career, Watsuji professed a love for Japan and promoted a very special place for Japanese culture.

A SKETCH OF WATSUJI'S LIFE

Watsuji Tetsurō (1889–1960) was a product of this period when Japan was coming of age. Like any other leading figure of Japan, he had to bear the cross of searching a way out of the difficulty that he and, by extension Japan, faced. In order to understand the background and development of his philosophical ideas in this milieu, a short sketch of some pivotal events, especially during his formative years, would be useful. Watsuji was born in a small farming village, Tobori, then outside of the city of Himeji, Hyōgo Prefecture on March 1, 1889, the year the Meiji Constitution was promulgated. The village is now part of the city of the same name. His father, a strict disciplinarian, was a taciturn and cheerless man at home, but a highly respected physician of Western medicine, who always maintained the highest standards of moral behavior. As a learned Confucian, he believed that "medicine was an act of benevolence (*i wa jinjutsu nari*)" and practiced this credo. He did not refuse to provide care on account of the patient's inability to pay; in fact, when he knew a family could barely feed themselves, much less pay for medical care, he would not only decline to accept a fee but also leave food at their doorway. He also accepted grains and other produce in lieu of payments.[2] He made house calls regardless of the weather, distance, or the time of the day. Watsuji's country upbringing and his father's thoroughgoing ethical attitude, as well as his calm demeanor and occasional temper, seemed to have rubbed off on the young Watsuji.[3]

After Watsuji finished his elementary school education, he attended Himeji Chūgakkō, a middle school located some six kilometers from his home. He could have lived in the school's dormitory but his mother asked him to commute from home because his help was needed there. He walked this distance to and from school for the next five-and-a-half years, rather than taking the available train. This was remarkable in view of the fact that he turned out to be sickly as an adult. Commuting to school took three to four hours every day and deprived him of social interaction with other children after school in Himeji and the village.

From early years, Watsuji demonstrated a great deal of sensitivity toward beautiful things and an enormous talent in academic subjects, especially in writing. A quiet and introspective boy, during his middle school days he found himself drawn to Shakespeare as well as to the romantic poems of Byron, Shelley, and Keats. He was strongly attracted to spiritual and fantastic worlds, which may account for an interest in his twenties in the philosophies of Nietzsche, Schopenhauer, and Kierkegaard.[4]

FIRST HIGHER SCHOOL

After finishing middle school, at age seventeen (1906), Watsuji moved to Tokyo to attend the First Higher School and received a first-rate education as one of Japan's most promising future leading intellectuals. Though prepared academically, Watsuji did not feel completely comfortable interacting with his classmates at the First Higher School—he was of provincial origin, introverted, and had a highly sensitive aesthetic disposition. Dormitory life proved to be somewhat challenging. As part of the customary hazing of underclassmen at the First Higher School, burly upperclassmen (usually school athletes) would "storm" dorm rooms. They would peel off the futon cover from sleeping students and shout homoerotic or offensive remarks. Some students were very intimidated by this and suffered a great deal psychologically, but even after appeals from students, the school did nothing to put a stop to it. Protesting these barbaric acts, Watsuji contributed a short essay in the school magazine calling for an immediate halt to this behavior. Later, he wrote in his autobiography that he felt terribly angry about the "storming," especially when he repeatedly heard, "*Shan da, shan da!* (He's a pretty boy!)."[5] This episode typifies Watsuji's personality—though he was sensitive and appeared compliant on the outside, he possessed a rebellious streak and resisted accepting standard practices and values uncritically. He was not one to cower under pressure; he would openly point out others' moral shortcomings when he thought he was on ethically higher ground.

THE TOKYO IMPERIAL UNIVERSITY AND GRADUATION

At age twenty (1909), Watsuji graduated from the higher school and entered the Tokyo Imperial University's philosophy department. He studied philosophy under Raphael von Koeber, whom he came to hold in the highest regard.[6] Soon after entering the university, Watsuji began to show a more serious interest in literature, poetry, and theater. He cultivated friendships with emerging literary figures such as Tanizaki Jun'ichirō (1886–1965), Kimura Sōta (1889–1950), Ōnuki Shōsen (a.k.a. Yukinosuke, 1887–1912), and the like, and participated in the founding of the literary magazine *Shinshichō* (second series). Watsuji also contributed to prominent literary magazines that pursued aestheticism, such as *Mita Bungaku* and *Subaru*. This period of his life, 1909 through 1912 or so, when he devoted much time to literature and drama was, according to his close friend Abe Yoshishige, Watsuji's "Sturm und Drang" period, a reference to Watsuji's devotion to literary activity (e.g., Goethe's romanticism) as well as to Watsuji's hedonistic lifestyle. This was his debauchery period when he tried his best to become a modern aesthete but determined in the end that he did not have the constitution for it. Watsuji wrote about this when discussing his literary friends in a passage in *Gūzō Saikō* (Resurrection of Idols, 1918), in which he recalled his struggle in choosing between *Sollen* (moral imperative; what one should do) and *Sein* (what is there now; pleasures of life):

> Why did I hate them so?
>
> I was not an aesthete like they were. I was only deceiving myself if I thought I'd thrown out *Sollen*. *Sollen* lived inside of me. To throw away *Sollen*, I would have thrown myself away. I couldn't deny that there lived an aesthete in me but I myself was not an aesthete. Thus, one year later, I came to a sense of deep remorse for acting as if I were one.[7]

At the end of this period of frustrating indecision and introspection of his inner self, Watsuji would choose to leave these friends and devote more time to the study of the ancient history of Japan. As part of the graduation requirements from the university, Watsuji wanted to submit a study of Nietzsche he had been writing, but Inoue Tetsujirō, his thesis supervisor, did not approve of this topic as a graduation thesis.[8] So Watsuji changed his topic and wrote about pessimism in Schopenhauer's philosophy in English so that Koeber could read it. He graduated in 1912 with a degree in philosophy and, in the same year, he married Takase Teru, a daughter of an import-export businessman in Yokohama.

This same year marked the end of the Meiji era and the beginning of Taishō, an era that many intellectuals sensed, if only vaguely, would be somehow be different from Meiji yet held unknown possibilities. A sense of anticipation was in the air. This was when Watsuji devoted a great deal of time to the study of Western philosophers, such as Nietzsche and Schopenhauer, in order to examine his own interiority. Contrary to the belief of some Watsuji scholars, this should not be thought of as Watsuji's Western phrase. Neither is it accurate to characterize it as Watsuji somehow "returning" to the study of Japan, as he had never left it. All philosophy students then were expected to study major European philosophers or ideas, so Watsuji's study of these figures was not at all unusual, merely expected. His studies of these Western philosophical figures served as case studies for an intense and agonizing introspection of his own inner being. When he emerged from this interior depth, he acknowledged that he held a special place in his heart for Japan. So it is more accurate to say that Watsuji held Japan's cultural history dear to his heart from a very early phrase of his formation as a scholar.

THE INFLUENCE OF SŌSEKI

In the development of Watsuji's scholarship and as a human being, Natsume Sōseki (1867–1916) cast a long shadow. Since his middle school days, Watsuji had always admired Sōseki. He even sat outside of the classroom window to listen to Sōseki lecture at the First Higher School. But it was around the time when Watsuji was still pondering which fork in the road to take—*Sollen* or *Sein*—that Sōseki emerged as a looming presence. Three years before Sōseki's death, in 1913, Watsuji made his acquaintance with Sōseki and began to visit his home, Sōseki Sanbō, for informal study sessions and socializing. There was a great deal of ceremony and deference involved in their relationship because of the distance in age and stature between these two people (in 1913, Sōseki was forty-six and Watsuji was twenty-four). In no time, however, Watsuji became a devotee of Sōseki and felt a very strong spiritual (and sometimes even somewhat romantic) love toward the literary figure.[9] Sōseki's presence was to have an immense impact on Watsuji's scholarship. In the last years of his life, Sōseki could no longer remain a believer in Western individualism, which he thought was too self-centered.[10] Watsuji also became critical of individualism and began to think about a different mode of being. One important thing that Watsuji took away from the association with Sōseki was his belief in ethical living. Sōseki believed, as a philosophy of life to live by, that one should pursue altruism and justice, setting one's own selfish interests aside in such pursuits. The path Sōseki advocated was not a self-serving, egotistic path for one's own benefit but an unselfish path sanctioned by Heaven's mandates (*sokuten kyoshi*). This maxim zcould just as well have come from Watsuji's own father, the first authority figure in Watsuji's life. Both men were telling him, in almost exactly the same words, how he should live his life. And just like Sōseki, Watsuji questioned the Western version of individualism and began seeking an alternate mode of human existence.[11] From early on, Watsuji defined the place for an individual in relation to family members, larger social units, and the emperor.[12]

THE CHOICE OF CULTURAL HISTORY

At a moral crossroads, Watsuji eventually chose *Sollen*, casting aside the rootless, decadent way of life of an aesthete. When he was twenty-five or so (about 1914), he began to harbor a strong dislike of his literary friends, as noted earlier, so much so that he distanced himself as much as possible to avoid interacting with them. As for the field of inquiry to which he could dedicate himself, he found himself increasingly drawn to the ancient cultural history of Japan. Watsuji's state of mind is mirrored in *Gūzō Saikō* (Resurrection of Idols, 1918), which was primarily a collection of short, highly introspective essays on a variety of topics. In this book Watsuji makes clear that his belief that Asia is a bona fide cultural sphere that should reaffirm its traditions and contributions to the world, and that Buddhism exerted a centripetal force that offered cohesion to Asian countries. Thus in spirit *Gūzō Saikō* may be thought of as a companion book to *Koji Junrei*.

There is another piece of writing of Watsuji that tells us a great deal about his state of mind. It is a letter addressed to his wife dated August 1, 1920 (when he was thirty-one). Watsuji wrote of his place in Japanese philosophy and touched on the defining spirit of the time. The occasion was his trip back to Himeji to undergo a physical examination for military service. He wrote on the train to Teru:

> The ancient history of Japan is not as great as that of Greece or other European nations. But I feel very attached to the ancient history of Japan, particularly when I think of the fact that this history represents our ancestor's souls and it runs, unbeknown to us, in our blood. And the other thing that interests me is that studying about Japan is not unlike excavating buried objects. The area in which we Japanese can do first-rate work may indeed be this research. The reason I say this is that, in the past, world culture invariably referred to Western culture, but, recently, Eastern culture has been gaining momentum, so much so that it now stands opposite Western culture. And in Asia, Japan is by far the most feared. Even if Japan were to fall into ruin some time in the future . . . Japan would no doubt be the talk of the world. And the culture of the Japanese people will leave conspicuous marks on world history. What culture has Japan produced thus far? In philosophy, it is no more than a copy of the West; the same applies more or less to the arts. Even the best in Japan cannot hold a candle to the best of the world. But, insofar as the study of Japanese culture is concerned, no Westerner is a match for the Japanese. In this field, a Japanese can do world-class research. So the more Japan is spoken about, the more this research will have enduring meaning.[13]

This letter was written a little over two years after Watsuji and his friends visited Nara's temples. *Koji Junrei* had come out a year earlier in 1919, and his next book, *Nihon Kodai Bunka*, was in the galley stage. In this letter to his wife, Watsuji might appear to be interested in only achieving fame, but that conclusion would be premature. In this passage, Watsuji acknowledged that Japanese philosophy had not yet contributed much to the world of philosophy, and he pledged his commitment to leaving a mark in cultural history that would endure the test of time. He had renounced selfish individualism—and this is borne out if one examines his entire life—and chosen Japan's cultural history as his field of scholarship.

This choice was seen as highly unusual and perhaps even ill-advised, as no other talented Japanese philosopher had chosen a topic that seemed so unrelated to Western philosophy as a serious field of inquiry. The prevailing expectation of any Japanese philosopher then was to study a Western philosophical figure or idea (e.g., Plato, German idealism). The Western orientation at imperial universities was so pervasive that works by Japanese philosophers were not even displayed in departmental libraries if such works were written in Japanese. Further, a philosopher was not taken seriously if he did not hold a position at an imperial university. Worse, unlike other systems and ideas from the West, such as political or social systems, which were more carefully evaluated before importation, philosophical thought in all stripes was brought from Europe with little modification. This situation with philosophy was encapsulated in a comment made by Karl Löwith, who taught philosophy at Tōhoku University during the prewar years. He remarked that the Japanese philosophical scene was like a department store of all things Western (from Plato to Heidegger) but held no organic connection to the Japanese people.[14] Thus, going against this entrenched practice of valuing Western philosophy and pursuing Japanese cultural history as an object of serious inquiry understandably was a great career risk for Watsuji.

For the several years after graduation from the Tokyo Imperial University, until 1920, Watsuji devoted himself to reading, thinking, and sometimes traveling (and writing for various publications to make a living). In 1915, at age twenty-six, he published a book on Søren Kierkegaard. *Koji Junrei*—which was his fourth book—signaled the end of his period of indecision. It was published by Iwanami Shoten in 1919, when Watsuji turned thirty.

PHILOSOPHICAL CAREER

This, therefore, was the chain of events leading to the publication of *Koji Junrei*. From here, Watsuji's professional life began to look up. He took a position at Tōyō University in 1920. In the same year he published *Nihon Kodai Bunka* (The Ancient Culture of Japan), which he himself thought represented a fine piece of scholarship. He took on editorial work for Iwanami Shoten's new philosophy journal *Shisō* (Thought) in 1921. Then, after three years at Tōyō University, and other teaching assignments at Tsudajuku and Keiō universities, he moved over to Hōsei University in 1922 (at age thirty-three). The list of the schools, as one can see, does not include any imperial universities. Although he was leaving his mark on cultural history, he was deemed undesirable at these universities due to his scholarly orientation. A change came in 1924. He was visited first by professor of religion Hatano Seiichi (1877–1950) and then by professor of philosophy Nishida Kitarō (1870–1945), both at the Kyoto Imperial University, inviting Watsuji to take a position at their institution. Watsuji declined their invitation politely, but Nishida was persistent. After a year of some serious and lengthy reflection and correspondences with Nishida, Watsuji accepted their invitation to take the position as professor of ethics. Watsuji had declined this offer initially fearing that he would not be able to continue his research in cultural history in the philosophy department at Kyoto (which at the time was awash with German idealism). After a year of negotiation, Nishida agreed to create a course of study in ethics, with the assurance that Watsuji would not have to give up his research in cultural history. During his time at Kyoto, Watsuji's concern about whether cultural history would be accepted as an academic discipline did not dissipate quickly. Various incidents there proved that his concern was not unfounded. Some students there were advised "not to become like Watsuji," a comment indicative of the concern that related to his specialty. Watsuji himself was conscious of such perceptions.[15]

ASPECTS OF *KOJI JUNREI*

Though *Koji Junrei* is written in a manner that makes it accessible to general readers, its background is quite complex. *Koji Junrei* is the place where Watsuji made intellectual as well as emotional connections among such elements as the place Watsuji sought for himself in society and where Japanese people and Japan's culture and history fit into a larger sphere in the world. As a man who came of age in the early twentieth century, he and other intellectuals agonized over the existential question of the meaning of life and how to live it. These very questions were originally posed in the West, but no satisfactory answers had yet been found. *Koji Junrei* was Watsuji's youthful attempt at laying bare his own answers to these fundamental philosophical questions. However, *Koji Junrei* also has more political and sinister aspects.

Watsuji writes in his own introduction to the revised edition in 1947 something that now may strike us as a bit odd. There he wrote: "By and by, the tenor of the times became such that the re-publication of this book would be imprudent." This passage was written in the late 1930s at the time when he was contemplating a revised edition of *Koji Junrei* and when the book had been out of print for some years, a period during which he had received numerous requests for it. Some requests, as he put it, came from "men who had been recently drafted into military service with little prospect of returning safely and who wished to visit Nara once in their life before deployment." What are we to make of this statement? Did the wartime authorities think that *Koji Junrei* was somehow harmful to the troops?

In hindsight, Watsuji's position on the role of Japan in world history is in line with that of interwar intellectuals who aligned themselves closely to militarism and the imperial household as the center of Japan as a nation. In fact if one reads Watsuji's lectures and writings, especially those written in the 1930s, his leaning to the political right cannot escape notice. Immediately after World War II, he was labeled a "nationalist," "conservative," and "official scholar for the imperial system," to name a few such labels.[16] Some called him the harbinger of *nihonjinron*.[17] So, one should expect that the reissuing of *Koji Junrei* would be celebrated by the authorities and not serve as a reason for the authorities to bring pressure to bear on Watsuji. The question is what was so imprudent about reissuing *Koji Junrei*.

ULTRANATIONALISTS OF GENRI NIHONSHA

There is ample evidence that Watsuji's writing became less welcome in the years leading up to World War II. Philosopher and Watsuji scholar Yuasa writes that, beginning in 1937 or 1938, when Watsuji was contemplating a revised edition of *Koji Junrei* at the suggestion of the publisher Iwanami Shigeo, right-wing politicians began taking issue with Watsuji's philosophy.[18] During World War II, his philosophy, especially his account of ancient imperial history in *Nihon Kodai Bunka*, in which the wording could be interpreted as suggesting instability in the imperial succession and presenting less than an impeccable personal character of an emperor, was branded as poisoned by Western thought.[19] The words and actions of his colleague Nishida, who was more politically active than Watsuji, were also monitored carefully. It can be assumed that the only welcome philosophy at that time would have been one in which the unbroken line of the imperial family was the true purveyor of Japanese culture and tradition (*kōkokushikan*) and one that described the Japanese culture as sui generis. For these reasons, ultranationalists such as Minoda Muneki (1894–1946) and Mitsui Kōshi (1883–1953) of the right-wing fundamentalist group Genri Nihonsha attacked *Nihon Kodai Bunka* and *Koji Junrei* in order to expose any offending descriptions. Though Watsuji's writing was never legally challenged as lese-majesty, it was certainly possible that ultra-rightists contemplated that idea seriously. For example, his colleague's scholarship was accused of this crime. In 1941, Watsuji was summoned to court to testify as a defense witness in a case involving Tsuda Sōkichi, a noted Waseda University professor of ancient Japanese history who was accused of lese-majesty. In particular, four books authored by Tsuda were being cited as blasphemous to the imperial family. Tsuda (1873–1961) was a major scholar of ancient Japanese history, who criticized using *Kojiki* and other ancient documents as reliable historical sources in the 1920s and consequently implied the instability of the ancient imperial throne. Hence, believers of *kōkokushikan*—the prevailing view of Japanese history as being centered around the imperial throne—took issue with Tsuda, who cast doubt on the historical accuracy of *Kojiki*.[20] Tsuda was known as an authoritative, highly influential scholar on Japan's ancient history, so much so that the news that he was being indicted for lese-majesty caused a no small stir in academia. As a defense witness, Watsuji offered his honest assessment of Tsuda's work from a scholarly perspective. Watsuji agreed with Tsuda on the questionable historical veracity of the descriptions in these ancient documents, but he stated that he believed that they were nonetheless accurate descriptions of the ancients' sentiments with regard to the imperial family. In the end, Tsuda was found guilty of the crime.

Watsuji himself was never formally charged by prewar censors and brought to court. He never retracted his comments on the hybridity of Japan's culture and people or on his idea of associating Japanese culture with that of Greece, both arguments that might have been challenged by right-wingers. Watsuji also never took back anything he said in *Nihon Kodai Bunka* or *Koji Junrei*. In the sense that Watsuji did not write something he did not believe in and for which he could not offer evidence, he was brutally honest. He would not stoop to writing or behaving in a way he believed to be untrue or immoral and therefore was always above reproach in this regard. And this remarkable strength and unwavering moral uprightness were already apparent when he wrote about "storming" at the First Higher School.

JAPAN'S CULTURAL IDENTITY

There is another piece of evidence in *Koji Junrei* that may help answer the question regarding the prewar censorship of this book. In *Koji Junrei*, Watsuji traces the ethnic and cultural origins of the Japanese to the Korean peninsula, China, and other parts of Asia, and he acknowledges that Japan's foundations were laid by the Chinese and Koreans. Going even further back into history, Watsuji finds that Japan's cultural heritage could be traced along the Silk Road, from Chang'an to northern India, to the western regions of China, and eventually to Greece. Watsuji states in Chapter 16 and indeed throughout the book that the Japanese ancestral people were, both physiologically and culturally, a hybrid of various ethnic groups. Watsuji seems not only to acknowledge this hybridity but also celebrates ancient Japan's international character. In fact, he believed that foreign influence was an asset to Japanese culture, and according to him, this occurred only before Heian (that is, up to the eighth century) and after the closing of the country ended (that is, Meiji and after).[21] What holds more importance for Watsuji in Japan's cultural history is not the ethnic or cultural makeup of people who immigrated to Japan or the geographical origin of practices and knowledge but what the Japanese people did to shape these primordial and foreign ingredients, to develop them, and to nurture them, in a way most befitting to the people and their environs. The easterly progression of Greek civilization, as Watsuji saw it, ended in Japan, and what is most significant for him was that the Japanese took the important and dormant principles of that civilization and coaxed them to bloom again.

As evidence, Watsuji traces *gigaku*, elements of architecture (e.g., the entasis of the

Tōshōdaiji pillars), the iconography of Buddhist images (e.g., curls on a Buddha's head), and other cultural elements back to faraway Greece. While one may think it is unremarkable that Watsuji recognizes traces of Greek art in Japanese art, for it is a generally accepted fact today, we should note that what Watsuji is saying about Greece is not merely an acknowledgement of its influence on Japanese soil; it is much more. Remember that Watsuji was writing this in 1919, only a few years after the rich cultural life in ancient cities on the Silk Road had come to light thanks to Albert von Le Coq's and Sir Aurel Stein's expeditions. Greece was the origin of the Western world's classical civilization, and Watsuji believed that the Greek spirit was embedded deep in Japanese culture.[22]

This adoration of Greece was not confined to Watsuji. Watsuji's contemporaries, such as the writer Hori Tatsuo (1904–1953) and the poet Aizu Yaichi (1881–1956) also recognized the privileged place Greece held in their psyche.[23] Watsuji, Hori, Aizu and probably others as well thought that the Greek spirit needed to be emulated in order for Japan to claim its place in world culture in its search for cultural identity in the modern era. In this formulation, the ancient city of Nara occupied a very special place in Japan in that it was the *Urheimat* of Japanese culture. Hori, for example, states this idea in a postcard to his wife, dated October 11, 1941:

> [Nara] is the place that is most Greek in Japan. The pillars of the [Hōryūji's] Golden Hall, nearly one thousand years old, are just like [the entasis in] Greek architecture. You can see the familiar honeysuckle design on the old doors to the building even today.[24]

In his musings, which were later published under the title *Yamatoji* (Road to Yamato), Hori also wrote about his adoration of Greece in the setting at Tōshōdaiji:

> I am writing this in the pine forest of Tōshōdaiji. I was strolling through the area of Yakushiji this morning, and I was ruminating on a poem by Mizuhara Shūōshi—*Jōmon no kuzurete iru ni ashibi ka na* (*Ashibi* are blooming /On the earthen gate that has now collapsed), and then, all of a sudden, I came here because an uncontrollable urge came over me. Now the autumn sun is shining on the Golden Hall and Lecture Hall, casting sharp shadows of the pine trees on the roof tiles and ancient pillars, the vermilion paint of which has now faded almost to white. The shadow moves with the sway of the trees in the light breeze; it is indescribably pleasant. This very place is our *Greece*. Right, if you get tired of living the life of a mouse, you should come here and spend half a day, whenever you can. In no time, you won't feel like writing novels. It's guaranteed.[25]

This is the same pine forest in *Koji Junrei* where, some twenty years earlier, Watsuji had enthusiastically written about the Golden Hall's classical beauty:

> It wasn't as if I did not know the beauty of this hall when it is viewed from the side. Some time ago, I had stood in the pine forest on the west side of the hall and looked at the building diagonally from behind, like today. I was completely taken then by the classic, commanding presence of the hall.

Aizu also held deep love for the ancient city of Nara and was no less passionate about Greece. One of his best-known *tanka* reads:[26]

Ōtera no	The round pillars of this great Tōshōdaiji
maroki hashira no tsukikage o	cast a shadow in the moonlight
tsuchi ni fumitsutsu	I think of the faraway past
mono o koso omoe	as I walk treading on theshadows

The faraway past Aizu was thinking about is not only his beloved ancient Nara but also the land from which Tōshōdaiji's architecture received its influence—Greece. Scholars of Aizu contend that Aizu's adoration for Greece was nurtured by his interest in the English poet John Keats, whose deep, sympathetic feeling toward Greek civilization was also well known. Here, we may recall that Watsuji also read Keats as a young man. Aizu's interest in Greece came from other sources too; he studied Goethe, Schiller, Shakespeare, the Italian Renaissance, and, most of all, the Greek humanistic tradition.

GOETHE

In addition to the reference to ancient Greece, *Koji Junrei* suggests another connection to the West: a remarkable parallelism to the work of a specific literary figure, Goethe. Goethe (1749–1832) was a man of great talent who excelled in all areas of humanistic and scientific learning, a true renaissance man of his time. Goethe's poetry, novels and plays, as well as his writings in science and legal studies, were a hallmark of Western civilization. His *Italian Journey*, both in terms of its visual imagery as well as the spirit embedded in the imagery, is the precise analogue of *Koji Junrei*. Stylistically, too, both *Italian Journey* and *Koji Junrei* were written in a diary form with insightful, unhurried, accessible prose that invites quiet rumination. If we look for more parallels, we are not disappointed. These two men's trips were significant in the development of their respective aesthetic and philosophical outlooks. One more point—their literary products, *Italian Journey* and *Koji Junrei*, had similar effects on their readers, as many readers had themselves traveled the same roads these philosophers took, with these publications in their hands.[27]

Watsuji's affinity in mood to Goethe in *Koji Junrei* seems unmistakable.[28] The chiaroscuro and Watsuji's romantic mood are noticeably similar to the following passage in Goethe's diary entry for February 2, 1787, in Rome:

> Nobody who has not taken [a walk] can imagine the beauty of a walk through Rome by full moon. All details are swallowed up by the huge masses of light and shadow, and only the biggest and most general outlines are visible. We have just enjoyed three clear and glorious nights. The Colosseum looked especially beautiful. It is closed at night. A hermit lives in a small chapel and some beggars have made themselves at home in the crumbling vaults. These had built a fire on a level ground and gentle breeze had driven the smoke into the arena, so that the lower parts of the ruins were veiled and only the huge masses above loomed out of the darkness. We stood at the railing and watched, while over our heads the moon stood high and serene. By degrees the smoke escaped through holes and crannies and in the moonlight it looked like fog. It was a marvelous sight. This is the kind of illumination by which to see the Pantheon, the Capitol, the square in front of St. Peter's, and many other large squares and streets.[29]

Compare this to Watsuji's description of his walk through Nara Park in Chapter 21, when he is walking up to Sangatsudō and the area around it.

> In the evening, the sky cleared and at night the moon brightly shined. I intended to visit N and walked leisurely through Nara Park. In the wide expanse of the park, I saw not one soul or one deer; the park was drenched in bright moonlight . . . The two roof layers of the gate were silhouetted dark against the moonlit sky, in such sharp contrast that it looked as if the gate had been bitten out of the sky. Underneath, from between the tall pillars of the gate, I could see the hazy moonlit sky, framed by the opening, which made its extraordinary size and grandeur all the more apparent . . . When I climbed the steps to the top to reach the Sangatsudō, my eyes, now accustomed to the darkness of night while walking among trees, were shocked by the bright moonlight again. The Sangatsudō was brightly lit by the moonlight and shined. What brilliance! That serene roof, seemingly weightless, shone silvery in the light. The beauty of eave lines that punctuates the silvery plane of light!

Not only does a similarity in imagery exist but also a spiritual parallelism. For an example of the latter, at the end of Chapter 6 Watsuji reflected on his stage in life and thought of himself as a person without a goal in life, sadly floating without a purpose. He states:

> Think of Goethe, who was extremely endowed with talent, I thought to myself. Even he regretted the fact that, when he traveled to Italy, he felt that he had not spent the necessary time to perfect his craft and that he hadn't taken the time to acquire the necessary skills for it.

We may recall that both Goethe and Watsuji took these trips to learn more about their own cultural roots by experiencing ancient cities firsthand—for Goethe, his roots were in

Rome and Greece, for Watsuji, ancient Nara. Spiritually the trips were a means to explore the cultures of the ancients, who were the ancestors of these authors. Goethe's philosophical orientation lies within the German literary movement *Sturm und Drang* in the late eighteenth century, which later developed into Weimar classicism and romanticism. Though Goethe's *Italian Journey* predated Watsuji's *Koji Junrei* by a good 130 years, in Watsuji's mind *Koji Junrei* and *Italian Journey* drew from the same spiritual fountain of Greek tradition. Thus we may say with some confidence that Watsuji's fleeting reference to Goethe is significant, as his interest in Greece lay deep in his mind. It is not at all farfetched to think that Watsuji was inspired by Goethe's work to plan a similar spiritual journey to Japan's classical Nara.[30]

Intellectuals active during Watsuji's lifetime (and even earlier), from Meiji on, starting with Fukuzawa Yukichi (1835–1901), engaged in spirited discussions about theories of civilization (*bunmeiron*) and speculated the rightful place Japan should occupy in world civilization. The distinction between the civilized and "barbarian" in premodern Japan was a dichotomy based on China on the one side and the barbarians and savages on the other. Parenthetically, it is ironic that in this Chinese formulation, peoples in the Korean peninsula and Japan were themselves classified as *tōi* (Ch. *dongyi*) "barbaric tribes to the east." In any case, during the premodern period, Japan sided with the Chinese world view. But soon, with the wholehearted intake of Western ideas in the modern period, Japan jettisoned China as its mentor and canceled its cultural alliance with that country. It then aligned itself with the Western nations. So the choice of the West makes sense. But a question about the choice of Greece may be worth closer examination.

This selection was motivated, I believe, by the fact that for Watsuji Japan needed a much stronger validation of its cultural and ethnic heritage than Great Britain and the United States could offer. Like many of his contemporaries, Watsuji regarded Anglo-American utilitarian views of life as culturally incompatible with his own.[31] Intellectuals were generally more drawn to ideas and systems emerging from continental Europe, rather than what was perceived as a more utilitarian and pragmatic tradition of Great Britain and the United States.[32] By tracing Japan's cultural roots to Greece, which "holds up" the eastern terminus of the Silk Road, as it were, Watsuji believed that Japan's ancient culture, as embodied in the ruins of Nara, could tap the great civilization at its source. Watsuji claimed Japan's culture to be in the same genealogy of civilization that gave birth to, some hundreds of years later, modern European nations, notably France, Germany, and Italy. If it could be shown that Japan had an affiliation with Greece, it would lend legitimacy to the idea that Japan wasn't so different from the West. This is evidenced in the notion, mentioned in a number of places in the text, that Japan is the last depository of this cherished classical spirit, while China, Korea, and India all unfortunately relegated that spirit to oblivion. A type of romantic admiration for the Greek humanistic spirit was therefore in play among intellectuals. By affiliating Japan's ancient culture with that of ancient Greece, Japan could also gain a powerful ideological tool. That is, since Japan's roots extend beyond the Asian context, Japanese culture is connected to the genuine, if ancient, center of world culture.[33] Therefore, Japan could leave, at least conceptually, the cultural land of Asia that had been dominated by Chinese studies and join the powerful West.

A TRIP TO EUROPE

In our effort to situate *Koji Junrei* within Watsuji's scholarship as a whole, it is important not to overlook the overseas trip Watsuji took in his third year at Kyoto. This trip came about in 1927, when he was chosen by the Japanese government to study in Berlin. On one of his side trips while in Germany, he traveled to Italy to see Roman buildings and sculptures.

This sojourn to Europe was significant in two respects, which may seem unrelated at first glance. First, Watsuji was able to read the first edition of Heidegger's *Being and Time*. He was impressed by the philosopher's analysis of time, because he undoubtedly could relate to the issue with which Heidegger was grappling and which Watsuji himself had agonized over just a few years earlier—how to live an authentic life.[34] No doubt Heidegger's book gave Watsuji food for further thought, but Watsuji was troubled that Heidegger made no mention of another factor that was just as significant as time, that is, the effect of land and climate on human existence.[35]

It turned out that Watsuji's trip to Berlin was cut short, to twelve months, due to his father's death, prompting his immediate return to Japan. Prior to this and during his travels to Germany, Italy, France, and London, however, Watsuji meticulously recorded his thoughts and impressions in a journal as well as in letters and postcards he sent to his wife Teru back home. Later, compiling these journal entries, he published *Itaria Koji Junrei* (Pilgrimages to Ancient Churches in Italy), which was not published until 1950. His ideas about geographical determinism expressed in this book as a complement to Heidegger's *Being and Time* would be incorporated into his ethical framework. *Itaria Koji Junrei* was very much like *Koji Junrei* (and Goethe's *Italian Journey*) in tone and spirit, though Watsuji was far more chatty in this book, in contrast to the rather somber, although not gloomy, tone of *Koji Junrei*. *Itaria Koji Junrei* is replete with ethnographic descriptions and comments regarding the connection between the land and the people's lifestyles. His travels in Europe and the ports of call on the way to and from Europe (namely, cities in coastal China, India, the Suez Canal, and so forth) formed the empirical basis for *Fūdo*, which exclusively dealt with the connection between geography and cultural characteristics.[36] The short trip to Europe thus yielded rich material to deal with the lacuna in Heidegger's writings.

The second significance of this trip was that it gave Watsuji a chance to validate his long-held conviction about the Greek humanistic tradition, which he discussed in *Koji Junrei* and elsewhere. In Rome, Watsuji was utterly taken by the statues of Niobe (Greek, 4th c. BCE) and the Venus of Sinuessa (Greek, 4th or 5th c. BCE). His praise for these pieces is reminiscent of his discussion of the main statue of worship at the Yakushiji temple in *Koji Junrei*. After praising the Yakushi Nyorai Bodhisattva in the Golden Hall of Yakushiji in superlative terms, he commented,

> This beauty is different from the beauty of the human body that we feel from Greek sculpture. Greek sculpture no doubt expresses ideal beauty as a reflection of a pinnacle of human desire, but in this Buddhist statue, we see something else, that is, a transcendent being in human form, which reflects our desire for reaching the "Other Shore."

Compare this to the following observation about the Venus of Sinuessa:

> This Venus statue is one without a head, shoulders, arms, or half of the chest, but the remaining torso and lower body are enough to convince us that this is a divine work of art. There is not a hint that the surface is anything but the "skin." All points within the body spurt out from within and come at us. The inside is perfectly expressed on the outside, and the outside perfectly reveals the inside. The statue does not represent "flesh" that opposes "soul," but flesh that is the soul itself, soul that is one with flesh. It is amazing that the beauty of human "life" and the profound power of "life" were actually put into concrete "form" as well as this.[37]

Watsuji was ecstatic because he was seeing the epitome of Greek culture in Rome just as he saw the pinnacle of Chinese and Indian traditions in the Yakushiji statue. For Watsuji, Greek and Japanese art shared a commonality in that they both captured the essence of the subject, albeit slightly differently. In other artistic creations, such as gardens, Watsuji claimed Greek and Japanese treatments of nature were based on the same universal principles. He observed how Greek gardens in Italy were situated and constructed. He then remarked that while gardens in England and Germany were symbolic of man's domination over nature, Japanese gardens were painstakingly maintained to look natural. He asserted that the Japanese garden was an idealized form of nature capturing its essence, just as a Greek sculpture embodied the essence of man (and the essence is manifested as visible on the outside). In the end, Watsuji equated Japanese gardens with Greek sculptures in terms of the universal principles of art. In other words, capturing the inner soul of man or the essence of nature is the universal attribute for great art regardless of locality or time. Since Japanese art has done this, he argued, Japanese culture is on par with the Greek classical tradition, the tradition from which European cultures draw their inspirations.

Watsuji wrote in *Itaria Koji Junrei* (Pilgrimages to Ancient Churches in Italy) that Romans were able to emulate the Greek spirit only in some of their sculptures and buildings, and he expressed a most thoroughgoing extolment of the Greek spirit. Reading *Koji Junrei*, the reader will undoubtedly notice Watsuji's line of thinking about this, as he argued that strains of Greek influence were lost as they traveled eastward. When these influences reached the terminus of Japan, they were met with favorable conditions and took root. It is easy to take the comparison of Greek and Roman cultures made in *Itaria Koji Junrei* and see the same argument in the case of China and Japan. For Watsuji, Italy and China are both heirs of the ancient Greek tradition but, in Asia, only Japan was able to make that tradition bloom.

POLITICS OF CULTURAL NATIONALISM

Watsuji repeats himself in *Koji Junrei* about Japan's special place in world history. He wrote that Japan was the last depository of the Greek humanistic tradition, so much so that the place of Japanese culture in world civilization is on par with Greek, Indian, and Chinese cultures. Japan's role is not confined within its small geographical area, for Japan represents Asia. Japan is Asia, Watsuji would say. Japan is important enough as a contender to stand against the West. This is the rhetoric that appears in his 1937 article, discussed below. Even if we accept his argument for the moment that Japan embodies more of the Greek spirit than does China or India, the countries in Asia that Watsuji said had lost their civilizations, Japanese culture could not be compete head-to-head with these, both in its pedigree and its contribution to world culture. It is a bit of a stretch then to endow Japanese culture with so many accolades as Watsuji did. Watsuji's aggrandizement of Japanese culture embodies the inherent danger of particularizing it and imbuing it with a chauvinistic attitude, especially toward other non-Western cultures of Asia. And this attitude seems to be cut from the same ideological cloth that supported Japan's overseas expansion.

This stance is no more apparent than in an essay entitled "Bunkateki sōzō ni tazusawaru mono no tachiba (The role of the persons engaged in cultural creation)," written in September 1937. This article was perhaps the most nationalistic of Watsuji's essays in which he made his cultural nationalist position abundantly clear. He stated that Western civilization had thus far ruled the modern world, but in a mere fifty years after the introduction of Western technology, Japan caught up with the West and demonstrated that Japan could compete with any Western nation in industrial and military strength. While India and China had lost their original and significant contributions to world culture, Japan still retained them and, because of this fact, Western nations must take Japan seriously as a threat. For the same reason, Watsuji argued, Japan was in a privileged and inextricable position to save millions of Asians from the colonial rule of Western nations. This role was the historical mandate and destiny of Japan. Thus, Watsuji reasoned that, if modern Western civilization were to be protected, Japan's prosperity would pose a danger to the West's wellbeing. Japan was therefore destined to find itself in a conflict with the West.

As for the role of those Japanese engaged in cultural creation, e.g., scholars and artists, they must protect the noble culture of Japan from destruction. This could only be done by integrating Japanese culture with the Greek tradition. And only by doing this would the totality of noble cultural spirit held by all cultures in world history unite into one. Watsuji then wrote:

> As a people with this responsibility in world history, the Japanese people not only have the right to develop but also to destroy anyone who tries to stop us from achieving this goal … [The mission of those engaged in cultural creation] is a mission of world significance, far superseding that of an individual's personal interest.

The last sentence is reminiscent of Sōseki's motto *sokuten kyoshi*. Finally, admonishing those who were too carried away by the prospect of Japan's finally entering into a world conflict to continue work, Watsuji suggested,

> [Not being able to focus on work] arises from the lack of strong, deep, and sustained willingness to dedicate oneself to this mission. Being excitable is a shortcoming of the Japanese; it is not a virtue. We hope that scholars and artists are not concerned with whether or not they cater to the public's views but, instead, strive for true cultural creation with persistent, strong willpower.[38]

This passage not only underscores Watsuji's commitment to the idea of Japanese culture's unique place, which is to be protected from Western powers' aggression as a symbol of Asia at large, but also foreshadows Japan's entry into the upcoming war. We can compare this essay to Watsuji's comment in Chapter 21 in *Koji Junrei*, where he observed that "the Japanese can easily be corrupted" (*Nihonjin wa daraku-shiyasui*). Watsuji quoted this remark made by a friend of his, who studied the system of monk-soldiers (*sōhei*), employed at various temples in Kyoto and Nara in the ninth and tenth centuries. Tōdaiji's *sōhei* fought against the *sōhei* of rival temples, causing irreparable damage to the temple complex and costing lives, all because of "petty," spur-of-the-moment inter-temple skirmishes. We are told that these battles were not about important issues—e.g., the interpretation of Buddhist doctrines or scriptures—they came from the jealousy of have-nots. Watsuji made this comment in *Koji Junrei* as if to admonish himself as well as the Japanese, just in the same way that, some twenty years later, he admonished scholars and artists in cultural creation to keep working on their craft during the feverish excitement of the times.

In general terms, Watsuji's point about corruption means that people may hold a deep, well-reasoned intellectual commitment, but once they are overcome by strong emotional and often irrational feelings, they may lose reason and act irrationally, with the result that it becomes impossible to follow through with intellectual commitment or rational decisions.

Watsuji would not have recognized rash behavior as a virtue, as he preferred actions backed by thoughtful reasoning. But aggrandizing Japanese culture to be almost on par with other world civilizations was uncharacteristic of the usual prudence he observed in writing. I say this because he himself stated, "The ancient history of Japan is not as great as that of Greece or other European nations," but in the same passage, he comes within inches of assigning Japanese culture a position of equal importance to Western civilizations. His conceptualization of the ancient city of Nara as an international melting pot of peoples, cultures, and ideas so persuasively presented in *Koji Junrei* gave way twenty years later to a more particularistic view of Japanese culture and people. Then, is it altogether untenable to regard his position, at least as it is presented in this 1937 essay, as evidence for Watsuji himself being carried away with the emotion of the moment? In this connection, we are again reminded of Sōseki's words that suggested pursuing Heaven's mandates and relinquishing self-centered concerns. Watsuji strove to live a life following Heaven's mandates by pursuing an ethically impeccable path, guided by the moral imperatives and the role of individuals in a larger community. However, acting altruistically or morally need not mean committing oneself uncritically to benefiting the community or to discarding democratic principles. In hindsight, Watsuji's ethical path could be called into question.

THE GIFT OF *KOJI JUNREI*

Judging from its amazing longevity and popularity, *Koji Junrei* has struck sympathetic chords in the psyche of the Japanese people from the time it was published in 1919 to today. Watsuji's *Koji Junrei* became widely acknowledged as the book that launched the post-WWII trend of visiting old temples in Japan as well as popular books bearing the words *koji* "old temple" and *junrei* "pilgrimage" in the titles.[39] Some well-known writers wrote their own versions of *Koji Junrei*. Even today, this 1919 book is frequently mentioned as the book to read for anyone contemplating serious visits to temples in Nara. Philosopher Miki Kiyoshi (1897–1945) recalled that Watsuji's *Koji Junrei* and *Nihon Kodai Bunka* were widely read and influenced young scholars like him in the 1920s.[40]

How should we best interpret the significance of Watsuji's *Koji Junrei*? *Koji Junrei* may be said to hold the position of a fountainhead, as it were, that anticipates the totality of Watsuji's scholarship. As examples of thematic threads that appear in *Koji Junrei* and are developed later, we can point to *Nihon Kodai Bunka*, which was a scholarly development of *Koji Junrei* (*Nihon Kodai Bunka* was probably prepared at the same time *Koji Junrei* was being written). The nascent idea of geographical determinism, found in nearly every chapter of *Koji Junrei*, would later appear in *Fūdo* (Climate, 1935) and reappear in *Rinrigaku* (Ethics, in three volumes published in 1937, 1942, and 1949. See volume three in particular.). The same idea was repeated in *Itaria Koji Junrei* (Pilgrimages to Ancient Churches in Italy). The

Greek humanistic tradition, especially sculpture, was used as a benchmark to evaluate Nara sculptures in *Koji Junrei* as well as in *Itaria Koji Junrei*. Watsuji's unwavering interest in the imperial system and its rightful place in Japanese history is obvious in *Koji Junrei* and would reemerge in more polished form in other publications. His interest in ancient Buddhism and Confucianism appearing in *Koji Junrei* was also elaborated in his later writings on these subjects. In summary, Watsuji comes across to the reader as a young scholar pointing out the significance of Japanese culture in world history, a topic which Watsuji would explore in a variety of later writings. In the myriad connections he makes in his publications, what is remarkable about Watsuji's philosophical framework is his consistent conception of Japan as a unit of culture and statehood and the consistency of the philosophical positions he took early on that underwent little change during his life.

Perhaps more appropriately, *Koji Junrei* should be viewed as a *zuihitsu* that recorded the intellectual and emotional impressions of ancient temples in the city of Nara, with which Watsuji had been intrigued when he took a course from Okakura Tenshin.[41] *Koji Junrei* is the first work that marked Watsuji's departure from a literary career and his foray into a serious, scholarly inquiry into the cultural history of Japan, although the book's mood is far less imposing than an academic tome.[42] *Koji Junrei* was first carried in the magazine *Shichō* in several installments, beginning with the August 1918 issue. The diary entry style is refreshing and projects a certain sense of immediacy as well as being suited to the *zuihitsu* style of writing.

As pointed out above, the late spring of 1918, when the events related in *Koji Junrei* took place, was toward the end of a time of intense introspection for Watsuji. Many of his reflections were recorded in *Gūzō Saikō* in torturously self-conscious style. It was also when Watsuji was about to emerge anew with a fresh orientation to life. The inner conflict is seen clearly in an early chapter in *Koji Junrei*, where he mentions that he had visited his father in Himeji right before the trip to Nara. There he felt unable to justify to his father the idea that visiting these temples would be important for his future path. Of course, his father's question should be interpreted as one asking Watsuji about his future directions in general, not about this trip in particular.[43]

What should we make of *Koji Junrei* as a whole? A precursor of Watsuji as a scholar? For many readers, the pleasure of reading this book lies elsewhere. The reader is struck by the fact that Watsuji was enormously gifted in communicating how he felt and what he thought when he came face to face with Buddhist images. Watsuji conveys to the reader arcane ideas, fantastic speculations, and the history of politics and society with his customary ease, aplomb, and knowledge. The reader can watch him experience a rapture, conceive a fanciful idea and then develop, explore, and wonder about it. The reader then joins Watsuji for an intellectual adventure of fitting pieces of a puzzle together. He paints a highly convincing, but also highly speculative, picture of grand ideas by making connections among historical facts and weaving them into layers of hypotheses. What he wrote about in *Koji Junrei* was indeed his impressions of Nara's ancient temples, yet his ideas reached back to social and political histories of China, India, and Greece, as well as their art and contributions to Japanese art. His knowledge of a wide range of subjects is nothing less than extraordinary, as are his skills in marshaling historical facts and imbuing them with fresh, if rather romantic, impressions of temples, images, the people he came across, and the surroundings. True to the Japanese "travel writing" genre, however, his prose is never heavy-handed. It is hard to believe that *Koji Junrei* was written when he was not yet thirty years old. When the reader walks, as it were, with the author through the book by his side, the reader is guaranteed to enjoy the same process of reasoning and discovery.

Another aspect of *Koji Junrei* is Watsuji's sprightly youth. It overflows every page of *Koji Junrei*. Watsuji is sometimes child-like and exudes a refreshing sensibility, often expressed in wordy, dreamy prose. His youth is pervasive and evident everywhere, but it does not come across as immature or unsophisticated. Nevertheless, it is with reason that he felt a bit embarrassed about the book when he reread it later, as stated in his introduction. He thought about revising it or rewriting it altogether, only to realize that he was unable to do so. It was, in fact, this very youthful, romantic prose inextricably embedded in *Koji Junrei* that made it so popular with readers. Still, the revised edition does differ from the original edition. The philosopher Tanikawa Tetsuzō has shown that Watsuji expunged exaggerated and emotionally charged language that peppered the original edition, but the revision appears to have been limited only to excising such overenthusiastic prose.[44]

In reading *Koji Junrei*, then, it is well to notice the many seeds of Watsuji's future ideas and ideological implications which were cultivated in his various later publications. While situating this work in proper historical perspective with Watsuji's later scholarship is undeniably useful, it is just as important, or perhaps even more so, to recognize on balance that the reason for the trend-setting longevity and arguably even the value of this book lie elsewhere. Here, we witness the man Watsuji Tetsurō thinking as a cultural historian, conceiving and developing a hypothesis, and testing its validity against historical facts. In reading *Koji Junrei*, then, we receive a great deal of joy as we walk through the ancient city of Nara with someone like Watsuji Tetsurō guiding us. This book is, in that sense, the ultimate guide to the city as well as to the man Watsuji himself.

Notes

1. Robert N. Bellah, "Japan's Cultural Identity: Some Reflections on the Work of Watsuji Tetsurō," *Journal of Asian Studies* 24.4:573–594. See also David Dilworth, "Watsuji Tetsurō (1889–1960): Cultural Phenomenologist and Ethician," *Philosophy East and West* 24.1:3–22. For an incisive analysis of Watsuji's formative years including the period of our interest, see William R. LaFleur, "A Turning in Taishō: Asia and Europe in the Early Writing of Watsuji Tetsurō," in *Culture and Identity: Japanese Intellectuals during the Interwar Years*, J. Thomas Rimer, ed. (Princeton: Princeton University Press, 1990), 234–256.

2. Watsuji Tetsurō, "Jijoden no kokoromi (An Autobiography)," in *Watsuji Tetsurō Zenshū* (Tokyo: Iwanami Shoten, 1961–1963), vol. 18, pp. 40–41. Hereafter *Watsuji Tetsurō Zenshū* will be abbreviated as *WTZ*.

3. Watsuji wrote that he inherited his father's irritable temper, which was usually under control, but occasionally exhibited as fits of anger. See "Jijoden no kokoromi," in *WTZ* 18:83 *et seq*.

4. Much information about Watsuji's early life can be found in his autobiography "Jijoden no kokoromi." *WTZ* 18:309 et seq. See also Yuasa Yasuo, *Watsuji Tetsurō: Kindai nihon tetsugaku no unmei* (*Watsuji Tetsurō*: The Destiny of Modern Japanese Philosophy), Tokyo: Meneruva Shobō, 1981, 15. This is an excellent, informative book on the life and work of Watsuji.

5. See "Seishin o ushinaitaru kōfū (The school tradition that has lost its spirit)," *WTZ* 20:41–52. Also see "Jijoden no kokoromi," *WTZ* 18:419–421. *Shan* is from German *schön* "beautiful." For a general description of First Higher School in Japan around this time, see Donald Roden, *School-Days in Imperial Japan: A Study in the Culture of a Student Elite* (Berkeley, CA: University of California Press, 1981).

6. Raphael von Koeber (1948–1923) left no small mark on the Japanese philosophical scene. Arriving in 1893 as a hired foreigner (*oyatoi gaijin*) and serving until retirement in 1914, he was the pillar of philosophical training for generations of young philosophers at the Tokyo Imperial University. His students included, in addition to Watsuji, Nishida Kitarō, Natsume Sōseki, Abe Yoshishige, Kuki Shūzō, Iwanami Shigeo, Abe Jirō, and many others. He emphasized a German brand of broad humanistic learning, which included Greek philosophy, medieval philosophy, aesthetics, and classical languages. He maintained a peaceful and calm demeanor as well as a sincere approach to academic learning, which was "perhaps reminiscent of a true Greek philosopher," as Watsuji put it, that was well insulated from the often cacophonous outside world. See "Kēberu sensei (Professor Koeber)," *WTZ* 6:5–39 for Watsuji's personal remarks on Koeber. See also the preface to "Homērosu hihan" (Homeric question)," *WTZ* 6:43–44. As for Sōseki's recollection of Koeber, see "Kēberu Sensei (Professor Koeber)," in *Sōseki Zenshū* 12:461–466. Tokyo: Iwanami Shoten, 1994.

7. *Gūzō Saikō*, in an essay entitled "Tenkō (Turn)," *WTZ* 17:22. For another very introspective description of his concerns around this time, see the essay entitled "Teishaba de kanjita koto (What I felt at the train station)" in *Gūzō Saikō*, *WTZ* 17:74–84. The pulls from *Sollen* and *Sein* which Watsuji felt around this time are also described very critically in "Jōyoku to jōka no yōkyū to (Sensuality and a demand for purification)" in *Gūzō Saikō*, *WTZ* 17:59 and "Hōtō musuko no kitaku (Homecoming of a debauched son)" in *Gūzō Saikō*, *WTZ* 17:52–58.

8. Watsuji had been working on Nietzsche for his graduation thesis for some time when he requested formal permission to write on him three months before his graduation. Inoue denied this request because he thought that "Nietzsche was too wild." Watsuji never held a high opinion of Inoue. See the interview he gave to the magazine *Kokoro* in the June 1 issue, 1959, entitled "Gensen o Saguru (In search of the source)." See *WTZ* 24:274. This unused manuscript was later published as *Nīche kenkyū* (A Study of Nietzsche) in 1913 and is now regarded as "epoch-making," unmatched by any work even in Europe, when it was first published.

9. In a reply to Watsuji's letter that expressed this romantic feeling, Sōseki stated that he was surprised to learn how Watsuji felt about him. See Natsume Sōseki, *Sōseki Zenshū* 24:209–211. Tokyo: Iwanami Shoten, 1997.

10. See Natsume Sōseki, "Watashi no kojinshugi (My individualism)," *Sōseki Zenshū* 16:581–615. Tokyo: Iwanami Shoten, 1995.

11. See "Sōseki sensei no tsuioku (A recollection of Natsume Sōseki)," *Gūzō Saikō*, *WTZ* 17:85–99.

12. See, for example, "Kikenshisō o haisu (Eradicating dangerous thought)," *WTZ* 22:141–151.

13. See Watsuji Teru, *Watsuji Tetsurō to tomo ni* (A life with Watsuji Tetsurō). Tokyo: Shinchōsha, 1966, 117. The translation is my own.

14. Quoted in Yuasa Yasuo, *Watsuji Tetsurō*, 27. Koeber apparently had a similar criticism of many Japanese philosophers of the time. See "Kēberu sensei (Professor Koeber)," *WTZ* 6:1–39.

15. For further insights into how Watsuji's chosen field affected his career and perception of his work, see Yuasa Yasuo, *Watsuji Tetsurō: Kindai nihon tetsugaku no unmei*, 79–106.

16. Yuasa believes that it was unfortunate that Watsuji spoke up to support the emperor system immediately after the war when national sentiment was against that, because it branded him with right-wing labels. By this time, the only remaining philosopher who commented in favor of the emperor system was Watsuji—Nishida had died during the war, and Tanabe was in self-imposed exile in Karuizawa.

17. *Nihonjinron* refers to a post-war discourse about the Japanese that focuses on issues of national and cultural identity and can be imbued with cultural and racial chauvinism. The stance generally taken is that the Japanese people and culture are unique in the world.

18. See Watsuji's introduction to the revised edition.

19. Watsuji wrote in his own introduction to the new edition of *Nihon Kodai Bunka* that, in 1937 or 1938, censors suggested changing a few items in the book, including the fact that Watsuji remarked that the image of Yamato takeru no mikoto, which he used for the book, appeared to be a composite of two images. The censors also took issue with Watsuji's Japanese translation of a description of ancient Japan in the Chinese historical document *Sanguo zhi* (Jp. Sangokushi) compiled during 189–280 CE. See *Nihon Kodai Bunka*, *WTZ* 3:3–5.

20. See Watsuji Teru, *Watsuji Tetsurō to tomo ni,* 260 et seq., which contains a description of how Watsuji felt about the military's interference with scholarly publications and a description of the general atmosphere concerning censorship. Tsuda had used philological investigation to separate mythology from historical facts in his description of the imperial family in the historical documents *Nihon Shoki* (720 CE) and *Shoku Nihongi* (797 CE), causing his writings to become the object of lese-majesty investigation by right-wingers. The Genri Nihonsha also condemned works of a long list of prominent scholars, including Minobe Tatsukichi, Nishida Kitarō, Takigawa Yukitoki, and others.

21. See, for instance, the essay entitled "Nihon wa nani o hokuru ka (What can Japan be proud of?)," *Gūzō Saikō*, *WTZ* 17:269–275. See also *Sakoku: Nihon no Higeki* (Closing of the Country: A Tragedy for Japan), *WTZ* 15. Writing in 1950, he proposed the idea that shutting Japan off from outside influences was detrimental to Japan's development and contributed to its defeat in World War II.

22. This line of thinking is evident in such works as *Koji Junrei*, *Itaria Koji Junrei*, "Bunkateki sōzō ni tazusawaru mono no tachiba (The role of the persons engaged in cultural creation)" in *Men to Perusona* (Masks and Persona), *WTZ* 17:441–444, among other places. See also William LaFleur, "A Turning in Taishō," pp. 234–256, which insightfully points out the parallels between ancient Nara and ancient Greece.

23. I thank Tom Rimer for calling my attention to Hori Tatsuo and Aizu Yaichi. Aizu's poetry is available in English in Michael F. Marra, *A Poetic Guide to an Ancient Capital: Aizu Yaichi and the City of Nara.* Baltimore: Modern Tanka Press, 2009.

24. Murao Seiichi, "*Koji Junrei* no kindai (Modernity in *Koji Junrei*)" in *Waka Bungaku Taikei* vol. 30, *Geppō* (Monthly Report) 25:4. Tokyo: Meiji Shoin, 2005. The idea that Hōryūji was strongly influenced by Greek elements (such as entasis) was suggested by architect Itō Chūta (1867–1954) in an 1893 essay "Hōryūji kenchikuron (Architecture of Hōryūji)," *Kenchiku Zasshi* (Journal of Architecture and Building Science) 7 (83):317–350.

25. Hori Tatsuo, *Yamatoji Shinanoji* (Tokyo: Nihon Tosho Sentā, 1997), 210. Mizuhara Shūōshi (1892–1981) was a haiku poet. He composed the haiku quoted here on the way to Shin Yakushiji during a trip in 1929, when he noticed a flowering *ashibi* shrub (Japanese andromeda, *Pieris japonica*) blooming where the low earthen walls were collapsing.

26. In Hasegawa Masaharu and Izumi Hisako, *Umi yama no aida, Rokumeishū* (Tokyo: Meiji Shoin, 2005), 191, the authors pointed out a similarity between Goethe's imagery and that of poet Aizu Yaichi. This poem is included in a collection of Aizu's poems called *Nankin Shinshō*. It is worth noting that Aizu founded the Nihon Girisha Gakkai (Japan Greek Association) in 1920.

27. Among the first travelers was Kamei Katsuichirō, who later wrote *Yamato Koji Fūbutsushi* (Scenes of Old Temples in Yamato) in 1943. With regard to *Italian Journey*, poet Johann Peter Eckermann (1792–1854), who was a close personal friend of Goethe and wrote *Conversations with Goethe* (Gespräche mit Goethe), traveled to Italy with Goethe's son in 1830 retracing Goethe's steps.

28. See Hasegawa Masaharu and Izumi Hisako "Kaisetsu" in Hasegawa Masaharu and Izumi Hisako, eds. *Umi yama no aida, Rokumeishū*, 326–355.

29. Goethe, J. W., *Italian Journey*, 1786–1788. Translated by W. H. Auden and Elizabeth Mayer (New York: Schoken Books, 1968), 156–157.

30. Watsuji wrote an essay entitled "Kyōrakujin (A hedonist)" in 1921 in which he advised medical doctor/poet/art historian Kinoshita Mokutarō (1985–1945) to emulate Goethe even more and implied that he himself regarded Goethe as his mentor. See *WTZ* 17:360–366.

31. For Watsuji's most trenchant criticism of the utilitarianism and culture of the United States, see his 1944 essay "Amerika no kokuminsei (National character of the United States)," *WTZ* 17:451–481.

32. J. Thomas Rimer elaborates on this point eloquently in *Culture and Identity: Japanese Intellectuals during the Interwar Years*. J. Thomas Rimer, ed. (Princeton: Princeton University Press, 1990).

33. Connecting Japan to Greece can be seen as a reaction to the sense of inferiority the Japanese felt during the Meiji period. This sense of inferiority was in part strengthened by Europeans' nineteenth century ethnic attitude toward the Chinese and Japanese encapsulated in the phrase "Yellow Peril." In addition to Itō Chūta, who detected Greek architectural elements at Hōryūji, a number of other intellectuals attempted to connect Japan to the European sphere, both culturally and ethnically. They include Shiga Shigetaka (1863–1927), who characterized the Japanese landscape as being the most beautiful in the world as he compared Japan's scenic features to those of Greece; Taguchi Ukichi (1855–1905), who touted the Japanese as being the most pureblooded of Indo-Aryans; historian Takekoshi Yosaburō (1865–1950), who proposed the idea that the Japanese race descended from the Phoenicians; and journalist Kuroiwa Ruikō, who also expounded on the notion that the Japanese were Indo-Aryans.

34. In 1922, Watsuji went on a white water rafting trip on the Tenryūgawa that drew him to ponder the very concrete question of what life was and how to live an authentic life. See *WTZ* 17:411–419.

35. Watsuji's dissatisfaction with Heidegger's *Being and Time* is expressed in his own introduction to *Fūdo*. *WTZ* 8:1–256.

36. *Fūdo* has been translated into English by Geoffrey Bownas as *Climate and Culture: A Philosophical Study* (Westport, CT: Greenwood Press, 1988).

37. *Itaria Koji Junrei* (Pilgrimages to Ancient Churches in Italy), *WTZ* 8:337.

38. "Bunkateki sōzō ni tazusawaru mono no tachiba," *Men to Perusona*, *WTZ* 17:441–444.

39. Postwar works by authors who followed Watsuji's steps both literally and figuratively and wrote books similar to *Koji Junrei* include Kamei Katsuichirō's (1907–1966) *Yamato Koji Fūbutsushi* (Scenes of Old Temples in Yamato) in 1943; Hori Tatsuo's (1904–1953) *Yamatoji* (Road to Yamato) in 1943; Yamamoto Kenkichi's (1907–1988) *Yamato Sangashō* (Mountains and Rivers of Yamato) in 1962; Shirasu Masako's (1910–1998) *Watashi no Koji Junrei* (My Pilgrimages to Ancient Temples) in 1982; and Itsuki Hiroyuki's (1932–) *Hyakuji Junrei* (Pilgrimages to One Hundred Temples) in 2006. Itsuki's work was made into a popular TV series. Photographer Domon Ken's (1909–1990) works entitled *Koji Junrei* (Pilgrimages to Ancient Temples) were published from 1963 to 1975 in five volumes. Furthermore, photographer Irie Taikichi's (1905–1992) entire portfolio may be said to follow Watsuji's *Koji Junrei* in spirit. In addition, any number of popular guidebooks to Nara's temples have been published.

40. Watsuji also published the Japanese translation *Kindai rekishigaku* of German historian Karl Lamprecht's influential 1905 work *Moderne Geschichtswissenschaft* (Modern Science of History). Miki credits this publication as being instrumental in securing a foundation for cultural history as a legitimate field of historical inquiry. In Miki's judgment, Watsuji stood out most prominently among the intellectuals of the 1920s. See Miki Kiyoshi, "Dokusho henreki (A personal history of reading)," *Bungei*, June through December, 1941, issues, collected in *Miki Kiyoshi Zenshū* (Complete Writings of Miki Kiyoshi) 1:369–432. Tokyo: Iwanami Shoten, 1966.

41. *Zuihitsu* is a genre of Japanese literature consisting of jottings, incidental writings, personal insights, ideas, and observations loosely organized around a theme. It literally means "follow the brush" and may be similar to "stream of consciousness" writings. Watsuji credited Okakura Tenshin with planting a passionate love for art in him. See "Okakura Sensei no omoide (Memories of Professor Okakura)," *WTZ* 17:352–354 and "Nishi no kyō no omoide (Memories of Kyoto)," *WTZ* 24:181–195.

42. See also LaFleur, "A Turning in Taishō," pp. 234–256, for an excellent analysis of how *Guzō Saikō* should be positioned in Watsuji's scholarship.

43. Watsuji continued to receive financial assistance from his father but tried to reduce his burden by taking on various writing projects. For other details of his life, from meeting his future wife to his death, from the perspective of his wife, see Watsuji Teru, *Watsuji Tetsurō to tomo ni.*

44. Tanikawa Tetsuzō, "Kaisetsu (Commentary)." In Watsuji Tetsurō, *Koji Junrei*, Tokyo: Iwanami Shoten, 1996, 271–287.

TRANSLATOR'S NOTE

Unlike other works, Watsuji wrote *Koji Junrei* in an easygoing style, and the translator has tried to maintain the same ease so far as practicable. To render Japanese words, the modified Hepburn romanization system was used throughout the translation. Different from the standard system, the letter *n* was maintained even when it was followed by homorganic consonants (e.g., *shinbun*, not *shimbun*). In addition, vowel lengths were indicated with a macron, and the moraic nasal followed by a vowel or the letter y was separated with an apostrophe (to distinguish, for example, *tan'i* "unit" from *tani* "valley"). Japanese words are set in italics. This system of romanization was followed for all Japanese words, except for those few, which were judged to be English words (e.g., Tokyo, kimono).

Watsuji provided a few of his own footnotes, which appear at the bottom of the page as footnotes in this translation. Translator's notes appear as numbered endnotes. Watsuji placed emphasis on certain words in the text by placing dots (*bōten*) next to words. In this translation, the emphasized text appears in bold. Other types of emphasis are indicated by different underlines. When published translations of the passages Watsuji quoted were available, they were used and cited in the translation. Otherwise the translator provided the translation.

Any deviations from the original were kept at a minimum. At the beginning of a chapter, Watsuji listed the topics for the chapter immediately after the heading. In this translation, the topical headings are placed in their appropriate places in the text to aid the reader. Some miscellaneous and supplementary information was added in the text itself, even when Watsuji did not place that information, such as the years of an emperor's reign, as in "Emperor Jitō (645-703, r. 690-697)" to help the reader. The historical orthography in some contexts (e.g., *Man'yōshū* poems) was changed to modern orthographic conventions. Watsuji consistently used the traditional Japanese and Chinese units of measure (the so-called *shakkanhō*) to give approximate dimensions and distances. In order for the translation to be read smoothly and understood easily by the English-speaking readers, these traditional measurements were converted to the nearest U.S. customary units (e.g., *feet*, *miles*).

Watsuji Tetsurō

Pilgrimages to the Ancient Temples in Nara

Koji Junrei

PREFACE TO THE REVISED EDITION

This book is an account of a trip I took with several friends to ancient temples in Nara and the vicinity in May 1918.[1] The account was first published in 1919, and this year marks the twenty-eighth year since its original publication. During that time, the original printing plates were lost in the Great Kanto Earthquake, and the new edition was printed in the following year, 1924. I had begun to wish I could revise it, but I thought it might be inappropriate to revise the account of how I had felt when I originally wrote the book. Thus, thinking that the book was never meant to be an academic treatise, I did not make any changes. Subsequently I moved to Kyoto to live for some time, during which I was able to visit Nara on occasion, and, when I did, I found myself becoming increasingly more embarrassed about this book. Thus I began to think often that I should take the time to rewrite it completely. I returned to Tokyo without finding an opportunity to do so. Then, several years later, in 1938 or 1939, the publisher informed me that it was time to reprint the book. Taking this as a welcome opportunity, I resolved to revise it. I asked the publisher to print the book in a manuscript format so that I could pen in revisions. I thought that although I would not be able to revise my original impressions that I recorded during my travels I could perhaps add my present thoughts in footnotes. This task was more complicated than I had anticipated. Though undeveloped, the account of my first impressions was organically connected to the rest of the book, making it difficult to make patchwork repairs. Thus the manuscript for the revision sat untouched. By and by, the tenor of the times became such that the republication of this book would be imprudent. In time I learned indirectly that another printing of *Koji Junrei* would not be practicable, and another five or six years passed with the book still out of print. So, until now, this book had been out of print for something like seven or eight years.

In these seven or eight years, unexpected events have taken place. That is, I received any number of requests for the book from all sorts of readers. There were a fair number of requests from readers to borrow the book so that they would be able to create their own facsimile by copying it longhand. I also received a considerable number of inquiries regarding how to obtain the book, many quite determined, from men who had been recently drafted into military service with little prospect of returning safely and who wished to visit Nara once in their life before deployment. Having felt somewhat embarrassed about the book, I felt totally at wits' end about my next course of action.

It was truly gratifying for this author to learn that the book was loved so much, but I wondered why this was so. Since the book was originally published, the field of art history has undoubtedly made advances, and many books have been written since. It seems to me that the role that this sort of guidebook once played is no longer needed. I myself would produce a very different book if I were to write a guidebook on ancient art now. In other words, this book would be out of step with the times. Despite this, why is it then that there is such a demand for this book? As I was pondering this conundrum, I came to realize that the book embodies something this author no longer possesses, namely youth and passion. It would be untruthful to say that during my ten years of living in Kyoto I did not contemplate a new edition of *Koji Junrei*, but I felt powerless to bring it to fruition. In other words, I no longer had the youthful passion that I had for the first book.

With this fact in mind, I began to realize the impossibility of making edits to this book with my present viewpoints and opinions. If the redeeming feature of the book is indeed synonymous with youthful passion, it is also synonymous with childlike unsophistication. Because I was unsophisticated, like a child, I was able to let my imagination soar as I wrote the book. Regardless of how much effort I might now put into it, my imagination would never be blessed enough for free, fanciful flight as it was in those days. It follows, then, that the deep impressions I received from ancient art more than thirty years ago and the variety of interests that they begot must therefore be preserved as they are.

In making a small number of changes, I took these thoughts into consideration and thus took the liberty of changing the old edition as needed. I made more deletions than additions, and I did so in order to bring my feelings at that time to the fore more clearly.

July 1946

The author

Note

1. During this trip to Nara, Watsuji wrote a number of letters to Teru, which provide more personal insight to Watsuji's thought. See *WTZ* 25:88–102.

Chapter 1

REPRODUCTIONS OF AJANTA WALL PAINTINGS

Right before my departure last night, I found just enough time to have Z show me reproductions of the Ajanta wall paintings[1] at his house.[1] The colors were more beautiful than I had expected from photographic reproductions I'd seen. We were pressed for time and did this hurriedly, so I cannot now recall my impressions of them precisely but, even so, they continued to come to my mind throughout the train trip. I said my farewells to my friends T and Mr. F. at the Kyoto Train Station and, as I sat alone in the dining car, the paintings came rushing back to my consciousness just as strongly as before.

One of my most unforgettable impressions of the Ajanta paintings was their particular color. The gradation of light and dark and saturation are very much different from those to which we are accustomed. This represents, most probably, a reflection of the land and people of a tropical region. Added to this were, I'd imagine, hot and transparent air that is extremely low in humidity, clear colors that contain no hint of moisture—these undoubtedly produced the particular colors of the paintings. What was most mysterious was a painting, done in the fifth or sixth century CE, which depicts a *kinnara* couple in the mountains and a celestial being playing music in the clouds.[2] Despite the fact that the figures and plants were depicted in very strong, saturated colors, the painting exuded a strangely cold and subdued feeling. Although the tree leaves were painted in deep green, almost black, they lacked any hint of light or air, something that would be unreal even in the shade of trees in the deepest depths of forests. I have always associated intense colors found in countries in hot climate zones with the dazzling light of these areas, as others have done, but I found the color scheme of this reproduction to be quite surprising. After reflecting on it a moment, I thought that this particular preference for cool colors was only natural to the Indians, who consider snow-capped mountains as the ideal earthly paradise. Those who have not been to India cannot be expected to understand how naturalistic these colors, lacking in nuance and air, are, but we

[1] The reproduction was the work of Mr. Arai Kanpō. Five or six years after this encounter, he died in the Great Kanto Earthquake as he worked in his art history office at the Tokyo Imperial University.

can infer from them the atmosphere or mood found commonly among the Indians of the fifth and sixth centuries. I speculate that the Indians then were not as cheerful as the Greeks at that time. Even in the mood of the Indians, who praised the beauty of the human body from the bottom of their hearts, we detect a tendency to prefer shadows to light, or, shall I say, a tendency to find more pleasure in the dark of the night and to fear broad daylight. This may also be surmised from not only the color scheme but also the faces of many figures depicted in wall paintings. There, both men and women generally have melancholic faces. The beauty of women's faces, which may be said to resemble that of sickly women, offers strong evidence for this idea.[3] The large almond eyes with a long and sharp slant somehow suggest a horrifying, hysterical gloom. The contour of the face, sharp and narrow from the lean build, and the fine lines that depict eyes, nose, and lips lack even a hint of fleshy ampleness. Not only that, it exudes a type of bewitching, gruesome, strange sort of beauty. Compare this to the paintings of healthy, fleshy Greek women, who are almost the embodiment of harmony. The difference between them is unmistakable.

CONNECTION TO GREECE

What I remember next about the Ajanta reproductions is the naturalism specific to India. I cannot remember which painting it was but it was a large painting—perhaps ten feet tall—of a woman with large breasts. Every part of the body—face, shoulders, arms, chest, and hips—was splendidly naturalistic. There, most certainly, I detected the eye of an artist who observed the woman's body closely and tried to tease out the secrets of her magnificent charm. This realism is attempted only with the woman's body; elsewhere in the painting it is absent. The composition is terribly unrealistic; fantastically shaped objects are placed all over the painting. Of course, in certain parts of the painting, there were areas that were both congruent and natural (by the way, I also understand that some paintings depicting Buddha's life and his narratives were done in a unified, fine composition), but, if I were to characterize the whole painting, I would say the composition was very symbolic, capricious, and not unlike something that we might see in fairy tales. It would be quite interesting to compare this to wall paintings in the Greek tradition found in Pompeii and other places, but I don't feel well informed enough to write about that. But one thing that is difficult not to notice is that the feelings that these two different types of paintings impart are quite dissimilar. I think depicting something naturalistically may be an artist's instinct, but the way naturalism works in each type of painting is very distinct one from the other. Painters working in the Greek tradition never forgot to paint something naturalistically, even if it was imagined, and stayed on the naturalistic foundation through and through. Indian painters, in contrast, while they were able to depict each of the bodies naturalistically, for the most part ignored natural placements of these figures. For instance, they painted very skillfully celestial beings flying through the air, as if those beings actually floated in the air, and yet they would be placed immediately above walking figures on the ground, without any consideration for the relationship between the two. I think this is because the artist failed to think of the naturalness of the entire painting ahead of time. That is, the composition did not come from the artist's contemplation before the painting was executed but it came from the requirements arising from the story itself. Something similar to this anomaly may be observed in Buddhist scriptures describing Mahayana mythology.

The relationship between paintings executed in the Greek tradition and the Ajanta wall paintings is not only a worthy topic of research in art history but must also be brought to light so that we will know better about the exchange of world cultures in that period. I am sure that there is any amount of research that has already been done by specialists about the technique, pigments, and other details, but, if I may make a vague speculation, it is not impossible, from the point of view of the history of the area and its invasion by Roman culture, to think that there was an **Indianized** Greek influence in the Ajanta paintings that was brought about by those Greeks who were part Indian and grew up with an Indian imagination. Even if the painter of the ten-foot painting I brought up at the beginning of this section were a native of India, we would have to acknowledge to a certain degree that this style of painting had India as its father and Greece as its mother. Without taking in the artistic spirit of Greece, this type of Indian art would not have been born. I think that the degree of digestion of the Greek influence there must have gone much further than in the case of Gandhara, and this permitted it to become extremely original.[4]

MEANING OF THE AJANTA PAINTINGS AS RELIGIOUS PAINTINGS

The reproductions of the Ajanta paintings brought another interesting issue to the fore. That is, why were paintings like these necessary as religious paintings? Religious paintings during the Renaissance can be considered either as a resurrection of ancient paintings in Christianity or as a liberation of humanity from the medieval age, but how do we explain the Ajanta paintings? What is at issue here is the seductive depiction of faces and bodies of women who appear as celestial beings and bodhisattvas and in scenes depicting romance. Madonna during the Renaissance was depicted with a well-endowed body and elegant face. There we find an artist's attempt to express the eternal Virgin's inviolable purity and boundless mercy as the mother of the Lord Savior, mixed with the expressions of Aphrodite, who was the incarnation of beauty. And of course some paintings were very successful in expressing this. But, in Ajanta bodhisattvas, we detect not even a faint suggestion of any attempt to express this purity or mercy. Neither do we detect the sense that artists strained to paint—by expressing either the youthful tension of life or the full, satisfied life—an idealized figure as Greek sculptors did of Aphrodite. It is as if artists who recognized women only as a counterpart to men and only as principal actors in seduction emphasized those parts that they felt were beautiful in the production of these paintings. This observation applies in particular to celestial beings, women in love, and women in stories. I do not think anyone who has seen how women are portrayed—with high, full breasts and full hips—would disagree with my assessment. What is expressed in these figures is neither a symphony of beautiful lines and planes, like the epitome of harmony, or a mysterious rapture that exalts the pleasure of the flesh to the level of the divine. Instead, what come rushing to the fore is the softness of the skin and the plumpness of the flesh. Why is it then that these paintings had to adorn the worship halls of Buddhists or be painted in the living quarters? Why is it then that practicing Buddhists in the mountains, who have cast away carnal pleasure and seek the truth and salvation from worldly desires, should acquaint themselves with these sort of painting day and night?

It is not right to categorize human life too strictly into such categories as religious, intellectual, or ethical. It breaks up concrete life into fragments and makes it impossible to grasp as a living entirety. Yet it is still necessary to take an aspect of life, separate it out, and closely observe its outstanding characteristics, so long as we do not forget that it is only one aspect of the whole. In this sense, religious life and a life of pleasure, though sometimes inextricably connected, must be carefully teased apart. The life of an aspiring Buddhist cannot escape this distinction. Worship ceremonies, halls of worship, and decorative art in Buddhism do not belong to the essence of religious life; in fact, they can all be removed from religious life. It is quite enough if one would move away from all types of artificial attempts in color and music and embrace only the devotion to and trust of the absolute being, as well as the practice of self-control, deliverance from hate, and the mercy taught by this absolute being—that's all that is needed. On the other hand, neither art meant for pleasing the senses nor art that enlightens one's spirit and cleanses the mind can draw in students of religion to the religious life, if they only take pleasure in the art. This is the reason why even in Buddhist congregations and Christian churches, religion, so long as it maintained a primitive, simple energy, never had much to do with art. Instead, religion expelled art because of art's characteristic relationship to the senses. This attitude is natural to those who wish to plunge into a life of religion with fervent passion.

Yet, we should not take lightly the fact that art has the power to elevate one's mind and cleanse it. Even if we were to concede that this artistic empathy exists in the realm of imagination and pertains little to the real life of those who enjoy it, such empathy may in fact stimulate one's life and motivate concrete action, for art has the power to make a person visualize the self at a **far higher** level beyond what is currently realized. For instance, if we employ music in a religious ceremony, it will surely carry a person to the so-called **temporary** relief from the bondage of this world that Schopenhauer talks about and stimulate people's desire to reach religious ecstasy and emancipation from worldly attachments.[5] That the Pure Land described in the Amida Sutra is landscape decorated by all types of art tells us how this was in fact put into practice. Thus, because of art's power to show all living beings in a **higher, attainable** spiritual realm, art had the potential to be used as a means with which to reach salvation. Yet, even when art was deployed as a tool, it had the power to stand on its own. So the fact that art in monasteries generated its own activity, as it were, is not unimaginable. The mysterious power of beauty undoubtedly made the worshiper feel the joy arising from religious practice. If we reflect only for a moment and realize that ecstasy achieved through art is far easier than the salvation arising from religion, this sort of situation can be understood very easily.

The Ajanta wall paintings provide evidence for the truth of this contention. The painters who produced these wall paintings were probably not constrained by Buddhist precepts. Likewise, I would think that the people who lived in these monastic quarters and praised Buddha in the worship halls probably did not feel a strong urge to sever themselves from carnal desires. The strange yet intense stimulation given off by various poses of men and women, lit only dimly by flickering lamplight, and any number of images of Buddha and such decorating the walls must have given way to an ecstatic intoxication.[6] If we were to assume that this sense was received as a religious feeling, this ecstasy would have arisen undoubtedly from the enjoyment of art; it probably did not come from a direct enjoyment that changes quickly into boredom and pain, as in the case of the non-monastic life.

This fact does not straightforwardly mean that people did not believe in Buddha. But what they believed in must have been a tolerant Buddha, who forgave everything and lead everyone to buddhahood; he wasn't a strict leader who commanded believers to follow precepts and devote themselves diligently to religious practice. This made it possible for the interior of a rock cave decorated by those paintings and sculptures to serve as a microcosm of the Pure Land and to give an opportunity for people to obtain a glimpse of the ultimate religious joy.

PAINTING OF A PERSIAN EMISSARY

Another issue comes from a relatively small wall painting depicting what appears to be an emissary, probably from Persia, which measured about three feet in height. The colors of this painting were completely different from all the others. The painting was executed in its entirety in delightfully harmonious, warm, and nuanced colors. The composition of a Persian man and four or five women surrounding him was highly skillful. The contour lines of human figures in this painting are considerably different from all others. In comparison to other paintings, some of which contain no contour lines and others only to a degree, we may say that this painting is characterized far more by contour lines. My friend Z pondered on why this painting was so superior to others, wondering if this painting might be in a special tradition among Ajanta paintings or if it might have been influenced by painting in countries in the western regions of China or paintings from Gandhara.[7] Clearly this painting imparts a special feeling and beauty. The opinion that this painting exhibits a Persian influence is probably based on these considerations. In Stein's *Ancient Khotan*, there is a photograph of a fresco of a naked woman standing in the middle of a lotus pond, and two Buddhas next to her.[8] The painting in the photograph feels clean and gives off a mood very different from Indian paintings but similar to the Ajanta painting of the Persian emissary.[2]

What captured my eye in the Persian emissary painting was the seductive expression worn by the woman who was positioned off of the right shoulder of the man. This is the sort of beauty not found in a painting of the Greek tradition, a type of feminine beauty specific to Indian paintings. It serves as the most representative example of the degree to which Indian men feared and loved women. This sentiment may be the same as the impression one gets from the myth of Venusberg in the Middle Ages, and the Greeks knew nothing of it.[9] The first transmission of this sentiment to places like Alexandria might have been through India. Men stood trembling for having to make this choice—take pleasure in carnal desire or save souls. The beauty of women that these men saw was precisely that of an erotic seductress. This painting depicts this beauty naturalistically and in a most typical manner.

But this painting is no religious painting. If a monk who had relinquished all carnal desires were to see this painting day and night, the painting would have been just as painful as sitting on a mat of needles. It is beautiful as it is bloodcurdling. It is that seductive.

May 16

Notes

1. Ajanta is located in Maharashtra, India. In its many rock caves dating from the second century CE, numerous examples of Buddhist art remain. His friend Z. refers to Hara Zen'ichirō.
2. *Kinnara* (Skt. *kimnara*) were originally demi-gods in Indian mythology, which were later incorporated into the Buddhist pantheon. As a part of *Hachibushū*, *kinnara* is one of the eight deities that protect the teachings of Buddha.
3. The beauty of a sickly woman refers to that which is found in a woman of fine facial features with gentle demeanor, who is pale from fighting some chronic illness.
4. Gandhara was a city in northern Pakistan and eastern Afghanistan in the Peshawar Valley that flourished from the sixth century BCE to the eleventh century CE. Buddhist kings of the Kushan Empire during first century to fifth century CE ruled this area where many stupas and stone statues of Buddhist deities were produced.
5. Arthur Schopenhauer (1788–1860) was a German philosopher who believed that one way to minimize the strife in our daily human condition is to obtain awareness through artistic and moral forms of awareness and asceticism. Watsuji wrote a graduation thesis on this philosopher for his degree in philosophy from the Tokyo Imperial University in 1912 (age twenty-three).

---

[2] Varnish was applied to wall paintings as a means of preserving them, but this painting, done on the ceiling, was left untouched, thus maintaining its fresh colors. We can say therefore that this painting preserves the original colors of Ajanta paintings.

6. The word "image" will be used for painted images of deities as well as sculpted statues and figures.

7. The western regions of China (Jp. *saiiki*, *seiiki*, Ch. *xiyu*) generally refer to Central Asia or Western Asia, sometime including India, which were located to the west of China proper.

8. Sir M. Aurel Stein (1862–1943) was a Hungarian archeologist-explorer who made four expeditions to Central Asia between 1900 and 1930. He wrote a report, *Ancient Khotan: Detailed Report of Archeological Explorations in Chinese Turkestan,* which was published by Clarendon Press, Oxford, in 1907.

9. According to a Teutonic legend, also known as the Tannhäuser legend from the fifteenth century, Venusberg is a name given to a mythical mountain in Germany. Somewhere in the mountain, hidden from mortal men, Venus, the Goddess of Love, lived in a cavern. Knight Tannhäuser, however, found it and spent a year worshiping Venus. After he returned to the mortal's world, he was filled with shame and sought forgiveness from Pope Urban IV. Tannhäuser, however, convinced that he was not forgiven, returned to the home of Venus.

Chapter 2

WISTFULNESS

I went home for a visit for the first time in quite a while and spent a night with my parents and my brother. I bid my farewells to them this morning. I felt a tinge of sadness after I boarded my train, and, as if to symbolize my state of mind, a May rain fell quietly outside of the train window and seeped into my heart. The phrase Great Mercy and Great Sadness came so close to describing how I felt.

Last night my father asked me, "What you're doing now—how much does it contribute to rescuing the decadent spirit?" I could not answer this question. I would have talked back to him four or five years ago. But now I could not help but lower my head in shame at the thought that prompted my father to ask me this question. My father is a man with a very strong passion for staying on the path. Not even for a moment has he forgotten the maxim that "medicine is an art of benevolent compassion," and in order to pursue that he has forsaken his own interest or pleasure and never looked back. A son of his has been quite unsteady in his own life, sidetracked all the time. My father's comment had a considerable impact on me, particularly because my own unsteadiness was something I had been thinking about giving up myself.

To tell the truth, it seems apparent enough to me that doing **research** in ancient art is not my intended path. I merely wanted to take this trip to enjoy the power of ancient art, to cleanse my mind, and enrich it. I need some studying before appreciating it fully. And it does not seem meaningless to me to write a travelogue of the trip for my colleagues and friends to tell them about the exquisite beauty of ancient art. Yet such work will not satisfy the need that dwells in the center of my heart. True, my interest in ancient art burns brightly, but my resolve had not extended so far that I would make it my sole work or my primary work. The rain continued to come down quietly. The view of Mt. Hiei, half obscured by misty clouds, suddenly reminded me of the tranquility of Kyoto that the train was now approaching.

(May 17)

NIGHT IN NANZENJI

This evening, I decided to decline an invitation from my friend T to go to the theater. Instead I sat down for dinner with my uncle at his house in Nanzenji, with Mt. Hiei visible from between the trees in the garden, sometimes obscured by clouds. I felt again the presence of something I must do before I indulged myself in art. But my heart rushed to the pleasure of art just like that of a debauched man. I sensed a hint of chill in my heart as I looked at this person, me, who was trying to leave this house in haste.

After retiring to bed, I opened a section of *Kasshi Yawa*.[1] A passage read:

> Empress Yang Guifei is ordinarily thought of as a slender woman, but a record dating from the Tenpō era states "Yang Guifei's had a body constitution which, by its own nature, suffered greatly in the summer from the heat. She always felt thirsty, so, every day she would place small fish in her mouth and suck on them, thereby releasing cool liquid to quench the thirst." This passage suggests that Yang Guifei was a fat woman.

The author Matsuura also expounded in this book that the ***nō*** theater originated from a theatrical form in the Song dynasty and the Japanese court music of ***gagaku*** from the music of masked theater popular during China's Tang dynasty. His writing is typical of this *zuihitsu* genre, which I find immensely enjoyable.

I heard water rushing. The stream comes into this garden from the main compound of Nanzenji, meanders through the azaleas, and pours into a pond. It then turns a water wheel and exits the house. The story is that Shingū Ryōtei, a scholar of Dutch studies, returned from Nagasaki and opened a small school called Junsei Shoin. Then he led a group of his students to build this pond and stream with the stones they carried from the Kamo River. The house he lived in still remains as it was then. Confucian scholar Rai San'yō (1780–1832) frequently visited this place during his last year or two of his life. He may have even slept in this very room I am now in. I heard that the water wheel was used to mill the rice that the owner of the house ate. The architecture of this building, in the shoin style, is quite undistinguished, but the pitch of the roof and construction of the veranda give a sense of serenity, a characteristic not often found in today's architecture. I cannot help but think that architects in the Tenpō era (1830–1844) were far superior to those of today.

Evening of May 17

Note

1. A collection of *zuihitsu* written by an Edo period daimyo essayist Matsuura Kiyoshi (a.k.a. Seizan, 1760–1841). He was the daimyo of the Hirato domain in Hizen Province.

Chapter 3

HOUSE IN NYAKŌJI

Walking across the compound of Nanzenji, we went to Mr. F.'s house in Nyakōji in the morning.[1] The sky was clear and the young leaves of Japanese maple trees shone brilliantly in the bright sunlight; Mr. F.'s brown house was buried in this greenery. From the second floor of the house, only a portion of the area where Miyako Hotel stood could be seen; otherwise the house was completely encased in billowing mounds of green leaves. It looked as if leaves of varying colors, no doubt due to the difference in variety, just sprang from the ground, overwhelming our senses like thunderous symphonic music. So after only five minutes or so of looking at this, we felt as if we had made a long, long journey from the human world. The fact that a quiet hideout like this could be located no more than ten blocks from streetcar tracks is a characteristic of Kyoto and, I thought, it has heavily affected the arts of this city.

This house had been formerly used as a boarding house for workers of a Kiyomizu pottery shop that was tucked hidden away in an alley on the hilly Gojōzaka road. Mr. F. by happenstance found the house during a walk and had the entire structure moved to this location. When he had the grubby boards and pillars washed and polished, he found that they made excellent material for a tearoom and sitting rooms. I heard that the main roofing *onigawara* tile was inscribed with the name of Dōhachi I, so the structure must date from the Bunka era (1804–1818).[2] The building was very well made, and it was easy to see that nothing was too minor to escape attention. In addition to the tearoom, the house has two sitting rooms, and one room on the second floor. It is a small house. Yet, it makes skillful use of the hallway and small nooks downstairs, imparting an overall psychological effect of living in a much larger house. Since it is so simple and unembellished, it would become boring if one lived in it for any length of time. Nonetheless it was quite interesting to see the house because it dated from the period when the culture of Edo reached its peak of delicateness.

VISIT TO THE NARA NATIONAL MUSEUM AND WALL PAINTINGS FROM THE WESTERN REGIONS OF CHINA

A little before midday, I visited the museum with Mr. F. and my friend T. Today, I found the artifacts, which Ōtani Kōzui brought back from Kucha and Khotan, to be extremely interesting.[3]

Judging from the fragments of wall paintings from the western regions of China in the exhibition, the paintings from this area seem technically far cruder than those from Ajanta. The drawing of two parallel lines formed noses and a long, slapdash line supposedly represented the eyebrow, making me wonder if they were produced half-jokingly. But how could they draw Buddhist paintings in jest? It's inconceivable that one would paint Buddhist pictures jokingly. So amateur painter monks probably created the works. The rendition of the eyebrows and noses were typical of amateurs but these paintings as a whole gave forth quite a bit of spirituality and possessed a pristine beauty.

The contour lines were rough but exuded a certain type of vibrant power. Wobbly contour lines imparted a true to life, fresh impression. The colors weren't contrived and maintained a refreshing tonality. I might also say that the human figures embodied a quality of freedom and artless immediacy not unlike those of the Post-Impressionists. I'd think that this naïveté would not have easily resulted from the technical skills of the professional painters who produced the Ajanta paintings. I could therefore sense the hand of amateur painters who, despite their lack of technical skills, were so enthusiastic that they were able to paint their own vision.

Monks who were ardent believers of Buddhism and who planned to spread the religion from India to Central Asia may not have considered the extremely aesthetic religious ceremonies in the Ajanta area to be anything more than a sign of decadence. And they might have thought that simpler art in the Gandhara area was more agreeable to their taste. We do not know what sort of paintings was produced in Gandhara. If we assume that they were naturalistic and clean, but were produced sometimes with an unrefined technique like the sculptures from this area, I think that it would not have been difficult for someone with certain innate artistic skills to imitate this style of painting. If a painter had been a professional, he would not have painted the hands of a bearded man, apparently a person of either Persian or Greek origin, in such a crude manner. The painter painted a line across the roots of the fingers on a hand just as though the painter had no more patience for the work. If a professional painter were to attempt the same, he would paint naturalistic fingers and hands in the same time these amateurs would take to draw their lines. The same can be said about noses, as I noted previously. If the artist had been intimately familiar with drawing human faces and known how to form a nose on the face, he could not have drawn it in that awkward a manner unless in jest. On the other hand, it did not look as if it was meant to be meaningless graffiti either. So I reached the unavoidable conclusion that it was most probably the artistically talented monks who had a taste for Gandhara art that produced these artworks in the western regions of China.

Those paintings, I thought, possessed a deeper spiritual content than their counterparts in India. They were a more profound type of beauty than beauty arising from sensual pleasure. For instance, the face of that bodhisattva (?) might indeed be technically far inferior to those in Ajanta paintings. But I felt that the bodhisattva face was more capable of moving people. When I looked at it carefully, I could say that it embodied a mysterious profundity that would draw a person into the strange ecstatic world of imagination. I found it extraordinarily difficult to put in words the delicate effect of the eyelids drawn with simple contour lines and the lips that parted in a faint smile.

BUDDHA HEADS FROM THE WESTERN REGIONS OF CHINA

There were four heads of Buddha among the excavated items at the museum that appeared to have received a quite a bit of influence from the Tang dynasty. I thought the following as I looked at these heads. If we were to study the eastern reach of Buddhist art, we would have to examine carefully the changes in which **eyebrows, eyes, noses, and ears were executed.** The reason why I propose this is that the ways these body parts were depicted must have changed according to the changes in peoples who served as models for this art as Buddhism spread through different ethnic groups. These groups would include the Aryan tribes of India, Asian peoples who mixed with the Greeks and peoples to the east of Greece—especially those with more Asian blood—the Turkic tribes, and the Mongolian tribes. I wonder if the gradual change in the location of a thin line drawn between the eyebrow and the eyelid shouldn't mean that the models for this were becoming Mongolians and Chinese peoples, who had puffy eyelids. Could long, narrow, and bow-shaped eyebrows also tell the same story? There are sculptures in Gandhara that were clearly modeled on Mongolian features, the technique of which was no doubt appropriated in Central Asia. The fact that the eyebrow still underwent a strong transformation as soon as it entered China could be explained, I think, by the change of models, as I explained above.

The issue of how the ideal for faces and bodies changes depending on the ethnicity of the artists is quite interesting in the context of the transmission of culture. For instance, paintings of Buddha became more and more purified and noble as Buddhism was transmitted eastward. This fact also raises an interesting issue that is worth pursuing; that is, how might this change correlate with the change of Buddhism teachings in these various localities. Another question is how this change related to the demands and internal issues of various ethnic groups then prevailing. These are all issues that definitely merit further thought.

BUDDHA HEADS IN GANDHARA AND THE MAITREYA AT KŌRYŪJI

The fact that art from the western regions of China became all the more noble and dignified when it arrived in China proper, befitting the mental image of the "Buddha," would become abundantly clear if we compared a head of Buddha among these four excavated items I mentioned above with the stucco head of Maitreya (or is it bodhisattva?) that now sits in the center of the Suiko Tenpyō Room of the museum.[3] While the naturalism of the head of Buddha from Gandhara would never fail to captivate our heart, it was no match for the supernatural majesty of the Maitreya. We should note above all the Maitreya is an image that retains the heritage of the Gandhara artistic style most prominently among all statues of Buddha in Japan. The body is fleshed out naturally. The large folds of the robe suggest their weight and possess delightful boldness and freedom. It does not suffer from the Chinese tendency toward decorativeness and manages to straightforwardly create a human figure. In my opinion, its potential as a molded stucco figure is utilized to the utmost. This is the sculpture that, among all the statues of Buddha, comes closest to sculpture of the West. But, despite its resemblance to the Greek style, the first impression one receives from this statue is of pure Buddhism. The powerful, dignified face is not that of an idealized human, but a face of a supernatural being in human form. This Maitreya statue achieved that which Gandhara art attempted but could not achieve. I think, insofar as this statue of Maireya is concerned, we can say confidently that Greek and Buddhist art was truly perfected in China.

(May 18)

Notes

1. It turned out that Watsuji purchased and lived in this house from 1924 to 1935, almost his entire time in Kyoto.
2. Takahashi Dōhachi I (a.k.a. Michihachi, 1740–1804) is the name of a well-known ceramic artist in the Kyoto area, who founded the Kiyomizu style of ceramics. Here Watsuji must be referring to Dōhachi II, who lived 1782–1855 and would have been active in the Bunka era. The Takahashi family still continues its art to this day.
3. Ōtani Kōzui (1876–1948) was a Buddhist monk who led expeditions to Central Asia between 1902 and 1910 and brought back a number of artifacts from the area. Kucha and Khotan were ancient Buddhist kingdoms in present-day Xinjiang, China.

[3] This stucco figure has now been returned to the Treasure Hall of Kōryūji.

Chapter 4

BATHING EAST AND WEST

I took a bath and was about to turn in for the night when a thought occurred to me. The so-called Western-style bathtub I used tonight was not as conducive to relaxation as a Japanese bath would be. When I sink into the soft chair next to a side table, with letter paper on top, I am more inclined to take up a fountain pen. This sensation is quite different from the one after experiencing a Japanese bath.

The Western bath is **business-like**; the Japanese bath is **pleasure-oriented**. The Western bath is no more than a facility to remove grime from the body, so in that sense it is no different from the toilet. In contrast, the Japanese bath is a place where one can enjoy, for instance, the way bath water feels to the body, the temperature of the water, the refreshed feeling after the bath, or even a feeling of intoxication. Although, in the West, the bath and toilet are placed in the same room, the Japanese do not feel this arrangement is altogether adequate, regardless of how clean the toilet might be, due to the demand of aesthetic sensibility that goes beyond cleanliness. This distinction is quite interesting to me, which promptly takes me to rambling thoughts about cultural history.

It has been pointed out that it is in the East where people take to the pleasure of the bath. In Asian countries with hot climates people bathe in cold water, but this, I think, has the same effect as warm water bath. I don't deny that people in the West enjoy bathing, but this statement may be true only about steam baths, which Westerners probably imported from the East. From what I hear, even the water from hot springs is actually drunk in the West, rather than used for bathing as in the case of Japan. In old literary works from China, the pleasure of bathing is intimately associated with the pleasure of drinking liquor and being with women and is characterized in terms of sensuality, but I wonder if there is a comparable art form in the West. Of course, in Rome, bathing was a serious matter. Bathing rooms, whether private or public, were constructed specifically for pure enjoyment, and public ones in particular were opulent and constructed with no expense spared. Under a round dome, marble was used everywhere. The buildings had cold-water baths as well as warm-water baths. They also had dressing rooms, not to mention powder rooms. The buildings were decorated with beautiful columns and sculptures as well as wall paintings. In them, people swam, bathed in warm water, took steam baths, talked, and so on to enjoy themselves. Although the Romans should be credited for starting this sort of bathing, they actually learned it from the Greeks. The Greeks, in turn, learned to bathe in their own homes from the Asians. The purpose of bathing for the Greeks was limited to healing the fatigue from war and strenuous exercise, at least in the beginning. It was in the mythical, luxurious country of Phaeacians in the *Odyssey* that people bathed for pleasure. When colonies in Asia Minor and southern Italy became more prosperous, this custom of bathing became more widespread. The Sybarites, who were the pioneers of extravagant luxury and licentiousness, made steam bathing popular.[1] Communal bathing also originated from Asia and gradually became as popular as warm-water bathing. Steam bathing was not without criticism—Hesiod and Aristophanes rather vociferously complained about its decadence, but their complaints had no effect whatsoever.[2] Immediately after Alexander the Great's rule, a public bathhouse was built in Athens; then bathing with people of the opposite sex became a common practice. In any case, the custom of bathing originated in Asia. It is fascinating, looking at things from the perspective of cultural history, to learn that Alexander the Great was astonished by the bathhouse King Darius had built.[3]

But the tradition of bathing for enjoyment waned in popularity after the Middle Ages in Europe. Of course, it was necessary to keep one's body clean by washing it, so a room for bathing was built in the house as well as in public places, but it seems to me that bathing was something that was "necessary," rather than "enjoyable." If one looks at the drawing of a bathhouse made by Albrecht Dürer, the women look hurried and intent on leaving as if they could not spend another minute there.[4] Many have painted the biblical story of Susannah bathing; none of these works express the sort of feeling about bathing we know to be true.[5] Although steam bathing exists with the explicit purpose of making the experience of bathing enjoyable, it is rare and not woven tightly into the lives of the people of the West. So long as the structure for bathing remains as it is, we may say that the Westerners do not appreciate the subtleties of bathing.

I do not have firsthand information about what happened to the tradition of bathing in China and India, but it is alive and well in Japan. The custom of bathing and the taste for it was, of course, learned from China and before that, the Japanese most certainly bathed in rivers. However, the sentiments expressed in Tang poems about bathing managed to find an affinity in the Japanese personality and, for centuries now, bathing has been deeply ingrained in the Japanese, excepting for, perhaps, vagrants. It does not matter how dirty the bathtub itself might be, the Japanese do not conduct any sort of business while bathing in it; they enjoy soaking in the water. Bathing is not taken as a decadent affectation, but it is considered to be a heaven-sent pleasure that is just as essential in the daily life of the Japanese as eating rice.

The exquisite beauty of women bathing in gently flowing water in a hot spring may not be appreciated fully by those who are not Japanese; nor, perhaps, would the beauty of the sheen on Japanese cypress that has absorbed bathwater be appreciated.[6]

To replicate the Japanese experience with the Western bath, one has only to build a drain in the bathroom floor, so that one can draw water in the tub to the brim. This improvement would take no time to implement. The fact that people do not take this simple step in the West makes me think that they do not have a highly sophisticated taste for bathing.

FROM KYOTO TO NARA

The train that takes one from Kyoto to Nara is dirty and shakes violently, making the experience unpleasant, but the scenery along the tracks amply makes up for it and then some. The gently sloping hills of Momoyama and Uji, covered with bamboo groves, tea fields, and persimmon trees, give a sense of unbridled tranquility. I could not enjoy seeing the billowing green of the tea leaves because the tea fields were totally covered with cloth protecting the plants. Nonetheless, the scenery was interesting as it was typical of a tea-growing area. The persimmon trees had already sprouted young green leaves, which covered up their awkward, craggy limbs, but I thought that the sight of these trees standing with lush leaves in the middle of wheat fields was a rare sight. It stands to reason that the literati-artist's taste would be nurtured in a place like this.

Another thing that I found interesting as I traveled on the train was that I sometimes encountered women who reminded me of sculptures from the Tenpyō era (710–794). I might just be hallucinating, but there is an intimate connection between the sculpture and the model on which it was based, so if one were to study the sculpture relating it to the physiology of women, we might be able to discern the degree to which this land had an impact on the sculpture to the Tenpyō era.

When we arrived in Nara, it was already dusk. I settled into this room. As I looked at the Wakakusa Mountains and green hills (though it was a bit late in the day to make out the color, to be honest), visible a little beyond Asaji ga Hara, I felt strongly that the feeling of this place was very much different from that of Kyoto. Nara is much more wide-open, straightforward, and unconcerned. My friend T was saying that perhaps because we spent two nights in that little secretive hideout in Nyakōji he felt a bit unsettled in Nara. Certainly, I could feel the difference between Nara and Kyoto from the scenery, which is the same difference embodied in the *Man'yōshū* and the *Kokinshū*.[7]

THE DINING ROOM OF THE HOTEL

In the dining room, we noticed a beautiful woman, who was sitting there by herself in front of the heating stove in the south corner of the dining hall. Her dark hair was swept up gently and covered her pale forehead, down to above the eyebrows. Appearing to be Spanish, she had large eyes and rosy cheeks. She wore a thin white top with low collar, which revealed the nakedness of almost all of her ample arms. A French family, which included a large man, who had a sickly pale face and long, dark hair, sat at the table next to the Spanish woman's. The man walked with a limp and it seemed that he had been wounded in a war. A Chinese woman, who wore no footwear, attended to the French family's two boys, who must have been something like four and seven years in age. The wife was still young and pretty, but she was no match for the typical virginal prettiness of her daughter, who looked delicate and quiet. This girl's neck was noticeably long. I have seen women with long necks in paintings but I had never seen one in the flesh. You might feel strange about my taking interest in these international scenes during a trip to Nara to visit temples, but I can say that I did not feel misgivings at all about how I felt. After all we are pilgrims of art, not of Buddha, who is the savior of all beings. Even if we were to feel like bowing down from the depths of our hearts in front of a statue of Buddha or be stricken by the bolt of Buddha's mercy, which would make us feel so deeply that we were reduced to tears, it would only be because we were overwhelmed by the art, which made use of Buddhist power, not because we converted to Buddhism in a strict religious sense. After all, we have not forsaken the senses of flesh to the degree that we can overcome every temptation and act only according to Buddhist precepts. So, in the dining hall, we let ourselves enjoy not only the palate but also pleasures of the world with the eyes.

After dinner, I went out to the veranda with my friend T. We could see many drunken men in a second floor room of an inn on the other side of a small pond. The men were having a grand, if too boisterous, time with geisha. I found it very interesting to see, through the green leaves, the dark silhouette of Kōfukuji and the flickering room light, with *shamisen* music wafting in the background, reflected on the same pond. We looked down on the surface of the water and continued to talk quietly

(Night of May 18)

Notes

1. According to Herodotus, the city of Sybaris (near the present-day city of Coscile in southern Italy) was known for its refinement and luxurious, opulent lifestyle. For other descriptions, see Athenaeus, *Deipnosophists* (The Banquet of the Learned), especially descriptions in book 12. C. D. Yonge, ed. London: Henry G. Bohn, n.d. Available from the digital library http://digital.library.wisc.edu/1711.dl/Literature.AthV3. Accessed May 30, 2009.

2. In Aristophanes' play *The Clouds,* one character, Strepsiades, states:

> Watch your mouth, and don't say anything disrespectful about sage and intelligent men, men so frugal that not one of them has ever cut his hair or anointed himself or gone to the bath house to wash; whereas you have been washing me out of house and home as if I were already dead! Now get a move on and take my place at school.

Apparently, some ancient authors thought that bathhouses as morally vile and disreputable and catered to the idle and lazy. See Aristophanes, *Clouds, Wasps, Peace,* Jeffrey Henderson, ed. and trans. Cambridge, MA and London: Harvard University Press, 1998, 123. About the popular perception regarding cleanliness, see the commentaries in Aristophanes, *Clouds.* K. J. Dover, ed. Oxford: Clarendon Press, 1968, 201–202.

3. Watsuji is likely referring to the time when the Macedonian king Alexander the Great fought against King Darius III of the Achaemenid Empire in 330 BCE, in which Alexander the Great emerged victorious and his victory led to the demise of the Persian Empire. According to the description in Plutarch's *Alexander* (John Dryden, trans., http://classics.mit.edu//plutarch/alexandr.html), the description reads:

> [A]fter [Alexander] put off his arms, [he] went to bathe himself saying, "Let us now cleanse ourselves from the toils of war in the bath of Darius." Here, when [Alexander] beheld the bathing vessels, the water-pots, the pans, and the ointment boxes, all of gold curiously wrought, and smelt the fragrant odours, with which the whole place was exquisitely perfumed, and from thence passed into a pavilion of great size and height, where the couches and tables and preparations for an entertainment were perfectly magnificent, he turned to those about him, and said, "This, it seems, is royalty."

4. Watsuji is probably referring to *Women's Bathhouse* by Albrecht Dürer (1471–1528), drawn in black ink, circa 1494.

5. The story of Susannah appears in the Book of Daniel in the Old Testament. It was a favorite theme of many paintings from the sixteenth century on. In the story, two elderly lascivious voyeurs observe Susannah bathing and make overtures. Susannah rebuffs the men's advance. In retaliation, they accuse her of infidelity. She is tried for promiscuity and is about to be put to death when a young man named Daniel saves her. In the end, the men are sentenced to death for their lie.

6. Traditionally, bathtubs were constructed of *hinoki* (Japanese cypress), fine grained and pale blond in color, which lends an agreeable, if faint, fragrance when it comes into contact with water.

7. The comparison is based on the fact that the poetry anthology *Man'yōshū* (after 759) was complied in Nara while the imperially commissioned poetry anthology *Kokinshū* (ca. 920) was compiled in Kyoto.

Chapter 5

PATHS TO THE CAPITAL PAST

My friend Z. and his wife arrived in the morning to join us. The first words out of Z's mouth were about the concert they attended in Tokyo the previous night featuring music by cellist Sykora.[1] Z delayed their departure from Tokyo because of this concert.

After settling down a bit, Z took no time to start pinning down the plan for our pilgrimage. We made up an ambitious plan whereby we would make a round of all major places in the span of ten days or so.

SHIN YAKUSHIJI TEMPLE

After lunch we set out to visit the Shin Yakushiji temple, traveling in rickshaws.[2] The road was full of potholes and exposed rocks. It eventually took us to more and more desolate places on the outskirts of town. At one point, low earthen walls ran on either side of the road, in a bad state of disrepair, some portion of the walls overgrown by quite a bit of vigorous green growth. When I see something like this, I become all the more aware that Nara is Japan's capital no more. I was used to seeing these low walls as a child, and I think those early childhood memories added a tinge of sadness to the way I felt about these fencing walls. The temple construction in the gable roof style, with many walls, had the same effect on me, because it aroused a similar sentiment. The roof ridges of houses around here were not perfectly level but appeared to have a slight rise at the ends, which I found to be very successful in projecting a sense of oldness. In other words, the same feeling one gets from the roof of Sangatsudō at Tōdaiji can still be found, albeit faintly, in the roofs of people's residences in this area.[3] Good architecture dating from ancient times, it seems to me, continues to give off a sort of aesthetic atmosphere.

We followed the narrow road that made me think of the old capital of Nara, now dilapidated, more and more. Then we came to a stop in front of a gate, where we could see a wheat field nearby. But, just standing there did not make us sense that anything much different from what we had seen so far would be waiting for us inside. We went in though a gate. We noticed straightaway that patches of fresh stucco for repair had been applied here and there to the sidewalls of a temple hall, a sight that took us a bit by surprise. We walked to the front of the hall and positioned ourselves at a spot where we could see the entire building. Our initial surprise developed into disbelief about why such a magnificent piece of architecture should be tucked away here. And that sense of surprise added an indescribable, refreshing immediacy to the ecstatic beauty of the building.

This building was reportedly built with the sponsorship of Empress Kōmyō (701–760). Since it was first built, it had been repaired a number of times, but it still exudes a cheerful and elegant harmony. This is not to say that the building does not have the healthy, sturdy disposition typical of Tenpyō architecture. The most persistent feeling one receives from looking at the building from the front is the sureness and solidity of Tenpyō architecture. I cannot think of any other architectural style in other periods that impresses us with more grandeur than this simple structure. Yet, the characteristic of this hall is **how light it feels**. This lightness, in turn, becomes tenderness, which permeates the entire disposition of this hall. This probably is due to the fact that the inside of this building had no ceiling, thus exposing the underside of the roof, which permits the building to be lower in height than otherwise possible. Having praised this hall, I should point out that at this temple, in comparison to this hall, the Yakushi Nyorai statue, the main object of worship here, and the statue of Kōyakushi in another building are far more noteworthy (*see fig. 1, photo section*).

In the main hall of worship, there was a circular altar, on which the Yakushi Nyorai (Healing Buddha) stood, around which the Twelve Heavenly Generals were situated. The face of the Healing Buddha is dark after being exposed to the smoke of incense. The large prominent eyes, unusual for Buddha statues, jumped out at us from that dark face. The face of this statue looked a bit unusual when viewed from the front because of the darkening from the incense smoke but, if we looked a little more carefully, it was not difficult to notice that it was a very balanced face with strong contour lines. This was all the more evident if we went around to the side and looked at the profile. The modeling of the muscle from the shoulders to the arms gave a sense of extraordinary strength and solid mass. It would be difficult to find a carved wooden statue that was as stately as this one. Not only was the whole statue carved out of one piece of wood, but we could also sense a very tight compositional unity in the work as a whole. The power to overwhelm the viewer that this statue possesses comes, I think, from the artist's extraordinary skills.

If we remembered correctly, Dr. Sekino said this piece belonged to the Tenpyō period in his lectures but we wondered today if this might not belong to the Kōnin period instead.[4] The strong and energetic way in which the clothing was carved made us think in that way.

We were not able to view the statute of Kōyakushi today.[4]

VISION OF SARNATH

On our way back, we walked on an unfrequented road through Kasuga Park. This ancient, wooded area is magnificent, no matter when I come here. All the trees had leafed by now and we could see tall Japanese cedar and cypress trees, seemingly untouched from ancient times, standing at attention. The wisteria was in full bloom. Its violet flowers could be seen even on branches of tall trees. I felt that the feelings of the people who wished to realize the vision of Sarnath in this wooded area were still wafting about among the flowers.[5] But the moment we stepped out to a busy commercial street, we came across entirely different scenes, with ordinary people enjoying themselves, typical of any "famous, tourist-trodden place." There I detected a feeling peculiar only to Nara. This contrast is not altogether displeasing, but it is nonetheless disconcerting in that this feeling and the classical feel we gathered from Sangatsudō and such are incongruent and do not seem to relate at all to each other.

We then went into the Golden Hall and Nan'endō of Kōfukuji, but I am sorry to say that we were too tired to form definite impressions of them. A wall painting in the Nan'endō, however, was worth seeing.

At the dinner table, as we looked out at the same kind of scenery as last night, we listened to Z.'s stories about his experiences staying in hotels in the United States.

(Night of May 19)

Notes

1. Bogumil Sykora (1890–1953) was a well-known Czechoslovakian cellist, who gave a concert at the Tokyo University of Music on May 18, 1918.
2. The foundation stone for Shin Yakushiji was laid in 747 CE at the request of Empress Kōmyō, who wished to build this temple to pray for the recovery of Emperor Shōmu (701–756, r. 724–749). The temple had as many as one hundred monks living there in the beginning. During the Heian period, the towers and other buildings were lost in natural disasters. Only a few of the original buildings remain today.
3. Watsuji describes Sangatsudō's architecture in somewhat more detail in Chapter 21.

---

[4] Kōyakushi is a masterpiece dating from the Hakuhō period (latter half of the seventh century CE). It was once stolen and lost its feet below the ankle, but it is not so bad that the loss affects the general impression of the statue. When we visited the temple for the first time, it was right after this theft took place. Then it was recovered and placed in storage with utmost care. Subsequently a new hall of worship was built to house this Healing Buddha, and it became possible to request that the doors of the small altar be opened so one could pray to this deity quietly. The Kōyakushi statue, lit from below by votive candlelight, was truly indescribable. The face bore a slight smile, the gentle undulation of the robe stuck fast to the body. Nowhere was there any evidence of artificiality. It was simple as though it was born as it was. Yet, at the same time, there was no obvious flaw. The statue is a result of tremendous simplification. The face looked very simple, almost primitive, but it was able to express an extremely delicate and profound feeling. The reader should experiment by shining light from different angles; from the simply carved face, the reader would certainly find rich, unexpected gradations of expression. Anyone who could carve like this was undoubtedly a master. This fact can also be discerned from the use of copper. It appears that the base was fashioned with a skill that is not altogether well developed, yet it has no trace of stiffness or defect. The technique was indeed astounding. In recent years, I should note, this statue was stolen for the second time.

4. Sekino Tadasu (1868–1935) taught architectural history at the Tokyo Imperial University from 1901. He is credited for his work with Okakura Tenshin on Nara-period architecture and for suggesting the name "Asuka period." The Tenpyō period as an imperial era spanned 729 to 749 but as a cultural period, it refers to the Nara period in general, 710–794. The Kōnin period may refer to the imperial era 810–824 but may also refer to the cultural and artistic period from about 800 to 900.

5. Sarnath (Jp. *Rokuyaon*) in the present-day State of Uttar Pradesh in India was a deer park where Sakyamuni was said to have taught the Dharma for the first time after achieving enlightenment in Bodhgaya several weeks earlier.

Chapter 6

THE ROAD TO JŌRURIJI

Today we went to Jōruriji.[5] We thought we could return to the inn not much after midday, so we asked the innkeeper to expect us back for lunch, but the trip took longer than expected. It turned out to be very interesting.

To the north, in the outskirts of the city of Nara lies Yamashiro Province—if I use the old name for the area. The boundary was not in name only because the area beyond it had a totally different feeling from Yamato, the old name for the Nara area. When we went over the Narazaka Pass, a complete change in landscape took place.[1] The road we took circled a small mountain half way up. The soil exposed at the surface was reddish and sandy, likely infertile. Except for spindly pine trees—I found the color of the bark rather attractive—there did not seem to be any trees at all. The pine trees grew in groups of several, visible below the road itself. Other than that, only nondescript trees, including some pines, no taller than three feet or so, were holding onto a precarious existence here and there, never spreading enough to cover the hillside. And among those clumps of trees, azaleas were in full bloom. This sort of landscape has a considerably different feeling from Mt. Mikasa to the east of Nara and other mountains to the south of it. To me, though, the bald mountain—arid and sandy—was not unfamiliar. In places like this, children would have great fun playing everywhere along the ridges. Spring would be the season for us children to collect young leaves of a particular kind of oak tree for wrapping rice cakes or, if we did not find enough of them, we looked for smooth and round leaves of rose bushes.[2] The azalea flowers, in pinks and pale blues, would help children to get excited about celebrating the Boy's Day festival. The weather wouldn't be too cold to play in the streams. Children would play in the mountains as if they were part of them, until the buzzing calls of cicadas made them a bit lonesome and beckoned them to go home. That's how it was for me some twenty years ago. I looked at the landscape for a long time as these boyhood memories came back to me, as if I were back home. This state of mind affected me in a strange way even after we arrived at Jōruriji.

Of course, it wasn't that we reached Jōruriji straight away. The rest of the way was still

[5] The temple is located in the village of Tō no O, the county of Sōraku, Kyoto Prefecture. It is less than four miles northwest of the city of Nara.

arduous. We came out from a wooded area to open land, went past some mountains, then through forested areas, then out into a clearing, where we could see some houses, apparently with some history and distinction, only again to travel farther on the potholed road. The road was **dreadfully uneven**, still wet from the rain last night, which made it difficult to ride the rickshaw. We spent time praising the beautiful contrasts in color between fields and the rice paddies but, after a while, we became impatient with the slow progress and stepped down to the narrow country road, except for Z.'s wife, who remained onboard. We walked, drenched in sweat, through oak groves and wheat fields, where wheatears were just about ready to come out. When we arrived at the village in the foothills, where the temple was located, Mrs. Z. judged that she could not stay on the rickshaw any longer. So she too had to walk a steep and narrow precarious road, strewn with small rocks, along with the rest of us. The road looked as if it might lead us to some farmer's kitchen. We had taken this road because the main road wouldn't have been passable due to a landslide there. So we were determined as ever to pass this hill but, mercifully, this part of the road was short. Then, it took us to another, flat stretch cut parallel to the ridge of the hillside. Greatly relieved, we kept walking, but this road continued on and on. On the hillside, we saw clumps of short pine trees and, in between, azalea bushes in bloom, same as before. We also came upon a place where *jizō* lined the road, then came to a spot where we could spy houses from between bamboo trees and clearly hear rushing water. There was an air of tranquility and mystery about the scene. We naturally concluded that we were almost at the temple, but the place turned out to be a watermill. The building near the top of the mountain, far in the distance, that we had spotted from the bottom of the mountain appeared to have been this millhouse. What a climb we made! We congratulated ourselves but another thought occurred to us—how much more? We continued on a slow, uphill walk, during which, at one spot along the way, we saw a huge boulder jutting out, hanging over the road. Then suddenly, the view cleared and we came upon a large flat area, which could apparently be used for growing wheat and rice. In it, there was a village, complete with groves and small hills. The view fitted the word "peaceful" to a tee but was totally unexpected so deep in the mountains. Jōruriji was situated in one corner of this village, perfectly befitting this tranquil setting. This was also unexpected and gave us a beautiful sense of serenity. So this was how the trip was; by the time we finally reached Jōruriji, we should have been back in Narazaka already.

JŌRURIJI

When I stood in the midst of a wheat field and looked at the charming, rustic view—the small gate of the temple, white walls, tops of pine trees peeking out from above the walls, I remembered that I had once seen a scene like this. Entering through the front gate of the temple, I first took notice of a quiet pond, nestled between the main hall and the pagoda, the color of its water, and the young reed stalks growing. Despite the fact that it was a sight of something unusual I had never seen it until now, the strangely transparent, deep, and cool color of the water was somehow familiar to me. The elegantly shaped main hall of worship, with the mountain looming behind it, was exactly right for this garden, and the small three-story pagoda stood in a part of the compound that was a bit higher than the rest. The pagoda had acquired a distinct coloration through age. These buildings were again both familiar to me. As I walked on the white sand in front of the main hall, I was not able to shake off this vague feeling of familiarity.

Where on earth did this feeling come from? Here was a quiet village not very deep in the mountains that has been secluded from the rest of the world. There, embraced in nature, an exquisite, small tower and a worship hall had been built. A charm pleasing to everyone permeated the atmosphere in the temple. It is, admittedly, a scene that may be simply too fleeting and ordinary for modern man. Yet, when our souls are in need of peace and rest, the hidden charm of this scenery moves something deep in our hearts. We always thought that the dream of Shangri-La that ancient people embraced—I think this fantasy found affinity with Pure Land Buddhism, resulting in the choice of this mountainous site, and the building of a hall by the pond—was simply the dream of ancient religious recluses that had no connection whatsoever to us. But when we came face to face with the temple in this mountain village that expressed this fantasy, we discovered that we did in fact possess something in our hearts that resonated with this fantasy. That took me by complete surprise. It occurred to me, however, that every one of us once lived in a Shangri-La, that is, each one of us was a child once in our lives! I wondered if this might not explain my feeling.

Buried in these stray thoughts, I found it difficult to concentrate on the nine sculptures of Buddha that lined the worship hall. My friend Z. pointed out to me the metalwork adorning the platform on which the sculptures were standing, which I also found worth noting. I also thought that the painting done on a piece of wood that looked very much like a candlestick holder, placed in front of each statue, to be interesting. I thought that the pale-faced *jizō*, although it was no more than that, was well done. Above all, though, the shape of this hall that stood in complete harmony with its surroundings was exceptional. It was wonderful to be able to see the golden statutes through the open doors of the hall. The setting, where nine large statues of Buddha are enshrined, buried in the gentle greenery, is fitting of the imagination typical of the time at the end of the Fujiwara period.[3]

It was well past midday. The wife of the priest of Jōruriji, who was working in the kitchen, was kind enough to feed us lunch. It was dark-colored rice served in chipped bowls. I felt sorry for Mrs. Z., who was unaccustomed to this sort of humble fare, but it was completely in harmony with today's trip.

KAIDAN'IN AT TŌDAIJI

On the way back we took shortcuts and saved time. We did not return to Nara until after four in the afternoon. Almost immediately we set out to see Tōdaiji, which promised us a totally different experience from Jōruriji. When we hurried over to Kaidan'in at Tōdaiji, the sun had almost gone down, casting dark shadows on the trunks of the large pine trees. In the empty lot next to the building protected by sturdy fences, lonely darkness foreshadowing the coming dusk hung in the air.

We stood on a patch of grass with small flowers in bloom and listened to the clank of a large lock unlocking. That made me feel anxious. Kaidan'in is just such a place. When we stepped inside, we first felt the large emptiness of a room mixed with depressing dreariness, then we almost let out a cry when we saw how everything was covered with layers of dust. There, in front of us, different from the nature we had just seen, stood a manmade structure, where the souls of men were buried in dust and dirt. On the stage of this building, hundreds, no, thousands, of monks must have received unforgettable and solemn Buddhist precepts that they promised to uphold. When I thought of this, the dust put me in a deeply sad, melancholic mood. This sadness was not anything like the warm and sensuous sadness I felt at the Jōruriji.

THE SHITENNŌ AT KAIDAN'IN

In the four corners of this dusty, empty stage stood the Four Guardian Kings (Shitennō).[4] And these are the greatest and most sacred sculptures of all time! I felt a bit of irony that was altogether peculiar. I myself prefer to see statues of this sort in their proper setting, but I didn't know what to think of this, now that I noticed the proper setting has been neglected to such disrepair. The authority vested in this practice of granting precepts had now lost much of its credibility. That might partially explain why, though the floor was covered with a cloth, we could simply walk about on the stage without removing our shoes. Regardless of how the practice had fallen out of grace, the greatness of these statues did not. Rather, now, the greatness is far more than that of the rest of the structure. The statues should never be left in this grime.

The four statues were true masterpieces in terms of the skills shown in both naturalistic and formulaic representation. The deep frowning face of the statue of Kōmokuten standing in the northwest corner of the stage was depicted in uncanny realism attentive to the smallest detail; not only that, the most sublimated form of the white hot tension of willpower was expressed in the face. The strength and grandeur of the statue came, not from the forced effort of attempting to express power as much as possible, but from a quiet but sharp eye toward realism as well as the sureness of technique that knew the balance between ostentation and modesty. So in this statue there was no evidence of the exaggeration often seen in sculptures of guardian gods in later periods. This quiet face, modulated by only faint suggestions, was far more effective in expressing the willpower of the subject and in articulating a clear artistic idiom than the face in which facial musculature was contorted in order to express all that was possible.

The body structure of this statue was most certainly based on that of a Mongoloid, or more specifically, it could be that of a Japanese. As soon as I looked at this statue, it made me think of a friend of mine. The particular muscles around the eyes, nose, and cheeks, and especially above the cheekbones and below the ears were familiar to all of us. The same could be said about the skin. I cannot honestly say that this was not a Chinese man, but I am certain this was not an Indian. Judging from the knowledge gained from excavated items in the west of China, this statue is not a man from that area either. It might therefore be reasonable to conclude that this sort of realism mixed with formulaic depiction probably developed, at the least, to the east of Yumenguan.[5]

I found the armor of the Four Guardian Kings to be of particular interest. The artist was able to express the texture of leather extremely skillfully. On both arms, right below the shoulders, a motif which appeared to be the head of a tiger or lion was positioned as if the large feline was spitting out the arm from its open mouth. Fangs and teeth in the mouth were delineated as well. And they looked like they were indeed very hard. The strap that held the chest plate hanging from the shoulders was no different from one we'd use today. The chest plate was tight against the chest and the stomach and it looked as if it would actually squeak if the statue were to come alive. I almost forgot that this statue was molded.

I wondered from which countries the battle-gear came. It is clear that the armor was not from India, judging from the cylindrical shape of the sleeves and the tight-fitting underpants worn on the lower body. This might resemble Greek and Roman armors in some respects, but it was clearly different. It could be similar to that of Persia, but I was certain that when Persia was in contact with Greece, no armor of this type existed. This meant that it came from either Central Asia or China. Skills in leather crafting could have developed in Central Asia, but the armor used in that area, from what I understand, was much simpler. All this points to the conclusion that this battle-gear in this style probably came out of China.

This conclusion begot another problem, which was this: the Buddha and bodhisattva statues were attired in Indian or even Greco-Roman clothing, so why was it, then, the guardian statues were in Chinese style? I offer the following answer: if one looked at the sculptures in Gandhara, there were cases in which the artist placed a Greek god or a bearded man who looked like a philosopher in one corner of a composition. Also among the excavated items from Khotan, there were pieces in which figures, clothed in Khotan clothing, were portrayed. I would venture to say that when visually depicting dramatic scenes like Buddha giving a sermon, as seen in Mahayana sutras, the figures of buddhas and bodhisattvas would be normally portrayed in the canonical style, but, when portraying the general public listening to an epochal sermon, the artists could only use their own imagination, which resulted in a situation in which different regions developed their own imagery. So it seems to me that the Twelve Heavenly Generals and Four Guardian Kings like these at this temple might be the result of the creative imagination of Chinese art.[6]

The practice of situating the Four Guardian Kings in the corners of a stage probably related closely to temple construction in China. I would surmise that Buddhist art took on a considerable number of changes in China. And art from the western regions of China, on which Chinese art was based, received much more influence from Gandhara than from India. So Buddhist art that was transmitted to Japan was art that had undergone a large number of changes.

THE MAIN IMAGE OF WORSHIP AT SANGATSUDŌ

From Kaidan'in, we trekked over to Sangatsudō.

I was always fond of the exterior of Sangatsudō but never thought that the main object of worship enshrined here, Fukū Kensaku Kannon, was on par with other main images in terms of its significance.[7] But, when we walked into the beautiful hall and looked up at it quietly, I was taken aback. It was as if there was a halo hanging where the statue stood. The radiating rays behind the statue, which I had thought were distracting, now appeared to fit superbly into the mysterious light drifting about in the twilight, and an indescribable, delicate harmony added to its beauty. The golden rays reflecting off the remaining spots of gold gilding looked as if they were not just an ordinary reflection in golden color but a special one that was beautiful and rich. The feature responsible for this, I assumed, was the interior, especially the incomparable look of age in the superbly crafted ceiling that brought it out to the fullest advantage. At the same time, however, the beauty of this hall would not feel right without the gold foil on the *kannon* in the center. That is, the *kannon* and the hall together formed a work of art. It was a result of a grand yet quiet symphony of color, light, air, and the broad and bold lines that crisscross inside the hall (*see fig. 2, photo section*).

The proportions of the main figure could not be said to be perfectly balanced. The shoulders, the arms, and the torso were solidly built, but, from the waist down, the balance was broken. The many arms, the radiating lines and the flame designs in them behind the back, the gently undulating heavenly robe, and the crown bejeweled and huge—each one of these worked well in an odd sort of way in harmony with the surrounding hall. I think the reason I did not see the beauty of this was that I was simply looking at individual parts rather than the entirety of these parts. Artworks dating from the Suiko period (593–628) reached a stage of simplification by cutting out what was unneeded, but Tenpyō art did not fear the partial mixing of the precious and the ordinary so that they would enliven the whole.

OTHER STATUES IN SANGATSUDŌ

I bowed my head to the Fukū Kensaku Kannon and Sangatsudō. I took my hat off to my friend Z., who had been enthralled by this *kannon*. I should add that what was beautiful did not end with this *kannon*. The surrounding statues were all exquisite. No one in their right mind would argue that the small figures on the side of Bonten and Taishakuten (also called Gakkō and Nikkō, respectively) were nothing less than masterpieces.[8] As for the other figures in the hall, different opinions were expressed. For instance, my friend Z. had nothing positive to say about the four guardian figures, but I expressed high regard for these relatively simple statues. I found the back one on the left to be appealing. Of course I admit that these were not as good as those at Kaidan'in, as they looked a bit stiff, but they were clean and straightforward and were not at all out of place in this magnificent hall (*see fig. 3, photo section*).

We discussed these things at some length after we returned to the hotel. Since so many unexpected events had occurred, everyone was animated that night. There was a group of four Westerners, apparently merchants, at the next table making one toast after another, every three minutes or so, several dozens of times altogether. We too were a bit excited and felt like celebrating like them. My friend Z. thought that most statues in Sangatsudō were largely insignificant and was steadfast in believing that Fukū Kensaku Kannon and the Bonten (Gakkō) were the only pieces worthy of being called masterpieces of the Tenpyō era.[6] I had a difficult time agreeing with this view. I think I would choose the Eleven-headed Kannon of Shōrinji instead, if I were to choose the best work from that era.

After each of us returned to our respective rooms, a deflating feeling, typical after excitement, came over me. I mentioned to my friend T, when we were talking about something else, what sort of work would be worthy of devoting one's life to it. I became envious of T, who was calm and purposeful and paid attention only to deepening his knowledge of the field of his choice until the time he could feel confident enough to become a professional. I felt like rootless water grass and I thought I must recalibrate my path. Think of Goethe, who was extremely endowed with talent, I thought to myself. Even he regretted the fact that when he traveled to Italy he felt that he had not spent the necessary time to perfect his craft and that he hadn't taken the time to acquire the necessary skills for it.[9] There was no way around it. I must chart my own path and make progress in it, one step at a time.

(May 20)

---

[6] Among the statues on the platform in Sangatsudō, the Nikkō and Gakkō bodhisattva figures and the Kichijōten figure, all of which were actually produced in clay, are excellent pieces of sculpture. My suspicion is that these did not originally belong to this hall. The statue called Shūkongōshin, situated in the same hall in a small shrine behind the platform and also likely constructed out of some plastic material, is an excellent piece of work. Looking back at the time when I was writing this passage, I focused on the balance between sculptures and the architecture surrounding them but not on these sculptures. If we were to remove them from the hall and examine them individually as sculptures, I'd think that these should be considered Tenpyō's best.

Notes

1. Narazaka is a long hill in the northern part of the city of Nara; it is now Narazaka-chō, Nara City. It is a steep hill that goes over Narayama and connects Nara to Kyoto Prefecture.
2. In his autobiography, Watsuji describes bald hills where he once played as a boy. See *Jijoden no kokoromi* (An Autobiography), *WTZ* 18:15. The sweets referred to here are called *kashiwamochi*. They are typically eaten on the occasion of Boy's Day (*Tango no sekku*) celebrated on the fifth of May. The cake itself has a sweet center, made of adzuki beans, which is covered with soft sweet-rice *mochi*, then wrapped in large oak (Jp. *kashiwa*) or rose leaves. Watsuji recalled in his *Jijoden no kokoromi* that the particular type of rose leaves used for this purpose was called *yakimochi bara* (lit. jealousy rose) because *mochi* stuck to the leaves, much like a jealous person would stick unwelcomingly close to the object of love. See *Jijoden no kokoromi*, *WTZ* 18:206–207.
3. The Fujiwara period is a cultural period dating from mid-to-late Heian or roughly the eleventh to the twelfth centuries.
4. These Four Guardian Kings (Shitennō) are guardians who watch over the four directions of the Buddhist world. They are Tamonten (a.k.a. Bishamonten, who watches over the north), Zōchōten (south), Jikokuten (east), and Kōmokuten (west).
5. The city Watsuji refers to in the original text is Gyokumon but it probably refers to Gyokumonkan (Ch. *Yumenguan*), a city about 60 miles northwest of Tonkō (Ch. *Dunhuang*), in western China.
6. The Twelve Heavenly Generals are guardian gods for Buddhist teachings. They are generally portrayed with armor, often guarding a Yakushi Nyorai (Healing Buddha). Among these twelve deities, perhaps Konpira (Skt. *Kumbhira*) and Taishakuten (*Indra*) are most familiar.
7. Also called Fukū Kenjaku Kannon, it is a bodhisattva with the power to lead all humans to salvation using its infinite net. It is often depicted with many arms and wearing a deer hide.
8. Bonten (*Brahma*) and Taishakuten (*Indra*) are Hindu devas that were integrated into Buddhism. In Japanese Buddhism, Bonten and Taishakuten, often appearing as a pair of statues, are considered to be guardian devas of Buddhism.
9. Goethe spent 1786–1788 in Italy to learn about Greek and Roman classical antiquity. In his letter dated February 22, 1788, Goethe wrote:

   > I realize more clearly every day that I was really born to be a poet, and that in the next ten years, which are all, at most, which I shall be allowed to work in, I must cultivate this talent and produce something good. The time when the fire of youth enabled me to accomplish things without much study is now over; I shall have the benefits of my sojourn in Rome to look back upon, even though I shall have to give up practicing the visual arts.

   See J. W. Goethe, *Italian Journey, 1786–1788*. Translated by W. H. Auden and Elizabeth Mayer (New York: Schocken Books, 1968), 472.

Chapter 7

FATIGUE

Having seen so many works of art within the span of one day, I returned to my room utterly exhausted, so that even speaking seemed tiring. I sat absentmindedly in a soft chair in the room to rest. When I had recuperated a bit, I washed my hands, changed my shirt collar and walked on the soft carpet to the dining room. Mrs. Z. had changed her attire on short notice and looked very sprightly. I was extremely hungry and the food was well prepared, so I had much more than my usual amount. Then we all started to talk with renewed energy. This was the time to discuss the works of art we saw today and digest the impressions we had just received. By the time we left the dining room, we were full and felt worn out from the events of the day. I went to the smoking room, but I only vacantly watched some Western women enjoying themselves.

I then returned to my room to take a bath. It then became entirely a bother to write down the day's impressions. It is best to capture these impressions when they're fresh, but it is also difficult to accomplish. The comments in my notebook became simpler as the day progressed.

NARA NATIONAL MUSEUM

It is unreasonable to think that we could see this whole museum in one morning. We should see at most two or three statues in one visit, so that we could see them to our heart's content until they soaked into our souls.

It appeared that my friend N was doing precisely this. We ran into him at the entrance, as he was coming out of the museum, having done his viewing for the day.[1] "I come here almost every day," he said. "If I am in a good mood, that is." Since he was an early riser, I was sure that he would walk around the park even before the morning dew evaporated, and go into the museum the moment it opened. He would spend countless hours sitting in front of a statue, as he felt the cool air of the cavernous museum on his slightly sweaty body. He had kept up this routine for over a month. Knowing that we were traveling, feeling always pressed for time, I felt a tinge of resentment toward N.

We said good-bye to N. When we walked up the stone steps of the entryway, we noticed that the doors of a display case in the entry hall for the Eleven-headed Kannon were open. Next to it, a man in Western clothes stood. He was in the midst of explaining "the beauty of the human body" to a museum staffer on the lower level. We were lucky that the doors were open, but this young man was a sore distraction. He gestured pompously with his body and jumped off onto the floor from the display platform. No sooner had he done so than he began preaching to a museum staffer there about "the beauty of the human body, specifically around the breasts." This explained why N walked out with an expression of disgust (*see fig. 4, photo section*).

We could not leave this area since we wanted to make the best use of rare opportunity of the glass doors being open. This was because the distorting imperfections of the glass and reflection of light on it were so very annoying.

In this connection, I would very much like the museum to improve the way they exhibited objects. I am sure that there were cost considerations, so we couldn't blame only the museum staff, but the way objects were exhibited took no consideration whatsoever of how viewers would see them. If everyone were as uncomplaining and diligent as my friend N, they could overcome the difficulty to a certain degree, but not everyone has the luxury of time. The least I'd ask would be that the museum rethink the order and methods in which objects were displayed, so that each one of the statues of Buddha would give us a distinct impression without interference from others. This would allow even those visitors who had little time for a visit to get a stronger and more coherent impression. Even more idealistically, I think institutions for public enjoyment such as art museums should be built much, much more luxuriously. This luxury wouldn't be anything like the luxury of a private person. That is, on the display platform in the entrance hall, objects which deserve one whole gallery to themselves were displayed in a confused, slapdash disorder.[7] It was impossible to even hazard a guess about how much disservice this jumble was to visitors. To rephrase my irritation in a way that people responsible could understand, I might say this: "This shabby clutter is a national disgrace to Japan. Because of things like this, Westerners do not respect the Japanese."

The word "national treasure" should be used to its fullest advantage. As native Japanese, it is our birthright to view these ancient artworks. And for us not to be able to appreciate them in an adequate setting is completely contrary to the idea of "national treasure."

---

[7] This was the case in 1919 or thereabouts. At that time, the Shōrinji's Eleven-headed Kannon stood facing the main entrance of the museum. Behind it, placed with its back to the *kannon*, stood the Kudara Kannon from Hōryūji. The Shōrinji Kannon was returned to the temple after several years. To visit this temple, which is located perhaps one mile from Sakurai, one would go past the Tō no Mine road and turn right at the crossroad and then go a little distance from the turn. The Kudara Kannon was also recently returned to Hōryūji, and it reigns over other deities at Hōmotsuden there.

THE ELEVEN-HEADED KANNON AT SHŌRINJI

Notwithstanding this irritation, I do think that the Eleven-headed Kannon of Shōrinji is unquestionably a masterpiece. I was a bit unhappy about how the shoulders were rendered, but the defect does not damage the overall impression. If we could situate this statue in a structure like Sangatsudō and balance it with the beauty of its surroundings, its fresh, rich elegance would shine to its full advantage.

It is widely known that Buddhist scriptures describe in great detail the shapes of Buddhas and bodhisattvas. No one would consider the Amida Sutra (*Amidakyō*) to be a scripture of Buddhist teaching. This sutra is, **first and foremost**, a description of various images of deities in the Pure Land. And, further, no one can call the Lotus Sutra (*Hōkekyō*) as not being a book about imagery. It is, **first and foremost**, a grand epic poem with Buddha as the main character. The Infinite Life Sutra (*Kanmuryōjukyō*) deals with the imagery **especially** in great detail. On the basis of these sutras, followers of Buddhism tried to see this imagery with their very own eyes. Grasping the image and virtues of Buddha was an important element in the inner life of Buddhists. Thus, it is easy for us to understand the importance of the stimulating and concrete role that "images of Buddha" played. It is from this sort of background that this image of *kannon* was produced. We do not know who the artist was, but no matter who it was, there is little doubt that he witnessed with his own eyes a clear image of Buddha.

Kanzenon Bosatsu, a bodhisattva who is all seeing and all hearing, possesses unimaginable power and infinite mercy to save all living beings from suffering. In order to be saved by him, one needs only to pray to him. Depending on the situation, he can take the form of Buddha or sometimes that of Bonten (*Brahma*). He can also appear in human or animal form. He helps all living beings to attain buddhahood and freedom from worldly attachments and provides peace. Given these characteristics, in what sort of shape should this bodhisattva be? First of all, it must have a superhuman dignity that no human can attain. At the same time, it should embody humanlike kindness and beauty. At the very basic level, it is not a human being. But, by manifesting itself in human form, it elevates the human shape to the level of divine purity and beauty. The iconography in Esoteric Buddhism goes even so far as to require that the image should have a water vase in the left hand and that the heads surrounding the main head like a crown should include one of a bodhisattva, one with an angry face, another with a laughing face, and so on, but these requirements are not an important part of the *kannon* imagery. Variation on the heads is acceptable, so long as the faces on the main head look a bit like a bejeweled crown on the head. The vase, too, isn't significant. If added, it may simply serve the purpose of giving the figure an artistic variation. What is important is the combination of superhumanness and humanness, as I said before, and here lies space in which the artist may let himself take flight into the realm of imagination.

Thus, this Eleven-headed Kannon may be said to be a crystallization resulting from a long, profound, and free conceptualization that has been nurtured by any number of sutras and carved images of Buddha. There we also witness a vestige of unlimited and unconstrained myths originating in India. I would think that peoples in the ancient Far East would not have had the predisposition to find purity and beauty in a half-naked body. We also find an influence from Gandhara, where artists injected the beauty of naturalistic representation into abstract imagination. The delicateness and sureness with which the human body is rendered and the beauty of the true-to-life fold of the robe had been absent in the artistic traditions of the Far East. In this figure, we also detect the intense admiration of the peoples of Central Asia living along the Ganges River, who longed for a paradise on earth in the far distance beyond the snowcapped mountains. I cannot imagine the strong fragrance arising from an ideal work of art that is not only naturalistic but also able to render something superhuman in quality as being separate from the threat of the monstrous desert where these peoples lived. Furthermore, the air of the Tang dynasty—the dynasty that attained the highest peak of culture in the Far East, served as the melting pot of distinct cultures, and used everything to its fullest advantage—envelopes the entire figure thickly. So a foreign influence did not remain just that. The admiration did not remain unrealized. The artist for this *kannon* dug out what lay at the depths of the human soul, explored the core of the human body, and found the mystery of human existence, which he then attempted to crystallize into a figure.

It is not recorded whether this great artist was Japanese. But I wonder if the people born during the Tang dynasty's melting pot culture or those who were nurtured by it did not feel a change in their emotional constitution when they traveled across the Yellow Sea and reached the Inland Sea of our beautiful country. Would the difference between the dusty, parched brown continent and Japan's green and luscious landscape, not unlike the features of a sixteen-year-old maiden, be not enough to cause a change in one's emotional perspective? If we were to assume a change occurred, the image that the inner eye of the artist saw must also have changed to some degree. For instance, take the facial expression of the *kannon*. It is no longer unfocused or vague, a feature typical of the continent; it is a bit more attentive and sharper. Can I not consider this as evidence of change? When we stand in front of this Eleven-headed Kannon, we obtain a direct, tangible feel that the imagery for it was conceived in this land of Yamato. Of course, it is not easy to separate the imagery from artist's natural disposition, but I cannot but feel an emotional closeness to the artist's disposition hidden in this imagery. It is nearly impossible to describe what this feeling is in detail but, when I stand in front of this figure, I do not sense even a hint of **foreignness** that I would normally feel toward items coming from the Tang dynasty.

The long, half-closed eyes, thick eyelids, sumptuous lips, broad nose—they are all idealized embodiments of familiar facial features. These characteristics are neither foreign nor unique only to supernatural humans, but the divine majesty and beauty that no human can possess is expressed in this statue. Visible through the half-open eyelids are the all-penetrating eyes of the *kannon* that can see man's soul and destiny. The closed lips, thick and sumptuous, possess a boundless power that can defeat the hardest swords and calm the most violent storms and floods. The round, fleshy cheeks do not suggest sensual pleasure at all, but are so noble that they would annihilate man's carnal desire. When we observed these facial features, simmering golden and floating on black lacquer, we could not but feel that this face is not that of a human being—it is unmistakably that of a *kannon*.

The fleshy body that supported this head also appears to possess the nobility of a *kannon*. This nobility is not solely due to the fact that the exposed surface of the *kannon* is simmering in black and gold. The modeling of the *kannon* body is **voluptuous** without being **fat**. The flexibility of the legs and arms is amply expressed in the soft folds of the robe and the roundness of the arms and hands, but in addition, this *kannon* also possesses a flash of steely willpower that underlies everything, all within. The entire figure of the *kannon*, which should of course be heavy, seems so light, as if to defy the law of gravity and float. I think these features are the basic elements that explain why the *kannon* gives us an impression of nobility.

The faintest breeze appears to strike the lower part of the *kannon* flowing slowly toward his back. This feeling is expressed in the direction of the folds of his robe that cling to his body. This treatment of the robe might be a standard technique for rendering a *kannon*, because he appears from thin air and it is difficult not to think of his appearance as motion. The rendering of the robe is so successful that it adds holiness to the figure that is not of this world.

The ornamental scarves that go around from the shoulders to the chest, then to the waist then to the arms, draping down by the legs to the base are extremely successful in providing curvilinear ornamentation that wraps around the entire figure. Perhaps the flowing robe also represents a delicate supplementary technique of suggesting the feel of the shoulders and arms to the touch. The difference in the arm positions between the right and the left interact with the symmetry of the scarves, which I thought gave the entire *kannon* a free, flowing, and pleasant rhythm without losing the balance.

Looking from the side, we are now taken by another surprise. The rendition of the shoulders, torso, waist, and legs is sure-handed and strong. This delicate balance is exquisite. This *kannon* is a work of a giant who knew the true meaning of naturalistic depiction. When we look at images of *kannon*, the first question that occurs to us is not the question of whether or not the artist was successful in naturalistic depiction. Despite this, if we should find superficial naturalism and clear unnaturalness, we tangibly feel as if the statue's divinity and beauty have been shattered. So, for this sort of statue, lucidity in naturalism is an essential condition. And this *kannon* underscores this principle clearly.

Despite these accolades to the *kannon*, I understand that it was found abandoned on the roadside some fifty years ago. I heard this from someone and cannot attest to the veracity of the information. The statue was apparently the main object of worship at a temple called Jingūji of Miwayama in the city of Sakurai, Nara. When the government attempted to separate Shintoism from Buddhism at the time of the Meiji Restoration, the statue, sadly, was abandoned at the roadside, at the insistence of the believers of ancient Shintoism. So the story goes like this. There was no benevolent person in the neighborhood willing to take the abandoned idol. In the end, this noble *kannon* lay covered with dirt in tall grass for days. One day, by happenstance, the abbot of a small temple called Shōrinji, a temple of the Pure Land sect, walked by it and discovered it. "How irreverent," he thought. "If there is no one to take it, I will take it back to the temple." So the *kannon* was brought to the Shōrinji temple.

Note

1. Watsuji's friend N is Naka Kansuke (1885–1965), a well-known poet and essayist, who was a few years Watsuji's senior.

Chapter 8

NUMEROUS IMAGES OF *KANNON* AND *KANNON* WORSHIP

I stood in the Suiko Tenpyō Room and was surprised by the sheer number of *kannon* statues displayed there.

On either side of the Shōrinji Kannon, Fukū Kensaku Kannon and Yōryū Kannon of the Daianji temple, and some other *kannon* statues stood. The Kudara Kannon, which had an air of transcendence about it, stood with its back facing the Shōrinji's Eleven-headed Kannon. Perhaps we should consider this statue as a statue of Kokū Bosatsu (*Akasagarbha bodhisattva*), rather than a *kannon*, but here we will follow the traditional designation and call it a *kannon*. The *Akasagarbha* statue of Hōrinji standing to the right of the Kudara Kannon holds a vase in its left hand just like the Kudara Kannon, and positions its right arm bent at the elbow with the open palm facing up. In terms of iconography, then, this statue may be considered a *kannon*. To the left of the Kudara Kannon, a small, carved *kannon* stood, on loan perhaps from the Yakushiji temple, unfortunately damaged considerably but still possessing a rare beauty. This statue gave us an impression of sensuality that was not unlike that of Venus. Behind this small statue, a small *kannon* from Hōryūji was displayed.

If we look at the southwest corner of the gallery, a feminine *kannon* figure of Daianji grasping a staff, a masculine *kannon* holding a lotus flower in one hand, and other *kannon* were lined up in a row. Against the north wall, *kannon* including those from Tōshōdaiji and some from other temples stood as if in formation. In the center of the gallery, several small Kondō Kannon figures from Hōryūji, wearing that mysterious smile, stood on a platform. The *kannon* from the Okadera, in a seated contemplative pose with the right leg over the left and the elbow of the right arm resting on the right knee, sat in quiet thought. It could be a statue of a Maitreya but the impression of this statue was still that of a *kannon*.

Excluding only a few statues—such as those of the Ten Principal Disciples of Sakyamuni, two sets of Four Guardian Kings (*Shitennō*), Taishakuten (*Indra*) and Bonten (*Brahma*), Yuima (*Vimalakirti*)—major statues of the rest of the collection were all *kannon*. This preference for *kannon* in the collection could be a result of the fact that these were relatively easily moved, so they naturally came together here. But, if one thinks about this for a moment, the greatest works of art during this Suiko Tenpyō era—and these include the Fukū Kensaku Kannon of Sangatsudō (at Tōdaiji), the Eleven-headed Kannon of the Shōrinji, the Shō Kannon of Tōindō of Yakushiji, the Kannon at Chūgūji, the Yumedono Kannon—are all *kannon*. We cannot ignore the masterpiece Yakushi Nyorai either, which is not a *kannon*. In any case, these non-*kannon* statues are a small minority. We might say that the preponderance of *kannon* exhibited in the Suiko Tenpyō gallery of the museum points directly to the popularity of *kannon* worship in the Suiko Tenpyō era.

The popularity of *kannon* worship is a good starting point for learning about the state of mind of the ancient Japanese people. This phenomenon is somewhat similar to the worship of the Virgin Mary in Christianity. In the popularity of *kannon* worship, we also detect a certain moment that would later transition to the worship of Amida Buddha and Pure Land Buddhism. This was a period in history in which people did not have many active means of self-expression, except composing *waka* and Chinese poems, thus the self-expression embodied in **idol worship;** in other words, the productive activity that shows up passively should be considered important and thus requires close examination. The fact that the artistic style and feel in which *kannon* statues were rendered in the Suiko, Hakuhō, and Tenpyō eras changed markedly should not be seen simply as an influence from abroad.[1] It should also be interpreted in terms of the fact that worshipers were attracted to new artistic forms and gained new means of satisfaction.

NATURALISM

The most marked change in the artistic style of *kannon* becomes apparent if we compare the Shōrinji Kannon and the Kudara Kannon.

In a preceding section I pointed out that the Shōrinji Kannon was based on naturalism. I think it is indisputable that naturalism is the foundation of any plastic art. But this naturalism is not as simple as the one for which **photography** serves as a typical example. This type of naturalism refers to the "work of the artist's eye" that is both free and able to express all sorts of nuance because it has been processed through the artist's disposition.

It is an artist's instinct to depict something naturalistically. And, at the same time, an artist possesses the freedom to emphasize certain aspects over others. Depending on the placement of emphasis, the work can be quite individualistic or typical of the genre. Depending on the trend of an era, one type of artist may be in fashion, but regardless of which style, the idea is that art is an effort to capture the essence of the whole by means of one individual object.

The *kannon* period in Japan was a period in which the products of art expended a large amount of effort to establish a formulaic representation. But, even in this work, the artist was free to vary the placement of emphasis in terms of naturalism. The difference between approaches with and without this emphasis is magnified in the Shōrinji Kannon and the Kudara Kannon.

KUDARA KANNON

In terms of whether or not it is founded on naturalism, the Kudara Kannon compares favorably with the Shōrinji Kannon. The clean and pure treatment of the Kudara Kannon's body, from the shoulders to the arms, and from the chest to the torso, as well as the silk folds that hang gently clinging to the legs are evidence of an artist's unmistakably sure eye that could discern reality. But, what the artist of this statue emphasized is almost diametrically opposite from that which the artist of the Shōrinji Kannon emphasized. Underlying this difference, we might imagine, are historical changes in ethnic groups and cultures as well as the resultant changes in artists.

The Kudara Kannon is a typical example of a style that came to Japan through Korea. Its origin was the Six Dynasties period in China (220–589 CE), but the influence itself can then be traced back to western regions of China and ultimately to Gandhara. Surmising from the fact the *kannon* looks almost entirely naked from the waist up, its origin may be traced as far away as somewhere in the middle of the Indian subcontinent. Yet, this Kudara Kannon, which should exhibit direct influences from Gandhara or India, reminds us more of many Han dynasty stone carvings, rather than of statues of Buddha from those two places. The air that surrounds the statue is not that of the western regions of China. That is to say, it seems clear that art from Gandhara or India was first **sinicized** (i.e., assimilated to Han dynasty culture), when it entered China. Although some of the art from the western regions of China remained unchanged without being sinicized, as shown in the stone carvings of Buddha at Dadong, what the Kudara Kannon represents specifically is a style that has been sinicized and not influenced by other artistic styles. Thus, we can say with some confidence that this style is a result of Chinese creation. I understand that the full use of the artistic spirit of Greek art in Chinese art did not take place until **more than two centuries after Gandhara art had declined**, and after the Tang dynasty monk Genjō (Ch. *Xuanzang*) led a full-scale effort to bring the culture of the Gupta dynasty of central India to China. So we may say that the sinicization came first, followed by an era of melting influences from various cultures, so the change in style is the opposite of the historical progression. Hence, this style embodies the change in Chinese culture, from the Six Dynasties period to the Tang dynasty (*see fig. 5, photo section*).

Having said this, I must admit that it is a bit difficult to make this Kudara Kannon an example of this transformation. The very linear treatment found in the carved reliefs at the Longmen site and other similar sites resembles that of the Yumedono Kannon, but the same cannot be said about the Kudara Kannon. What interests me about this is the stylistic meaning of this very linear treatment. The Kudara Kannon seems consistent in giving the impression that it is made of hard and sharp curvilinear lines, as if they were combinations of hard-as-steel lines and curves produced from bent steel plates. It expresses simplicity and clarity. Yet it is also broadly appealing and meaningful. It does not exude attention to detail, but this does not mean that it lacks a delicate sensitivity. The artist was attentive to achieving a unity of various parts of the body, but, rather than aiming at the beauty of form, the artist aimed at something that is abstract suggested by the form. In other words, the subject matter of "*kannon*" is not expressed through the beauty of the bodily shape, but by way of something mysterious hinted at by the body. An example of this is the eternal quietness expressed by the hanging folds of the clothing: owing to which, there is not a hint of the lower body underneath. The artist, therefore, was intent on capturing the meaningful form on the surface and pursued it to the end, rather than digging into the physical features of the body and extracting mysterious beauty from it. I think that it is another place where a feature of Han dynasty style is made visible.

This analysis only half-explains the beauty of this *kannon*. It was neither the passion nor the ideology specific to the Han people that motivated the Han dynasty artistic style to rise from within and be applied to the creation of this work of Buddhist art. Because of the invasion of barbarians from the outside, the Han people's blood and passion were in a violent chaos. It was the time when, in addition to the heartfelt admiration they'd always had for harmony and gentle-manneredness, they began to feel a flash of new sensitivity that had been unknown to them. That was not unlike a presentiment of the spring, a tacit knowledge that flowering plants are slowly emerging from the ground. In this way the Han people began to masticate and digest the cultures from India and the western regions of China. Along with this development, a longing love for foreign lands also sprang up. Deities from foreign lands, capable of embracing all living beings with their boundless mercy, finally slipped into the deepest recesses of the Han people's psyche.

The abstract "Heaven" changes into the more concrete "Buddha." We feel this marvel from the Kudara Kannon. The beauty of the human body, the nobility of mercy—the people in transition who accepted these tenets were just like innocent, newborn children finally comprehending how supernatural beings are expressed in the shape of a human. Perceiving a supernatural being tangibly, as someone close to one's soul—being able to actually see it with one's own eyes—was an event undoubtedly equivalent to a world-changing event for the Han people. They looked at the human body in a completely new way and felt human emotions with a new heart. There they also found an entirely new, immeasurable profundity as well as a symbol for the Pure Land. And as a crystallization of that emotional movement, they produced **statues of Buddha in their own Han style**.

I should be careful here. By saying the foregoing, I do not mean to imply that a Chinese produced the statue. Here I am speaking only about the meaning of the artistic style in which the Kudara Kannon was created. It was created in only one of the available artistic styles in China at that time. But when it arrived in Japan, this style would exert a very decisive role; the Japanese found a strong affinity to the experience embodied in this style.

The strangely mysterious and pure feeling that one receives from the Kudara Kannon comes from an uncomplicated marvel that I related in the foregoing. The round and pure arms and the smooth beauty of the chest that is completely free from impurity were not produced by an artist who was accustomed to the beauty of the human body but by an artist with a heart that was surprised by the discovery of the bottomless beauty of the human body. The face of the *kannon*, with a faint smile, is familiar and gentle; it is suggestive of our admiration that has been crystallized, yet it is somewhat eerie. We cannot understand why the *kannon* looks like this without presupposing the *kannon*'s unblemished heart, a heart that could no longer think of anything other than mercy, one that borders on abnormal stubbornness. We can feel this especially magnified when we view the *kannon* from the side, particularly in the profile of the long, gentle face and in the odd bending of the thin body.

It is foolish as well as useless to give a reason why the *kannon* looks this way by trying to guess the artist's state of mind; instead, one should first consider the technique of sculpting available during the Six Dynasties period. At the same time, I find that this is the only way to explain the feeling of the Kudara Kannon. I cannot conceive of the idea that the beauty of life embodied in the *kannon*, still as the deepest pool of water, could be produced by less than a perfect artistic technique.

Note

1. The Suiko era generally refers to the Asuka cultural period (from the end of the sixth century to the seventh century) and, in some cases, more specifically to the reign of Emperor Suiko (r. 554–628). The Hakuhō period is a cultural period from about 645 to 710.

Chapter 9

SCULPTORS OF THE TENPYŌ ERA AND RŌBEN

The names of sculptors from the Tenpyō era are for the most part unknown. In my understanding, in those days a large temple would support either a good sculptor or a group of sculptors. A monk could have also done double-duty as a sculptor. For this reason, it may be difficult to dismiss straightaway the possibility that the monk Rōben (689–773) was not also a skilled sculptor. The theory that the statue of Rōben in the Rōben Hall is **a work of Rōben himself** is a bit farfetched, since it is dated to the Jōgan era (859–877), but this in itself cannot serve as evidence to show that Rōben was not a sculptor.[1] The architecture of Sangatsudō and the sculptures contained within this structure, all associated with the monk Rōben, are all masterpieces. This in turn provides evidence that Rōben was a person with an extraordinary understanding of art or, at least, had at his disposal a group of highly talented artists. If it is true that the sitting statue of Rōben is a work done by him, Rōben is truly a first-rate artist. On the other hand, if we suppose that the sculptors under his supervision or the disciples of these sculptors produced this statue, we can say that Rōben indeed trained the country's best sculptors. The artistic and technical skills in naturalism used in producing the statue of Rōben are rare in both the Tenpyō and Jōgan eras. I would think that if Rōben could actually sculpt a work in his own image at that level of technical skill he could have built Sangatsudō and produced the Shōrinji Kannon. I have no doubt that the fact that a group of artists affiliated with the Tōdaiji temple constituted the core of Tenpyō art is because artistic geniuses always stayed close to Rōben. I think casting large images of Buddha is also related to this. I believe that the account, related in the historical document *Genkō Shakusho* and others, that it was Rōben who convinced Emperor Shōmu to build a huge image of Buddha in Nara is true, although it is impossible to know if Rōben, or some other genius, was the **first** person who conceived the gigantic hall and the huge cast image of Buddha.

At least twenty years passed after the completion of the bronze statues of Yakushiji and the wall paintings of Hōryūji before Sangatsudō was completed. It took another ten years before the plan to cast the image of Buddha came into existence. And it was ten years later still that the Buddha was consecrated in a ceremony, ready to be prayed to. So if we assume that there was a genius sculptor, we must also consider these historical dates and his age. The existence of a genius sculptor is more important than the prevailing social and political trend of the times. The fact that we observe a significant change in art after the Tenpyō era may be due to influences from abroad but more likely was due to the death of this sort of artist.

MONDŌSHI

Although we may never know the names of these artists or how they lived, we can certainly detect individual characteristics in their works. Let us take a group of objects like the Shōrinji Kannon and those in the Sangatsudō and consider this as one group. Then, compare this group to another group of works, such as the statues of the Ten Principal Disciples or the Eight Deities that protect the laws of Buddhism (Tenryū Hachibushū) at Kōfukuji. Or compare a group of carved objects at Daianji with the carved wood images at Tōshōdaiji. Still another comparison, one which is more detailed, would be to compare the Yōryū Kannon and the Four Guardian Kings (Shitennō) at Daianji to the Eleven-headed Kannon at the same temple. What we find in these comparisons are surely not mere differences in technique but differences in artists' individual characteristics.

The various works at Kōfukuji are said to have been produced by a sculptor by the name of Mondōshi from Gandhara. We cannot be certain about this, but there is no doubt that one single artist produced the images of the Ten Principal Disciples and the Eight Deities that protect the laws of Buddhism. The artist was most probably an extraordinary talent, and a superb technician. But his technique in naturalism was only superficial. Thus, although his works are skillfully executed, they are not majestic.

We must recognize this artist's talent not in his ability to crystallize the mysterious, profound vision, but in his extraordinary ability to render naturalism or, in some cases, his ability to go beyond naturalism and create a fresh formulaic representation. Whether or not an image he created was a disciple of Sakyamuni or a protector of the Buddhist laws (a member of the Hachibushū) is beside the point. The works by this artist, if we look at them as simply works depicting the daily lives of monks and warriors, are superb works that were produced only rarely. The artist had the skill to create all manner of faces. This uncanny ability to capture an expression or a facial feature, and other highly developed skills and subtle dexterity are, without resorting to exaggeration, characteristics that are enough to amaze anyone. He was particularly skillful in depicting the face of the Ryūō, a protector of the Buddhist law.

I think what we see here is the artist's predilection for naturalism. If we base our judgment on this, it is not impossible to think that this artist was a man from Gandhara who had been trained in China. But so far as we know, no works in either China or the western regions of China that resemble the works of this artist have been found. However, that dexterity, sharp perception, and the beauty of his works do not remind us of the wide open plains of the Eurasian continent but, rather, of the nature of an island nation, where art is much more integrated. So it is not unimaginable that this artist was a very unusual product of Japan. If we were to direct our flight of imagination in this direction, the name Mondōshi would give rise to a truly fascinating and thought-provoking mystery.

THE ARTISTS AT DAIANJI

Works at Daianji do not give the impression that they were made by an extraordinary talent as do those at Kōfukuji discussed above. The figures are full in some places, and we can also observe that the artists bravely confronted significant artistic issues in a straightforward manner. However, the criticism that their naturalism is superficial is quite justified. The view from the side of the Yōryū Kannon gives an impression of a very stable and beautiful harmony and solid strength, but it somehow lacks a pleasant, lingering aftertaste. The round arms, for instance, were not produced with a delicate sensibility. The Four Guardian figures are devoid of any obvious flaw and the faces are just about perfect, but the figures as a whole are ordinary and leave us wanting something a little more.

Daianji was built by the monk Dōji some time before Sangatsudō was built. But it is not known if these statues were built at the time of the construction of Daianji. If I were to trust my instincts, I would think that they are much newer than the temple. The evidence that they postdate the temple is that the material is wood, and the artists apparently tried to express a clean, clear-cut feeling that the dry lacquer technique could not manage. We would also have to agree that the naturalistic technique seen in the Daianji statues was a little too advanced for the period of the building's construction. Considering these points, I cannot say this with perfect confidence but the artists might have consciously tried to outdo the masterpieces of the Sangatsudō group. Unfortunately, however, their enthusiasm was successful only on the surface. Their vision was much more indistinct than that that seen by the Sangatsudō artists. As the exterior surfaces of these figures became more naturalistic, the overall impression became more and more bleached of freshness.

An artist who learned from Sangatsudō pieces and pushed the limit of innovation in his own way probably was the person who produced the very feminine Eleven-headed Kannon of Daianji. The head of the Kannon was replaced at a later date, so we naturally must exclude this from our discussion, but the rest of the body is a woman's body executed very naturalistically. This observation is particularly evidenced in the chest and the hips. Here I see the artists at least began to pay more conscious attention to the human body. We do not see the dignity that we expect of a *kannon* in this image; however, we recognize a beauty that makes us think of the Roman goddess Venus. If we were to remove the head and the arms from this statue and look at what remains just as a woman's body, I would have to say that it is far more attractive than the rest of the Daianji statues.

ARTISTS AT TŌSHŌDAIJI AND AT HŌRYŪJI

The carved and unfortunately damaged figures of Tōshōdaiji were produced using a technique similar to the one used for the Eleven-headed Kannon just mentioned above, but the impression it gives is much less defined. It was more than six or seven years after the Great Buddha of Nara was consecrated that Ganjin, who traveled from Tang China, created a center for artists at Tōshōdaiji. This event marked the beginning of the late Tenpyō period. Even if we were to assume that these wooden figures were done in an artistic style prevalent during the Tang dynasty's Emperor Xuanzong's reign (685–762, r. 712–756), we should expect this style to appear considerably different from that used during Dōji's time, some thirty or forty years before. Unfortunately, we can only praise the newly arrived sculptors' disposition far more enthusiastically than their technical skills. Take the images of Daijizai Ō (Skt. *Mehesvara*) and Sakyamuni, for instance. They are full-figured but lacking in strength. The image of Sakyamuni, in particular, executed in a new style in which the thighs are particularly large and the clothing adheres tightly to the skin, cannot but give a slack feeling. On the other hand, that may have been an expression of the artist's individuality.

I would also imagine that Hōryūji, as well, had a group of influential artists. In this Suiko Tenpyō gallery, the Four Guardian Kings (Shitennō), produced in stucco, Bonten, Taishakuten, and other images in the five-story pagoda are on display, having been made available on loan from the temple. I can sense a commonality, at least among the molded figures and the Four Guardian Kings. I might say that this common feel is a sense that they are neither hurried nor adventurous, as if the artists very much enjoyed producing them, making them indeed very pleasant to look at. As is clear from the molded figures of a small girl and a woman, the artists demonstrated a secure naturalistic technique but, around these figures there hangs an illusory and fantastic air. The Tamonten and Kōmokuten figures, two of the Four Guardian Kings, are excellent works with regard to naturalism. If I were to express my personal preference, I think these Four Guardian Kings are superior to the Ryūō figure at the Kōfukuji temple.

NIHON RYŌIKI

This may sound a little odd but, when I come close to a figure, which for example could be lacking arms, I sometimes feel overwhelmed by the indescribable life energy radiating from it. Even a figure that exists only in my memory has a familiarity to it, and it conjures up old memories, as if I'd known it for a long time, just like a living human being. So, it is quite possible that ancient people somehow had a vision of statues of Buddha. Also I can almost understand how monks and nuns could have fallen in love with statues of Buddha. *Nihon*

Ryōiki, though it is written in an unsophisticated style, is interesting in that it describes these feelings of the Tenpyō people very tellingly.[2]

A PHOENIX AND A CELESTIAL BEING ON THE CANOPY OF HŌRYŪJI

Among the items of special interest on loan from Hōryūji to the museum are the figures of a phoenix and a celestial being that were removed from the canopy in the temple's Golden Hall. The phoenix maintains a pose in which it has just alighted, spreading high three large tail feathers. The feathers exude a very special feeling—they look very hard, like steel, yet appear flexible like true feathers. The bird's large feet, sculpted roughly and actually too large for the body, together with the enormous beak that seems to occupy more than half the head, give an impression of being oddly easygoing and powerful, and convey an intense feeling to the viewer. It is simple, masculine, and refreshing. Straight lines and nearly straight curvilinear lines, like the ones I mentioned in our discussion of the Kudara Kannon, form the phoenix's body. In addition, this bird also exudes a free, rhythmical sense that one sees in quickly executed black ink paintings.

The celestial maiden sits quietly on a lotus platform with a lute on her lap. Its simplicity is no less than that of the phoenix. Just as the phoenix is disproportionate, the face and arms of this musician are especially large. The face, puffy in its lower part and thus very noticeable, has long eyebrows that continue from the nose. It has extraordinarily large upper eyelids and very elongated eyes as if to balance the eyelids, and a large mouth as if to draw all of a viewer's attention—every part in sight is enlarged. Yet, strangely, there is a sense that nothing is exaggerated. It is simple, sincere, and carefree. It gushes with a certain emotion—a lovely and quiet familiarity. In addition, because the eyes and mouth are so large, they give a certain odd impression that is a mixture of coquetry and dignity. I have in the past felt that it was this figure that possessed an emotion specific to the Japanese people. But when I looked at the rubbing of a carved relief from the Longmen site, I also detected the same sort of image there. This must mean that this figure arose from the emotion common to both the Japanese and the Han peoples, but it is executed in a particularly pleasing way. In this sense, this figure belongs to our ancestral peoples.

After one looks at these works, the artist living in the times when the canopy at Hōryūji was made and the artist contemporaries at Hōryūji are, I must confess, truly awe-inspiring.

IMAGE OF YUIMA AND THE BUDDHA PRESSED IN COPPER

Aside from the works at Hōryūji that I discussed above, there are a number of others that are noteworthy. For instance, the molded sculpture of Yuima (*Vimalakirti*) is a delightful masterpiece that is well worth our admiration. I think this sculpture was produced in a style that developed out of the Gandhara style. The same artistic lineage can be assumed for others like **the Bonten and the Taishakuten at Sangatsudō,** referred to as Nikkō and Gakkō by the temple, and **the figure of Sakyamuni** (or could it be a Maitreya?) at Kōryūji. The development of this artistic style should perhaps be credited to the Chinese, but we know of no artwork in China that shares this style. So naturally we do not think the impression that these statues give is somehow Chinese; I am led to think, instead, that the tradition did not take root in China and that it was the Japanese who inherited this spirit for naturalism. To reflect on this further, I think that this sort of grand art was no more than short-lived fireworks arising from the melding of ethnic groups and cultures. If the ancestral people of Japan had been endowed with the power to nurture this artistic tradition properly, they would have been able to assert the right of Japanese culture with considerable confidence.

The copper images of Buddha done in *repoussé* relief at Hōryūji are not large but are exceedingly beautiful. Though it is without distinct details, the image of Amida Buddha in particular, which is the main object of worship, is reminiscent of the wall paintings at the same temple. This image in relief was imported from the Tang dynasty. It may somehow be related to the wall paintings.

Notes

1. The Rōben Hall in Watsuji's terminology refers to a building called Kaisandō, which commemorates the first head of the Tōdaiji, Rōben, and houses the seated figure of this man. This building is located near Nigatsudō in the Tōdaiji temple compound.
2. *Nihon Ryōiki* is a collection of Buddhist stories written in the Kōnin era, compiled around 822. See *SNKBT* 30:88–89 for the original version of this story.

Chapter 10

GIGAKU MASKS

The large and strange-looking masks displayed in the museum were once used for the silent, masked dance, called *gigaku*, performed during the Tenpyō period. Among these, a few exude a particular type of beauty that jolts us out of our inattention and transforms it to astonishment.

Originally, as I understand it, these masks were not born out of a heightened desire for artistic creation but out of what we might call a secondary desire for parody. The carving technique the artists used to express human emotion by means of formulaic patterns, however, is quite amazing. First of all, the technique is based on strict naturalism. Second, it is able, seemingly with ease, to capture the very essence of a facial expression and elevate it to an expressive pattern. Thus, if the artist intended to express the emotion deep inside of a person, the artwork would become a great work of art. On the other hand, if the aim was to express what was visible only externally, such as humor, ugly habits, or a passion for material objects, the product does not seem as valuable. Some human expressions resemble those of a monkey. If an artist captured the pattern for this similarity, we might be surprised by the artist's ability, but we would be unlikely to receive any artistic impression. In contrast, when we see gradations of sadness or joy that spring out of the human heart in clear form, as we do in these masks, we feel a strong joy as if encountering an inexhaustible spring of life.

The expressions on these masks are not only formulaic but are also quite exaggerated. But this must come from the original impetus for the mask production for the dance—to make them clearly visible, by means of exaggerated expressions, to as many people in the audience in a very large performance space as possible, some seated very far away. The exaggeration, therefore, is not necessarily based on the artist's dearth of creativity. As a result, these masks do not convey a sense of emptiness that would normally arise from exaggeration, but instead give a strange sort of life energy that comes out of particular spatial relationships. We can see this immediately if we compare these Tenpyō masks to dance (*bugaku*) masks such as *chikyū* and *nasori* and the like produced during the Kamakura period.[1] The masks produced during the Kamakura period are much lacking in creativity, and we only see an exaggeration that has nothing to do with a true feel for life. This may be a reflection of a people who were living a chronically sickly life, as if their center of existence had moved to a peripheral nerve. What the producers were trying to achieve here, I believe, was not the vision they obtained from coming into contact with the core of life as it is. It was merely a shadow of fantastic nightmares that attack the tired mind. There is nothing human about it. The mask of a woman is far less human than the Tenpyō mask portraying a *tengu* (a mountain goblin). So the artistic impact of the Kamakura masks is far more diminished.

EFFECT OF *GIGAKU* MASKS

Some time ago, I was able to examine closely a superb dance mask from the Tenpyō era at the home of Mr. H. The mask had a very pleasant, calm feel, arising from the carefree, leisurely treatment of the facial features, executed without missing fine gradations. The eyes, nose, and mouth were boldly and skillfully shaped, yet without harming the natural beauty inherent in them. The pleasing and harmonious rhythm is created by the gentle undulation of expressive creases in the skin and the smooth curves for the highs and lows of the face. And, the skin that looks flexible and fleshy is full of vitality! When I looked at this mask, an unclouded, cheerful feeling—a feeling that is at the same time tinged with relaxed weariness from an enrapturing experience—quietly seeps into my soul and permeates it. I feel the same radiation of life energy from these masks that I get when seeing someone in person. And since they are only sculpted objects and not human beings, they always give me this eerie feeling.

Then, Mr. H. put the mask on. When he did this, the mask suddenly seemed to take on a new sort of life. When Mr. H. moved his head, it looked as if the expression on the mask became animated by its own will. I was totally astonished, utterly taken by this unexpected impression of the mask.

When the mask was laid on a *tatami* or I took it on my lap, I felt that it was not in its rightful place. I realized that we were used to observing it as an object independent and removed from the context for which it was produced. It was impossible for me, until the amazing moment when Mr. H. put it on his head, to imagine the mask, which was four times the size of a normal human face, to be somehow connected to a human being. But when the mask was placed in its rightful context, that size, oversized as it was, was not at all too large. Rather, because of the size of the mask, it did not look like a human had put on the mask. It was as if an artistic mask had acquired a human body, to such an extent that a very interesting impression unimaginable to modern human beings was created. It was at this point that I finally understood why this mask was made so large. I then remembered that masks for Greek plays were also oversized, and thus realized that there was a necessary relationship between the effect of these masks and their size.

The fact that masks were much smaller later tells us that there were significant changes in the dances and plays in which these masks were employed.

Because of the very strong impressions I received from these masks, I came to harbor the idea that the stage performance that employed these masks during the Tenpyō era consisted of music and dance. When I looked at these masks rather carefully, I could almost feel the role each of these masks played in these performances.

PERFORMANCE OF *GIGAKU*

The performance of *gigaku* was described in *Shoku Nihongi* in various places.[2] According to this record, it was performed not only at Buddhist memorial services held at large temples but also at imperial ceremonies and banquets. It also appears that there were special occasions just for *gagaku* performances. It is recorded in *Shoku Nihongi* that Emperor Shōtoku "traveled to the Yamashina temple, and heard **Lin-yi** and **Wu music** performed," which I think is an example of the last category.[3] Unfortunately *Shoku Nihongi* only makes mention of the performances and tells us nothing about what the contents were. How was this masked play performed, and what was the music like? We can only learn the answers from other historical documents. What is useful here is *Yōroku*, a summary of events kept at Tōdaiji, which owned the masks. Let us now try to reconstruct the performance as best we can, using our imagination.

PERFORMANCE OF *GIGAKU* AT THE GREAT BUDDHA'S CONSECRATION CEREMONY AND THE STAGE

First of all, the stage. Yōroku's description of the consecration ceremony held for the Great Buddha of Nara in 752 contains no specific description of the stage, but a chapter entitled "Kaigan kuyōki (Record of the consecration ceremony)" in *Yōroku*, dated Jōgan 3 (861), provides a rather specific description of the stage's structure. This consecration ceremony, taking place more than one hundred years after the original Buddha was cast, was performed on the occasion of the successful repair of the Buddha's head that had fallen off. Of course, during these one hundred years, a number of changes in culture in general, and significant changes in music, in particular, took place. Therefore we cannot make an educated guess about what might have occurred in the Tenpyō era using this description alone; it will help us some in our effort here, however. First of all, the stage was set up **on the outside**. That is, it was situated in the large open space in front of the Great Hall in which the Buddha sat.[4] This location apparently was the same during the Tenpyō era. It would have likely been the case, judging from the description, that musicians stood in two groups, one on the right and another on the left, in front of the hall. The stage was a high platform constructed of wood.

The dimensions were 80 feet square, there were high banisters on all sides, and four framed pictures, one for each side, were hung. Eight small pine trees were placed on the east and west corners of the stage and a small altar was set up[5] on the east and west ends of the stage. In addition, two scaffolds were erected to hang banners made in fine embroidery. Also, a signage pole from which a banner measuring 33 feet high hung was erected somewhere near the stage. Added to this was another, smaller stage, measuring 20 feet deep and 40 feet wide, which was constructed on the south side of the second level of the Great Hall.[6] It is doubtful that these structures still existed during the Tenpyō era. At least on the occasion of the consecration ceremony, we know that the *tōka*, a type of mass step dance, was performed directly on the ground.[7] In *Shoku Nihongi* a description of the *tōka* reads "The east and west sides sang out, standing apart in the yard."[8] A separate stage may have been built for *gigaku*, but details are not clear.

In addition to the stages, tents were erected. For the aforementioned Jōgan ceremony, three such tents were set on both the east and the west sides, and these served as seating areas for musicians, imperial emissaries, and members of the high-ranking nobility.[9] According to historical records, for the Jōgan ceremony, "the highest-ranked Buddhist priest, who was in charge of the consecration ceremony, the monks who delivered sermons, and the readers of Buddhist scriptures entered on palanquins with white canopies held high above them and were then seated in the tents." It was also recorded that "other lower-ranking monks and novices entered from the south gate and were seated in one of the tents on the east or west side on the north end."[10] For the ceremony held during the Jōgan period, walkways, some roofed, were constructed to accommodate one thousand monks but these walkways were not constructed during the Tenpyō ceremony, which might have been the reason for erecting this many tents.[11]

AUDIENCE BEFORE THE GREAT HALL OF BUDDHA

The open space in front of the hall, which accommodated the stage, was filled with masses of Tenpyō people, who wore deep, single-color robes for the occasion. According to the records, several hundred more than ten thousand monks and nuns attended the ceremony. Added to this, unquestionably, were officials of all ranks, upward of several thousand, and, of course, a multitude of common people who came to see the spectacle, even though not all of them could have entered the compound. There, colorful clothing filled the entire area, except of course the buildings of Tōdaiji, which would have appeared to be floating on the sea of colorful people. The Great Hall, in which the statue of Buddha was housed, was not as small and unseemly as it is now. A row of eight pillars now hold up the building in front, but originally there were twelve, making the front of the building nearly twice as wide as it is today. At the time of this ceremony, after one passed through the Second Gate

(Chūmon), one could see the construction of two towers, accompanying the main hall, was being finished: one on the east side and another on the west side, each measuring more than 320 feet high.[12] It strains our imagination to fathom the scale of these structures. The early summer sun shone mercifully and provided warmth to these grand buildings and the innumerable attendees.

ACTING ON THE STAGE

The consecration ceremony ends. The recitation of the scriptures ends. Then the various musicians enter. They come into the compound through the South Gate, make two circular rounds in front of the Great Hall, and stand in two groups, on the right and left.[13] Then the attention of the people is focused on the stage. The first dances to be performed are ones indigenous to Japan. The first of these, according to *Shoku Nihongi*, was *Gosechi no mai*, which *Yōroku* (Records of Tōdaiji) described as a dance led by a female singer and thirty dancers.[14] The dance probably was the one "with loud stomping of feet," which alluded to the mythological event in which dancing lured Amaterasu Ōminokami out of the mountain cave.[15] This set of dances was followed by the *Kumemai* dance, which involved two groups of twenty dancers. One group was led by Ōtomo, playing *koto*. Another group performed a sword dance and was led by Saeki.[16] The latter dance was an old-fashioned dance of warriors in military clothing. This performance was then followed by a *Tatefushimai* dance, done by forty performers. This was also a dance of soldiers, said to have been performed by dancers who each held a shield in one hand and danced in rhythmical steps.[17] The next was *tōka* (also called *nyokan tōka*). One hundred and twenty women in two groups performed this step dance, as they sang.[18] According to one theory quoted in *Shaku Nihongi*, the song ends with the refrain *yorozu tose arare*, so it is thought that this type of dance was generally referred to as ***arashi bashiri*** from the time of Fujiwara period on.[19] Since *bashiri*, which derives from the Japanese word ***hashiri*—"running"**—has the same meaning, one can well imagine what this dancing was like. When these dances and songs had been performed, they were followed by Tang music, and then by Goryeo music. The order of performance was as follows: one dance performed with classical Tang music, one dance performed with contemporary Tang music, three dances performed with Lin-yi music, one dance performed with Goryeo music, one dance performed with Tang miscellaneous music, three dances with Lin-yi music, one dance with Goryeo music, one dance performed by a female dancer with twenty other dancers and performed with Tang music, three dances performed with Goryeo music. Then these are followed by Goryeo women's music—by the time these performances were complete the sun would be already setting.[20]

COSTUME FOR *GIGAKU*

We are interested in making a guess at what the music and dance were like. The *gigaku* masks were undoubtedly used for some of these performances—at least for three performances described as Lin-yi. I have been told that the masks used for this occasion still exist in the Shōsōin Imperial Storage House, and I would venture to say that those are of the same type as the ones I saw. The costumes too are said to still remain in Shōsōin, so I have been told, at least, but details are scanty.[21] According to a catalogue compiled in Tenpō 4 (1833), Shōsōin was said to hold "various clothing, a variety of ancient cloths" and "clothing and dust."[22] I hear that an inestimable amount of old cloths disintegrated into piles of dust. It is probably very difficult therefore to separate out the costumes used during this ceremony. In the record of the Jōgan consecration ceremony, the following items were listed: "women dancers' costumes, Tang robes, Tang clothing, bodhisattva clothing for monks."[23] Also the same record lists materials apparently used for making the clothing, including "1,050 feet of **cloth**, 530 feet of **silk cloth**, 9 feet of **brocaded Tang cloth**, 66 feet of **thin silk fabric**, two sets of clothing dyed in indigo, ten pairs of shoes," but it is not clear if these reflect the Tenpyō era's clothing.[24] This is because the list was prepared during the Jōgan era, which was after the death of Kōbō Daishi, and marked the beginning of a significant change in people's lifestyles.[25] The item described as "**Tang clothing**" above simply indicates its stylistic origin and it does not necessarily mean that the clothing retained the Tang style faithfully. So it is preposterous to think that these remains dating from the latter half of the Fujiwara period could serve as a basis for conjecture about the clothing style of the Tenpyō period. Thus, what is most reliable is to make a guess from paintings dating from the Tenpyō period. The clothing depicted in these paintings appears to be made of soft materials and draped onto the body, allowing the contour and the external appearances of the body as well as the musculature to be seen easily by the viewer. We would think that the costumes used for the masked play might have been of this type, and the play with an Indian theme in particular must have been of this type. For the Jōgan ceremony, the monks who attained the bodhi rank, as I understand, were dressed in attire seen in Buddha statues. During the Tenpyō period, when Tang dynasty fashion was most influential and sought after, it would not have been unnatural at all to design costumes with influences from the western regions of China, India, Persia, and so forth.

ACTING TO LIN-YI MUSIC

A section entitled "Kuyōki" in *Tōdaiji Yōroku*, the aforementioned record compiled during the Jōgan period, tells us a bit about acting. At high noon, Lin-yi musicians of Tōdaiji, dressed in man-bird costumes, walk in two files of east and west quietly from the stage to the hall, holding offerings. On the stage a large white elephant stands. In a seat built on the elephant's back, a monk dressed as Fugen Bosatsu (Skt. *Samantabhadra*)—only scantily dressed and showing light skin—sits in contemplation just as this deity would appear in sculptures and paintings. When the men dressed in the man-bird costumes come back from presenting the offerings to the Buddha, this bodhisattva begins to dance to the singing of the scripture. The men in man-bird costumes in two files stand facing each other and dance as they play music. The next performance was music from the Hu Kingdom (it could have been *kogaku* "ancient music").[26] The Tamonten appears leading fourteen demon deities (or accompanied by a main follower and twelve yaksha in another account).[27] The pairs of demons would bring out a large peach, a large pomegranate, lotus seeds, aconite, and a large silk screen. There would be one person holding a bow, another a spear, another an axe, another a staff. At the same time, celestial maidens, symbolizing good fortune, would enter followed by twenty other maidens. Of these twenty, sixteen would each carry a stem of an artificial flower, and others would carry a wish-granting jewel, a brush, and a fan.[28] We may assume that the yaksha (Jp. *yasha*, Skt. *yaksa*), celestial maidens, would be have been dressed as they appear in paintings and sculptures. They too are divided by east and west, in two files, and proceed from the stage to the front of the image of Buddha, where they make offerings and then return to the stage. The main followers of the Four Guardian Kings and yaksha then stand in the southeast corner of the stage. The sixteen celestial maidens divide into two groups and perform a dance. This performance is followed by celestial music. The Daijizai Tennō comes onto the stage accompanied by sixty celestial maidens.[29] Twenty of these maidens in celestial costumes come onto the stage holding containers full of artificial flower petals, while the rest play music. They then divide into two groups, one on the east side and another on the west side, and sing in praise of Buddha:

> Buddha sits peacefully ruling over the universe
> Buddha manifests himself in all universe
> Buddha is serene and shows himself in everything
> Buddha's universe is vast and permeated with Buddha's laws[30]

When the singing is done, the maidens then scatter the flower petals. The petals float through the air. The maidens then dance. Then they exit.

NEW PIECES OF *GIGAKU*; INDIGENIZATION

The dance performances continued from early to late afternoon, but at this point let us not go further into these performances. Instead let us consider the three examples I cited in the above passage. The first two dances were described in *Yōroku* as new pieces and we think that the last one, considering the fact that the Kegon Sutra (*Flower Garland Sutra*) was used for the song praising the Buddha, also was one prepared specially for this occasion. The records in *Yōroku* state that the artists were dancers and fifers of Tang, so they may have been officials of the government's *gagaku* department.[31] Although it is highly reckless of me to discuss this without giving due regard to choreography and music, I contend that the format must have been not too different from a stage production that is now called *tableau vivant* in view of the structure of this dance music. This would have been a natural and simple expression of the vision obtained from the scripture and Buddhist statues, and it should not be regarded as an expression of the artists' creativity. Coincidentally, the beginning of the Jōgan era was when Heian monk Eshin'in Genshin was in his declining years and, during this time, there was a very special vision of Amida Buddha's descending from heaven to welcome the deceased to the Pure Land.[32] The same sort of tendency in religious belief can be detected in the aforementioned acts during the ceremony. If this is indigenization, I agree. Indeed, a vision of the Pure Land had been already incorporated into Japan by this time. Accordingly, these dances were more befitting of the smaller and less remarkable masks of the later period than the larger *gigaku* masks. This line of reasoning leads us to conclude that, from the record in the "Kuyōki" (Record of the consecration ceremony) section of *Tōdaiji Yōroku* written in the Jōgan period, we are no closer to finding out the details of *gigaku* music performed with masked play performances during the Tenpyō period.

DEVELOPMENT OF LIN-YI MUSIC

Perhaps twenty to thirty years before the Jōgan consecration ceremony, masked plays from the Tenpyō era became clearly differentiated from the *bugaku* of the Jōgan period, when a large-scale music reform was implemented after the death of Kōbō Daishi, sometime around the reign of Emperor Ninmyō.[33] Around this time, only the music from Goryeo prospered, and masked plays and Lin-yi music lost their independence. Subsequently, a new type of music from Tang (called *kakko* music) became popular, which, in addition to Goryeo music, formed what is now called *gagaku* (court music), which was formed from these two musical types.[34] As a result, a **number of new works and arrangements of old works** were created. Thus a style of **Japanese-style foreign music** came into existence. This also allowed for quite a bit of foreign influence to come into the types of music called *kagura* and *saibara*.[35] Judging from this, we can say that Japanization around this time consisted of selecting musical and dance influences that suited only the taste of the Japanese and nurturing the development of these musical elements (note the Japanese here include those immigrants originally from outside of Japan, but who, by the middle-Heian period, had become almost indistinguishable from the rest of the Japanese due to racial mixing). So, musical elements that could be valuable were cast aside if they failed to meet the taste of the Japanese. Having fallen out of favor, the silent, masked dance of *gigaku* thus became totally inconsequential.

Lin-yi music was originally dance music developed in India, and is said to have grown within the **religious system of Brahmanism**. If we carefully examine the Lin-yi music played for the Jōgan consecration ceremony, we can see that the music lost its Brahman flavor because of the reform during the reign of Emperor Ninmyō (r. 833–850). So, we must note that,the frequently performed ***bugaku*** music perhaps a hundred or two hundred years after the Jōgan period must have been totally different from the original, even if it held the same label of Lin-yi music. According to *Bugaku Yōroku* (Records of Dance Music), in numerous musical performances during the late Fujiwara period when this type of music was at the apex of popularity, Ryōō (on the left) and Nasori (on the right), which are important numbers in Lin-yi music, were performed at the end of the performance program, with only a few exceptions.[36] And it was not rare to find Koinzu and Batō, which were both types of Lin-yi music, being played in the middle of a performance program.[37] However, judging from various descriptions, all these types of Lin-yi music were extraordinarily constrained by a number of detailed rules. For instance, during the Jōgan period, a simple but free flight of imagination was permitted. After the Jōgan period, that sort of freedom had become totally out of the question. The Kamakura period was a time during which those other masks were also created, so I do not think that the people then had any accurate understanding of these ancient dances, but I would imagine that the tradition from the end of the Fujiwara period would still have been maintained.

DISADVANTAGES OF TRANSMITTING THE SECRETS

Zappi Betsuroku (Separate Account of Miscellany), a record written by the student of music Fujiwara no Takamichi, offers a glimpse into the world of music around this time.[38] The reason why Takamichi wrote this book was that he felt antipathy toward the practice of *hiden sōshō* (transmission of secrets) that he perceived as obfuscating to music. "This secret is a secret of the family so it goes without saying that I must uphold it, but I do not think it is reasonable," he asserted. Nonetheless, the fruit of his own interest did not fall far beyond the reach of his family's proverbial tree. He states this about Koinzu:

> I understand that this is a very unusual dance that is highly esteemed and treasured. If I performed this dance, I would be promoted to a higher rank and receive an imperial gift. From the look of it, it is not all that different from others and one would wonder why there is such big ado about this, but I understand that there is some secrecy surrounding the entering and exiting from the stage when dancing.

It is the family tradition of this dance at the end of the Fujiwara period that Takamichi then spoke of with considerable passion. For instance, Takamichi quoted one of Masazane's diary entries, "Tadatoki danced the Koinzu dance. There were elements in the dance that were not in the family tradition. He danced as he pleased; he is indeed an outrageous man."[39] Despite a family tradition that severely stunted the life of this art, the dancers made more fuss about learning this family tradition, paying little attention to a wide-ranging examination of the dance and music themselves. So Takamichi made comments such as the following: "As for things that do not have backing in the family tradition, stories of what people say about them never go away; the whole dance becomes diluted." And as for the Bosatsu dance, Takamichi remarked,

> Until about the time of Ex-Emperor Shirakawa (r. 1072–1086), a dancer of Tennōji performed this number. But there were few other occasions for this dance. The group was once asked to dance at a grand Buddhist event, but they were reluctant to do the performance. So this sort of dance was not transmitted further to new learners, eventually fading out. I understand that it no longer exists.

This is a fitting end to an art form that was wedded so strongly to the old ways in terms of minute technical details. What remained as dance music at this time was no longer that of the Tenpyō period, which had been an energetic, grand form of art.

If we simply look at the fundamental difference in artistic temperament between *gigaku* masks from the Tenpyō period and those from the Kamakura period and if we also recognize the deep chasm between them in their respective ability to grasp the essence of life, I would think that the reader would come to the same conclusion about points made in the foregoing discussion without a moment of hesitation.

GIGAKU MASKS AND BRAHMAN MYTHOLOGY

Next, let us ask the question about how we can imagine the dance music for which these Tenpyō *gigaku* masks were used. A short answer is hidden in the masks themselves. Using these masks, masked and silent *gigaku* performances were staged during the Tenpyō period. According to legends, either **Bosatsu** or **Buttetsu** brought to Japan Indian dance music as well as forms of Lin-yi music described variously as Bosatsu dance, Bosatsu, Buro, Batō music, and so forth. These various types of music were played at the consecration ceremony of the Great Buddha of Nara, receiving an enthusiastic response from the audience of nobility and common people alike, as it is chronicled in volume two of *Tōdaiji Yōroku* (Records of Tōdaiji). According to research done by a scholar by the name of Okabe, the Batō dance draws its inspiration from the slaying of a serpent by King Pedu in the Rigveda legend. Okabe thinks that the word Batō is a transliteration of Pedu or a transliteration of the name of the famous white steed, Paidu, that the king received from the Twin God Asvin, and this steed helped the king to kill the serpent. In *Bukyoku Kōden* (Oral History of Dance Music), a chronicle compiled at the end of the Ashikaga period, it is stated:

> [T]his Batō music was brought from India, more specifically, from the Brahman tradition.[40] According to one theory, the Vietnamese monk Buttetsu brought this over to Japan. The evidence for this is said to be stored in Tōshōdaiji. It is also said that this music is a portrayal of a jealous empress.

The word *ama* in Ama dance comes from the word *amma*, meaning "mother," and refers originally to the God Shiva's wife Durga.[41] The Ama dance supposedly depicts Shiva and Durga in extravagant merrymaking. In *Bukyoku Kōden*, however, this music is described a bit differently, as follows:

> This music is considered to be ancient music. Its dance is performed with masks. It also makes use of solemn spoken parts. Emperor Ninmyō commissioned Ōto no Kiyokami to create this work during the Jōwa era, sixty or seventy years after the death of Emperor Kōken. The work was not entirely new. The new version changed the music's original words. The new version was called *On'yō jichin kyoku*.[42]

Because it says that words were changed, it must mean that there were words to change from, which in turn means that, if there were words set to dance music, it must have involved some acting. Here, the impression of the *gigaku* masks provides an important clue to this conjecture. That is, one of these masks must represent King Pedu. Similarly, one of them must portray Ryōō. One of them must also be the God Shiva, and another the wife Durga. And actors wearing these fantastic masks, I have no doubt, acted out fight scenes between the horse and the serpent, and extravagant parties of men and women.

In addition to these listed above, there are several other types in Lin-yi music, such as Karyōbin, Bairohajinraku, Raryōōjujinraku, Koinzu (a.k.a. Suikogaku). Brahman myths may be able to offer an explanation about what they are.[43]

LIN-YI MUSIC, MUSIC FROM THE WESTERN REGIONS OF CHINA, AND THE TRADITION OF MASKED PLAY

The many *gigaku* masks cannot be accounted for by **Lin-yi music** alone. Let us therefore go back to ***kuregaku*** mentioned in the phrase ". . . heard Lin-yi and Wu music performed."[44] Wu music or *kuregaku* is said to have been brought to Japan by Mimashi, a Paekche man, during the era of Emperor Suiko (r. 592–628), but we do not know if this music was the same as Wu music in the Tenpyō period. In any case, *kuregaku*, which is often mentioned in comparison to **Lin-yi music**, is believed to have originated in **the western regions of China**. In the section on the country of Kucha in the book called *Daitō Saiikiki,* there is a statement that reads: "*gigaku*, played with **wind and string instruments**, was very much welcomed in many countries," which implies that this *gigaku* is the type of *kuregaku* that was brought into Japan.[45] Note here that we know that there was **no tradition of playing drums strapped to the waist or the use of masks at any time before the China's Six Dynasties period** (222–589 CE). Furthermore we know these features are a musical tradition of the western regions of China. If we assume that *gigaku* came from China, it no doubt came from the western regions of China. Lin-yi music was in the tradition of Indian music that came to Japan from the south across the ocean, so the *kuregaku* that is often mentioned parallel to Lin-yi music must have undoubtedly came by the land route from the western regions of China. ***Gigaku* from the western regions of China**, like all art forms in this area, was formed with influences from India and Greece. It is therefore not impossible to conceive that even **masks** came from the Greek tradition via India. Some people would snicker about tracing all masks to Greece but it is quite conceivable that Greek drama came into northern India and Central Asia, as we shall see later. The fact that such instruments as ***rikkin*** (standing harp), ***fue*** (flute), and ***dobyōshi*** (cymbals) were among the musical instruments used in *gigaku* cannot be overlooked in this regard.

It would be fascinating to find out what sort of music *kuregaku* was, because it is connected to **the tradition of masks**, which started in *sarugaku*, then was transmitted to *dengaku* and then to the *nō* theater. This is because it was from *gakuko*, **a class of people specializing in making *kuregaku*, living in the village of Morito in the county of Shiroshita in Yamato Province**, that a new type of *sarugaku* later developed.[46] Even after *gakuko* gave away their business of playing *kuregaku* to other groups of musicians, both on the left and the right, they still played *sangaku* with drums and flutes. According to one theory, this *sangaku* originated as a mixture of a comical act from Japan's ancient times called *sarukau* (alternatively, *sarukō*) and a comical act from Tang called *sangaku*. This mixture of these two performing traditions came to be known as *sarugaku*, because of their phonetic and conceptual similarities. It is quite plausible that the resident musicians in the village of Morito injected ***gigaku*** into *sarugaku*, which after all was their livelihood. Masks, at least, did not come down to us from *sarukau* or *sangaku* because, so far as we know from graphic depictions of ***sangaku***, performers of this comic form did not use masks. ***Nō* masks**, then, in turn, serve as evidence for us to conclude that *gigaku* was absorbed by and survived in *sarugaku*.

SARUGAKU AND *DENGAKU*

Sarugaku was centered around comical short performances. It included dances and acrobatics as well as comical sketches with a storyline. One can say that ***kyōgen*** descended from this *sarugaku*. According to *Shin Sarugakuki* (Records of New *Sarugaku*) by Fujiwara no Akihira, who lived at the time when *The Tale of Genji* was being written in the early eleventh century, one can find such acts entitled "Kyōwaranbe no sorazarei (Fables of children of Kyoto)," "Azumabito no uikyōnobori (An easterner's first travel to Kyoto)," "Fukuhirohijiri no kesamotome (Fukuhirohijiri goes looking for his priest robe)," "Myōkōni no mutsukigoi (A devout nun begs for diapers)," and the like, all of which were either "acrobatics" or "comical sketches."[47] Fujiwara no Akihira made critical remarks in his book about each of the *sarugaku* comedians, making comments such as "as soon as such-and-such actor comes onto the stage the audience begin to laugh by merely looking at him," "such-and-such actor is subdued when he comes onstage but as the play progresses, he goes into a state of feverish excitement." It is not entirely inconceivable that this comedic act descended from the tradition not of **comedic acts** and **acrobatics** of the aforementioned *sarukau* or *sangaku* but the tradition of *gigaku*. In view of the fact that the main venue of performance for *sarugaku* was in the village of Morito, and Morito must necessarily have been the original place from which the Ōmi and Tanba *sarugaku* styles originated, it is difficult not to make this sort of speculation.

Although *gagaku* existed with the support of the imperial family, *sarugaku* found its source of support from Buddhist temples and Shinto shrines. The former underwent change in accordance to the taste of the nobility. The latter, on the other hand, changed according to the demands of the general public in the middle or lower social classes. Given our current knowledge about how meaningful festivals at Buddhist temples and Shinto shrines were for the people in Kyoto during the Fujiwara period, it is fair to say that *sarugaku*, which played an important role in these festivals, was just as important as *gagaku* as a cultural symbol.

In addition to *sarugaku*, there was also ***dengaku***. Scholars do not all agree about the origin of *dengaku*, but it appears certain that *dengaku* originated as a cheerful dance among the farming class, although we do not know whether it had a direct relationship to a form of dance called ***tamai*** (*ta* "rice field" + *mai* "dance") in ancient times. Because *dengaku* as an entertainment act developed much later than *sarugaku*, we should not dismiss outright the idea that *dengaku* developed out of *sarugaku*. In the aforementioned *Shin Sarugakuki*, the author Fujiwara no Akihira acknowledged that *dengaku* was a *sarugaku* act. Although it is true that *sarugaku* was a comical act performed by professionals, *dengaku* was not. It was an entertainment form for farmers, in which farmers themselves took part, that is, they themselves performed dances, thus leading *dengaku* in a different direction. In a volume called "Onmogi (Rite of passage for women courtiers)" in *Eiga Monogatari*, the following description of ***dengaku*** appears, written in the same historical period as that described in *Shin Sarugakuki*.[48] That is, in *Eiga Monogatari*, *dengaku* is depicted as a musical troupe that performed in the countryside when rice seedlings were being planted and for the procession on the rice-planting day.[49] In this record, we find the following description: Fifty to sixty young women, wearing loose white clothing called *mokoromo*, white woven hats, heavy pinkish white makeup on the face, and with their teeth dyed black with *ohaguro* black teeth dye, proceed to a field in a file where rice planting will take place.[50] Following these women is an old man who directs the planting. He wears a scruffy kimono with the front open, with the tie cords dangling, wearing a large tattered woven hat and high clogs, and marches in a grand manner. Following this man are oddly figured women. These women wear old, dirty, and raddled red kimono made of boiled silk, white makeup, and ornaments in the hair. They wear high sandals and woven hats on their heads. A *dengaku* troupe comes next. This consists of about ten "humorous males" who have strapped **a strange-looking drum called *dengaku*** to the waist, and play the drums to the music produced on flute and ***sasara***.[51] They sing and dance to this music, "apparently taking pride in this act and enjoying it immensely." At the end of the procession, men holding tubs and stacked boxes, presumably filled with food as well as other curious objects, line up. At last, when everyone arrives at the field and the rice planting begins, the *dengaku* troupe, which had been a bit quiet up to this point, begins to play their instruments to their hearts' content, sing, and dance and proceed to create a huge commotion. It is quite clear to me that the purpose of this act was to make the farmers' work less dreary, and it is reasonable to assume that farmers sang songs in rhythm with the *dengaku* troupe as they planted rice seedlings. This type of art of the common people, in its very literal sense, expanded its influence from time to time. For example, a tremendous *dengaku* craze occurred in Kyoto seventy years or so after the depiction of *dengaku* above. According to *Rakuyō Dengakuki* (Record of *Dengaku* in Kyoto), we learn that "no one knew where this craze came from but it appears to have begun in villages and then reached the nobility class."[52] The record then relates that all sorts of people, whether they were monks living in dormitories, administrators, or even soldiers, formed *dengaku* groups and danced, visited temples to worship, and wandered around in city streets. People would hop around on a *takaashi* (pogo stick), play waist drums, hand drums, copper cymbals, and wood whisks (called *binsasara*). Men dressed as women would walk around the city. And all this took place throughout the day and night. Hopping on the *takaashi* was presumably a *sarukau* act but I wonder if it is not possible to conjecture that this is in the tradition of *cothurnus* of Greek plays.[53] As for the waist drums, I conjecture that they were drums that came from the western regions of China, hand drums probably derived from tambourines, and cymbals from cymbals in the West. The description in *Rakuyō Dengakuki* continues in the following manner. The rich who joined the *dengaku* craze spent extraordinary amounts of money to dress themselves in gold and silver embroidered clothing and put on ornaments made of precious metals. Courtiers and soldiers wore their formal attire or armor, and they danced and played drums, leaping and spinning in groups. *Kebiishi* put on colorful dyed clothing, which the law prohibited them from wearing, and whirled and twirled around in the street in broad daylight.[54] Even guests who visited high-ranking courtiers at the palace also formed groups and set out to the street. Added to this were mobs of monks, makers of Buddhist images and scrolls, and such, **donning hats and wearing beautifully brocaded overcoats**, and dancing **a type of Lin-yi dance called Ryōō and Batō**. Many of the high-ranking administrators even dressed themselves in short jackets made of rice straw, with flat woven hats made of reed on their heads, holding nine-foot tall fans, as they set out to the street. Even more insane were the lower ranking administrators, who pranced around practically naked, save for red loincloths, with their hair untied and wildly flowing, wearing a type of hats worn by farmers.

"It looked as though everyone in the city had gone mad." The description ends with a quip that "it was more than certain that this craze was caused by the spell cast by the fox." This sort of craze was most certainly temporary but one can palpably sense the power of *dengaku*. *Dengaku*, however, was no more than a sort of masked dance party. It was decidedly simpler than *sarugaku*. We should notice that it is generally acknowledged that it was monks who brought Lin-yi music to *dengaku* and this prepared the ground for the appearance of *dengaku hōshi*.[55] In the next era, we witness an emergence of two types of ***nō*—one in the tradition of *sarugaku* and the other in the tradition of *dengaku*.** This in turn suggests a professionalization of *dengaku*, in other words, evidence that it became more similar to *sarugaku*. Because these professionals were **monks**, I think that they engendered certain types of themes and ideas in *dengaku*. Furthermore, **if compared with** *sarugaku*, *dengaku* embodied almost no hint of religion.

NŌ, *KYŌGEN*, AND *GIGAKU*

I was once given to daydreaming about the relationship of Indian plays to *nō* chants and *kyōgen*, when I was reading *nō* chants and *kyōgen* scripts. The connection was no more than a flight of fancy. Yet, if we trace back **the tradition of masks** that flowed into the *nō* tradition, as we have seen thus far, there is no doubt in my mind that its origins can go at least as far back as the *gigaku* performed during the Tenpyō era. Even if we were to assume that *nō* and *kyōgen* developed entirely on Japanese soil, the ideas and themes embodied in them clearly would come from Chinese and Indian cultures, so much so that it is unavoidable to think that its dramaturgy too would have derived from these cultures. If we think in this way, it will be possible to examine *nō* and *kyōgen* closely and speculate about *gigaku* during the Tenpyō era.

In comparison to *gigaku* masks, *nō* masks are based on entirely different principles. Similarly, it goes without saying that the *nō* theater is entirely different from *gigaku*. Thus it is possible that certain valuable qualities of *gigaku* disappeared during the *nō* theater's development. Speaking in broad terms, then, we may say that great arts during the Tenpyō era did not develop and evolve as they should have. Even if we assume that *nō* and *kyōgen* were the results of long development, we cannot immediately conclude that they were superior to *gigaku* during the Tenpyō period. As we can clearly see in sculpture, painting, and poetry, it is quite possible that *gigaku* was far better as a play than *nō* or *kyōgen*.

GIGAKU, PERSIAN PLAYS, GREEK PLAYS, AND GREEK PLAYS IN INDIA; BRAHMAN AND GREEK CULTURES

I have incubated this fantasy of mine, that *gigaku* was related to Greek dramas, from looking at *gigaku* masks themselves. However, if we can ascertain that *gigaku* came out of **Indian music** and **music of the western regions of China** as I have proposed above, this fantasy will no longer be a mere baseless speculation.

BRAHMANISM AND GREEK CULTURE

Some readers may think that Indian music and music of the western regions of China, transmitted to Japan as *gigaku*, consisted of **music** and **dance**, devoid of dramatic structure. In this musical tradition, however, performers dance the Shiva and Durga dance, accompanied by "lyrics." Given this, I cannot help but think that this combination inevitably gave rise to a type of drama.

Now then, how can we make a claim that a particular play from India and the western regions of China is in the same tradition as a Greek play? Here we cannot bring out visual evidence like sculpture but I would argue that the relationship between them is almost identical to the relationship in sculpture. It is known that Greek plays were staged frequently in northern India, Bactria, and Persia beginning at the time when Alexander the Great led a military campaign to the east.[56] Bactria, a country established by the Greeks, was located to the west of a mountain range in Central Asia. Persia held close ties with the Roman Empire, and naturally there was a great deal of Greek influence in Persian plays. It is known that after the Sassanian dynasty was established in 226 CE Persian kings wrote Greek-style tragedies and that they were staged before the altar where Dionysus and Roman generals were enshrined. Elsewhere in northern India, Greeks established a kingdom in the first century BCE, which also influenced Buddhism a great deal.[57] For instance, Buddhist **scriptures** written at the beginning of the Christian era and after, **especially Mahayana scriptures**, underwent a great deal of change due to the influence of Greek art. It is safe to say that **the rituals of worshiping Buddha** also were reorganized artistically owing to the same Greek influence. Brahman culture also received much influence. Since this culture shared the same roots with Greek culture, it was more readily influenced by Greek culture. Brahmanism, which had taken on an extremely metaphysical and speculative nature in the fifth or sixth centuries BCE when the Upanishads were being written, lost some influence to Buddhism, which embodied a more solid relevance to life. The tradition of worshiping **very human-like deities**, not unlike Greek deities, however, remained very strong and influential with the people, and this gave birth to the cult of Vishnu, Shiva, etc., even after the beginning of the Christian era. The Yuezhi entered northern India and conquered it, and soon after this event, the king of the Yuezhi became an enthusiastic worshiper of Shiva. Then, King Kanishka I of the Kushan Empire—who we know now as an ardent supporter of Buddhism—entered northern India. After the period of King Kanishka's and his successors' reigns, the next king again returned to the worship of Shiva. We may say that Mahayana Buddhism characteristically incorporated both contemporary and old Brahman mythology because it was a new religion formed in northern India, where the god of Shiva was highly influential. At this time, I would imagine that the cult of Shiva had received an influence from Greek religious practice. As evidence for this, I point to the heavily Brahmanistic Indian religion of the Gupta dynasty, which ruled northern India after the Yuezhi left. This religion was quite distinct from the older Brahmanism and also closer in character to the worship of Dionysus and Aphrodite. In addition it had some features reminiscent of secret ceremonies in the western regions of China. It is possible to think, however, that the features of Indian secret ceremonies were first adopted in the western regions of China, transformed, and adopted back into India. Whatever may have been the case, it was now impossible for Indians to resurrect pure Brahmanistic culture. That is, although they finally regained the right to rule northern India where Greeks and the Yuezhi had coexisted and ruled the region for more than 500 years, they could not have recreated purely Brahmanistic culture, even if they tried. The art of the Gupta dynasty is the pinnacle of Indian art, and this is precisely because a fusion of cultures over a long period of time is crystallized in it. If we were to extrapolate from these observations, it should not seem outlandish to link Greek tragedies and the cult of Dionysus directly with Indian plays and the cult of Shiva. We see traces of Greek tragedies in the structure of Indian plays. Some Indian plays begin with a prayer to the god of Shiva. Originally, Dionysus and Shiva were manifestations of the power of life, and related to destruction and reproduction. They are not identical to each other owing to the different historical times and places where they originated. Likewise, Indian plays are not identical to Greek tragedies. What influenced Indian plays was not the principle of a Greek tragedy; rather, it was the brilliant concreteness of illusion, the sharp sense for sensual beauty, and the entire spectrum of other **naturalistic and humanistic characteristics** of Greece. With regard to plays, we must remind ourselves that Greek plays that came into India were principally new plays written during Greece's Hellenistic period. If we subscribe to the idea that a characteristic of Indian culture is its supernatural and super-humanistic nature, I would think the culture is most unsuited for writing plays, but even if this was not the case, I think Indians were not suited for playwriting because they are naturally given to excessive fantasy. It so happened that newly written Greek plays were no less naturalistic than modern plays. I think it is through this naturalism and the powerful influence that it exerted on Indian culture that an Indian theme could be made into a drama. Plays written by Kalidasa during the height of the Gupta dynasty in the fifth century CE were reputedly masterpieces that no work in Europe—between the Hellenistic period and the Renaissance—could favorably compare.[58] Despite the fact that his plays deal with Indian life in which people always try to transcend nature and man, Kalidasa's method of depiction is never supernatural or superhuman. It has been said that Kalidasa's ability to portray human nature compares favorably to Shakespeare's. It is patently clear that these dramas that were not Indian in a strict sense were influenced by Greek plays. In other words, India was achieving something at this time what was achieved in Europe one thousand years later.

INDIAN AND GREEK PLAYS

It is natural to assume that thriving Indian drama resonated as far away as the western regions of China by land and Indochina by sea. By this I do not mean that only Kalidasa's masterpieces were passed on to these areas. Among those transmitted to the outside of India, some undoubtedly were not the greatest creations. It is also possible that some of the transmitted plays were simple ones that did not require professional actors. In addition, we must also allow for the possibility that since these plays accompanied missionary work for Buddhism they may have been those that particularly suited this purpose. It is probable that India and China interacted before the time of Emperor Taizong of the Tang (599–649). The height of the Gupta dynasty corresponds to the era of the Northern Wei dynasty (386–534), and during this period, a considerable number of people from the western regions of China visited Northern Wei, and this interaction flourished especially after Emperor Taizong extended the reach of the Tang dynasty to the west. After the expansion, culture from the western regions of China, and this included Buddhism of course, poured in. It is safe to assume that Indian plays were part of the influx of culture.

During the rule of Emperor Xuanzong of the Tang, even more foreign culture was enthusiastically imported.[59] On the dinner table of the nobility, people saw Indian, Persian, and Roman dishes, which became highly praised. Women of a certain rank vied with one another to wear clothes from the west of China, probably semi-Greek in style. Toward the beginning of China's Tang dynasty, in the Tenpō era, in other words, year 12 or 13 of Japan's Tenpyō era, even the common populace seemed to have preferred a clothing style from the western regions of China.[60] Women's clothing in particular, as one can see clearly from the design of *yong* dating from this time, very much resembles Greek clothing.[61] Further, it is recorded unambiguously that around this time **a new style of music originating from the western regions of China** was held in high esteem.

CULTURAL INTERCOURSE WITH CHINA AND JAPAN

Such was the situation with the Tang dynasty, which flourished during Japan's Tenpyō era. Of course, this Tang China was admired by the Japanese people. Around this time, promising students traveled to China in droves. Tang visitors often arrived in Japan. Indians and Persians came, as did, no doubt, Indian plays.

It is still unknown, however, if Indian drama in fact arrived on Japan's shores as plays. People of Japan were interested in Buddhism. In India, where Buddhism was born, however, its influence was in decline. Buddhism flowed into countries that embraced it **with more hospitality**. China received it with open arms. So able monks and talented artists migrated toward the east following the flow of Buddhism. Brahmanism, however, was not evangelistic, and it probably held no desire to propagate itself outside of its home country.

Thus I cannot think of a reason why full-fledged Indian plays should have reached anyplace outside of India. I would contend that the elements from Indian plays that were adopted were limited only to those absorbed into Buddhist ceremonies. In this sense, then, *gigaku* cannot be considered to be a play in its fullest sense. Even if we were to assume that *gigaku* was a no more than a pageant, we mustn't forget that in the background behind *gigaku* were fully developed Indian plays.

Notes

1. The Kamakura period stretched from 1185 to 1333. *Chikyū* and *nasori* are two of some ten different types of masks used for *bugaku* performance, which are somewhat smaller than *gigaku* masks but are considerably larger than *nō* masks.
2. *Shoku Nihongi,* also called *Shokki* for short, was a history of Japan written under imperial commission. It was completed in 797 and chronicles the previous one hundred years of Japan's history.
3. The Yamashina temple is the present-day Kōfukuji temple. The record of Emperor Shōtoku's (718–770, r. 764–770, known also as Emperor Kōken when she ruled 749–758) attendance appears in the entry dated for the eighth day of the second month, Jingo Keiun 1 (767). See pp. 151–152, *Shoku Nihongi,* vol. 15 of *Shin Nihon Koten Bungaku Taikei* (hereinafter abbreviated as *SNKBT*). Tokyo: Iwanami Shoten, 1989–2005. Lin-yi (a.k.a., Lini or Champa) was a country in the southeast part of the Indochina peninsula, which flourished from the seventh century CE to about 1832. Wu was a Chinese kingdom in 222–280 CE, and its capital city was in Jianye (present-day Nanjing).
4. As Watsuji states elsewhere, much of the detailed information presented here may be found in *Tōdaiji Yōroku* in the Hiramatsu Bunko Collection at the University of Kyoto Libraries, available in digital form, accessed June 9, 2009.
5. The altar mentioned here, *raiban*, in *Todaiji Yōroku* is believed to be a small, elevated platform equipped with a lectern in front, a gong on the right, and an incense burner on the left, on which a monk or nun could sit and offer prayers. For descriptions of other items on and near the stage, see *Todaiji Yōroku*, 83, vol. 1, *et seq*.
6. This structure may have been built in the place where there is now a large roofed window on the south façade of the Great Hall of Buddha. The stage apparently jutted out from (or was open to the outside of) the "mid-level" of the building.
7. In the annotation provided for *Shoku Nihongi*, *tōka* was known as *arare bashiri*, a word that suggests that the dance was a quick-paced foot dance.
8. See *Shoku Nihongi*, *SNKBT* 3:118–119.
9. *Tōdaiji Yōroku*, 83.
10. For these details, see *Tōdaiji Yōroku*, p. 83 *et seq*.; see also *Shoku Nihongi*, *SNKBT* 14:498–499.
11. See *Tōdaiji Yōroku*, 83, for the description of the Jōgan ceremony.
12. Later, these towers as well as many other Tōdaiji structures were destroyed in warfare and from fires caused by lightening strikes. The towers were never rebuilt.
13. *Shoku Nihongi*, *SNKBT* 14:119, 498–499
14. This dance was performed for the imperial harvest festival. See *Shoku Nihongi* in *SNKBT* 14:499.
15. According to the legend recorded in the *Kojiki* (Record of Ancient Matters, 712), Susanō no Mikoto had been responsible for all sorts of misconduct. Other deities complained about Susanō, but the Goddess Amaterasu refused to discipline him and eventually went into hiding in a stone cave, which resulted in all manner of curses falling upon the land. Concerned, all deities then assembled to discuss how they could lure Amaterasu

out of the cave. The *Kojiki* states that in the end the deity Ama no Uzume danced a dance that was highly boisterous and comedic. Curious about the commotion outside, Amaterasu eventually opened the stone door to take a peek, and she was then taken out of the cave. This restored sunshine and peace over the land.

16. Ōtomo no Ojimaro was a court official between 774 and 782 with the rank of *kunaigyō*. He led a troupe of *koto* (Japanese zither) players. Saeki no Matanari (?–757) was a court noble who led a troupe of sword dancers for this occasion. *Kumemai* is an imperial court dance performed usually by four dancers, accompanied by music and singing. A modern version redolent of this dance may be viewed at the Kashihara Jingū shrine in Kashihara, Nara.

17. In this dance, also known as *kishimai*, *tatefushi* (*no*) *mai*, and *tatafusemai*, the dancers, clad in armor, lay down their shields, symbolizing their obedience to the laws of Buddhism (or to the emperor). The dance described here was led by Haji no Sukune and Fumi no Imiki (*Shoku Nihongi*, *SNKBT* 14:499).

18. *Shoku Nihongi* in *SNKBT* 14:499.

19. *Shaku Nihongi* is an interpreted account of the *Nihongi* compiled by Urabe no Kanekata at the end of the Kamakura period between 1274 and 1301. For details, see *Shaku Nihongi*, *Shintō Taikei*, vol. 5. Tokyo: Shintō Taikei Hensankai, 1986. The phrase *yorozu tose arare* means "may the emperor live a life of ten thousand years." The dance itself involves rhythmical foot dancing and singing. This lively dance may be fitting for the Sun Goddess Amaterasu's emergence from a rock cave, but its origin is attributed to popular, secular dance originating in the Sui and Tang dynasties in China. See *Shoku Nihongi*, *SNKBT* 12:296. The Fujiwara period refers to a cultural period from the mid- to late Heian period.

20. Tang miscellaneous music likely refers to non-*gagaku* music.

21. Indeed, many items used for the original consecration ceremony conducted in 752 are still in storage at Shōsōin. See Matsushima Junsei, *Shōsōin hōmotsu meibun shūsei* (A Collection of Labels for Items Stored in Shōsōin). Tokyo: Yoshikawa Kōbunkan, 1978.

22. A catalogue was created during the repair work of Shōsōin in Tenpō 4 (1833).

23. These items are listed in *Tōdaiji Yōroku*, vol. 1.

24. These items were apparently only a small part of a large amount of goods, services, and money, which were donated for the occasion. *Tōdaiji Yōroku* recorded these items Watsuji mentioned as having been donated by the Fujiwara no Asomi clan (vol. 1, p. 76). In the original text the following is given: "320 *tan* of cloth. 8 *hiki* of silk cloth, 9 *shaku* of brocaded Tang cloth, one *hiki* of think silk fabric." A *tan* was a bolt of cloth that measured approximately 11 inches by 33 feet. One *hiki* equaled two *tan*. One *shaku* is equal to about one foot in U.S. Customary unit.

25. Kōbō Daishi, also known as Kūkai, lived 774–835 and founded the Shingon Sect of Buddhism.

26. Hu was a name for the five "barbarian tribes" that ruled an area to the north or west of China proper and were powerful during 304–439 CE.

27. Tamonten is one of the Four Guardian Kings of Buddhism, along with Jikokuten, Zōchōten, and Kōmokuten. They each rule over a number of lesser deities (rendered as demon deities here), including Yasha and Rasetsuten, which are ruled by Tamonten.

28. The jewel is symbolic of the jewel of Buddhism (*nyoihōjuhō*) that can grant all manner of wishes. The brush (*byakuhotsu* in this text), also called *hossu*, is made of animal hair, with a handle, that was probably used to drive away worldly attachments. It is not clear what type of fan was used.

29. Jizaiten (a.k.a. Daijizaiten, Skt. *Mahesvara*) was originally an Indian deity of creation that was brought into Buddhism.

30. I thank Eiji Suhara for his help with this translation. The original text comes from the Flower Garland Sutra, *Taishō Shinshū Daizōkyō* (hereafter *TSD*) T0279.10.0204c28-29.

31. *Gagaku* refers to dance and music played for the imperial court, consisting of traditional native music and music from the continent and Korean peninsula. *Gagakuryō* was a department that trained musicians and performed music at official functions.

32. Eshin'in Genshin was a Tendai monk, who lived from 942 until 1017.

33. Emperor Ninmyō lived 810–850 and ruled 833–850.

34. *Kakko* music, or *Kakko gaku*, was a type of percussion music that came from China. Music around this time (and this designation still continues today in *gagaku* [court music]) was divided into two types, "right" and "left." On the left was music from China, India and Lin-yi. One the right, there was Goryeo and Bokkai (part of present-day northeast province of China) music.

35. *Kagura* was instrumental music involving woodwinds and string instruments and percussion instruments to keep rhythm, was played at Shinto shrines. *Saibara* was vocal music accompanied by a similar set of instruments.

36. *Bugaku Yōroku* can be found in volume 10 of the series *Gunsho Ruijū*, compiled by Hanawa Hokinoichi. Tokyo: Gunsho Ruijū Kanseikai [Kantōsha], 1951. *Bugaku Yōroku* contains programs of Buddhist ceremonies, musical performances, and banquets. The Fujiwara period refers to a cultural period during late Heian.

37. *Koinzu* (also pronounced *konju*) is a type of dance "performed by a single man using sweeping gestures. He dresses in a fringed tunic and pantaloons, a *ryōtō* costume, and carries a short stick with a rounded ball at the end." The masks portray a bleary-eyed drunkard. *Tōzu* is the expression of a "terse, red-faced man." http://www.aisf.or.jp/~jaanus/deta/k/konju.htm.

38. *Zappi Betsuroku* is a collection of essays and episodes about how to play various pieces of music written by Fujiwara no Takamichi (1166–1237). Takamichi was born to a musician's family and learned to play the four-stringed Japanese lute called *biwa*, and to produce and repair the instrument. *Zappi Betsuroku* is collected in volume 19 of the series *Gunsho Ruijū*, compiled by Hanawa Hokinoichi. Tokyo: Gunsho Ruijū Kanseikai [Kantōsha], 1951.

39. Fujiwara no Masazane (1059–1127) was a high-ranking court official and a poet. He was involved in the compilation of *Ruijū Utaawase*, a collection of *waka*.

40. The Ashikaga period is a cultural period during the Muromachi period, 1392–1573.

41. Not all sources consulted agree that these deities are related to each other in this way.

42. *Bukyoku Kōden* was a book written by Toyohara Muneaki (1450–1524) on dance music. See volume 19 of the series *Gunsho Ruijū*, compiled by Hanawa Hokinoichi. Tokyo: Gunsho Ruijū Kanseikai [Kantōsha], 1959. Ōto no Kiyokami (?–839) was a court musician, who also arranged and composed. The Jōwa period spanned the years 834–848 during Emperor Ninmyō's reign. *On'yō jichin kyoku* would be something like "music to pacify the land using the sorcery of a Ying-Yang diviner's power."

43. *Karyōbin* (a.k.a. *Karyōbinga*, Skt. *kalavinka*) is apparently a dance performed in a bird costume, typically performed by four dancers. It is often performed in Buddhist memorial services. *Bairohajinraku* (a.k.a. *Hairohajingaku*) is a type of Tang music and belongs to the *gagaku*'s "right" section. The dance is performed usually by four dancers dressed in armor. *Raryōōjujinraku* is performed by one person, who portrays the entrance of the Ran Ryōō (Ch. *Gao Zhanggong*, ?–573) into the battlefield, fighting against the Northern Zhou army in 564. *Koinzu* (a.k.a. *Konju*) is a dance performed by one person and portrays the king of Hu dancing after drinking. Hu was name for the five "barbarian tribes" that ruled an area to the north or west of China during 304–439 CE.

44. *Shoku Nihongi*, *SNKBT* 15:152–153

45. *Daitō Saiikiki* (Great Tang Records of the Western Regions, Ch. *Da Tang Xiyu ji*) is a narrative account of the Chinese monk Xuanzang's journey from Chang'an, China to India between 626 and 645. See Xuanzang, *Da Tang Xiyu ji* (Xi'an, China: Shanxi ren min chu ban she, 2008), 12.

46. Though "Morito" is more likely, the village name could be read "Toto." The system of giving a distinct social class to musicians originated during the Northern Wei dynasty (386–534).

47. Fujiwara no Akihira lived from 989 to1066. He was a Confucian scholar and writer. See Fujiwara no Akihira, *Shin Sarugakuki*. Tokyo: Heibonsha, 1983.

48. The *Eiga Monogatari* is an eleventh century historical narrative dealing with imperial history from approximately 900 through 1092.

49. For the original description, see pp. 111–112, vol. 2, of *Eiga Monogatari*, in *Nihon Koten Bungaku Taikei* (hereafter referred to as *NKBT*). Tokyo: Iwanami Shoten, 1957–1967.

50. *Mokoromo* could be read *mobakama* in another source. It appears to have been loose "dress-like" clothing worn on the upper and lower body like a skirt.

51. *Sasara* consists of two bamboo sticks, each about one foot long. One stick is split into narrow strips two-thirds of the length. The other stick has saw-tooth notches. The split stick or whisk is rubbed on the saw-teeth of the other stick to make noise.

52. *Rakuyō Dengakuki* was written by Ōe no Masafusa (poet, bureaucrat, and Confucian scholar, 1041–1111) to record the *dengaku* craze that occurred in the summer of 1096. *Rakuyō Dengakuki* is collected in volume 19 of the series *Gunsho Ruijū*, compiled by Hanawa Hokinoichi. Tokyo: Gunsho Ruijū Kanseikai [Kantōsha], 1951.

53. *Cothurnus* is a high, thick-soled, and laced boot worn by actors in Greek and Roman tragic drama with the sole padded with cork to give elevation, authority, and importance to some actors. What Watsuji refers to as *takaashi* here could have been a single-pole stilt, ridden like a pogo stick, by *dengaku* performers.

54. *Kebiishi* were officials in charge of public safety, enforcing laws in the city of Kyoto during the Heian period.

55. *Dengaku hōshi* were professional *dengaku* performers dressed in monk's clothing. Some of these performers may have actually been Buddhist monks.

56. Bactria occupied a region in the present-day Iran and Afghanistan. Alexander the Great defeated King Darius III of the Persian Empire in 330 BCE, heralding the beginning of extremely vibrant Greek culture in that area.

57. This was so-called the Indo-Greek Kingdom that flourished in northwestern India in the last two centuries BCE.

58. Kalidasa (dates unknown) was a highly regarded writer of plays and poetry in classical Sanskrit, who lived during the Gupta dynasty. His stature is sometimes compared to that of William Shakespeare.

59. Emperor Xuanzong of the Tang dynasty lived 685–762 and ruled 712–756.

60. China's Tenpō era (Ch. *Tienbao*) spanned 742–756.

61. *Yong* were clay, wood, or metal figures, many in human shape, that were buried with the dead in China beginning in the Warring States period until the Ming dynasty (roughly from the fourth century BCE to the end of the nineteenth century).

Chapter 11

VAPOR BATH

Within the temple compound of Hokkeji, there is a bathhouse associated with a bathing legend about Empress Kōmyō.[1] It is the so-called *karaburo*, or waterless, vapor bath. Up until now, I did not know the existence of this "vapor bath," but when I was riding a rickshaw on the hilly Narazaka road the other day I learned about it for the first time from the rickshaw man. This bathhouse was a long, narrow building that looked like a roofed corridor, located midpoint on the hill, where I could overlook the Great Hall of Buddha of Tōdaiji across a narrow valley. The legend has it that engineers, carpenters, and laborers and such who became ill during the casting of the Buddha or the construction of the Great Hall of Buddha convalesced in the bathhouse. Today I quite accidentally happened to lay my eyes on that legendary "vapor bath" at Hokkeji.

The bathhouse is located in the garden to the east of the main worship hall and appears to be rather small, measuring about 18 feet square. The structure inside of the building took me quite by surprise. The floor was covered with tiles. In the center, there was a platform about three feet high off the floor level, on which a small house, complete with a roof and clapboard walls, was constructed. The entire structure was constructed as if it were **nested boxes**, that is, a box inside another box. In other words, a bathhouse was fashioned inside another bathhouse. The sides of the bathhouse on the inside were constructed to resemble the louvered window shutters in Western architecture, and the whole bathhouse resembles a small weather instrument shelter at weather stations. Naturally it is dark inside. In order to reach this second bathhouse, one climbs three or four steps, and enters through a low, narrow entrance as one stoops. It appeared that a small number of people, five or six at most, could sit inside without feeling too cramped. This area was the so-called bathing area. It was designed so that steam would fill this area as it was fed through the spaces between the floorboards. In other words, this was a veritable steam bath.

It is unknown if this construction informs us about how bathhouses were built in the Tenpyō period. For instance, the fuel hole on the east side of the building, where fire was fed to produce steam, was constructed of brick like a Western furnace. Farther in the corner on the northern side of the building, a cylindrical tub encased in concrete was found, reportedly still used regularly by the nuns in the temple. If we were to assume that this sort of improvement was made over the last one thousand years bit by bit, it would be undoubtedly dangerous to speculate about the original form on the basis of this bathhouse. I wondered, though, if at least this "**structure as a steam bath**" might not be close to the original. Is it not possible that, at the very least, **a steam bath** that resembled this one existed during the times of Empress Kōmyō?

THE LEGEND OF EMPRESS KŌMYŌ

Above the crossbeam at the entrance to the inner bathhouse, a framed picture of Empress Kōmyō hangs depicting her bathing the sick. In the picture, one sees sick people inflicted with leprosy sitting in a room much like today's public bathhouse. To their side, Empress Kōmyō stands erect, clad in a layered formal court kimono. It is bit anachronistic, thus amusing, to see a Nara period empress in late Heian clothing. The fact that a modern bathhouse is portrayed in the presence of this steam bath was beyond amusing; it was ironic. Yes, if truth be told, we must admit that we imagined the legend Empress Kōmyō's bathing of people to be exactly in this way. If we suppose that bathing was done in a steam bath, there are a certain number of preconceptions we must reevaluate.

It has long been known that steam baths are an effective means of medical care. Even today, steam baths are meaningful as a type of physical therapy. Thus it is not unimaginable that during the Tenpyō period inflictions of severe hysteria and other diseases that caused weakening of the body were treated by steam baths and found to be effective, even if only in a minor way. If this was the case, making steam baths available to the public would be the same as operating a charity hospital. It is then quite conceivable that Empress Kōmyō, who upheld the idea of benevolence as an ideal, would bathe the sick in a steam bath. In doing so, she might have shown a great deal of enthusiasm, so much so that her attendants might have had to restrain her from actually providing help with bathing in this very bathhouse. The legend does not stop at simply relating a story of the empress bathing the sick. The story related in *Genkō Shakusho* and other documents is as follows.[2] When Empress Kōmyō was feeling a bit overconfident, now that the Great Hall of Buddha had been finally completed, she heard a voice in the palace room one day encouraging her to administer bathing. As a result, she had a bathhouse built. At this time, she also made a pledge that she would "wash one thousand lepers with her own hands." Of course, the attendants tried to stop her, but she would not hear of it. Thus, finally, when the empress had washed nine hundred and ninety-nine lepers, she came upon the one-thousandth. This patient was disfigured considerably, so badly that "the room was filled with the smell of the rotten flesh." The brave empress hesitated but thinking that her pledge would be fulfilled with this leper, she mustered courage and began to wash the leper's back with her imperial hands. The sick person then spoke:

> I have been inflicted by this terrible disease and have suffered from the pox for many years. A good doctor once told me that if only I could have someone suck the puss out, I would surely be cured. Of course, there is no such merciful a person in this world who would do this for me, so my disease worsened to the current condition. Your Majesty, with your benevolent heart, saves everyone equally, without regard for class. Would Your Majesty please save me, too?"

The empress was the representative of the aesthetic sense of the Tenpyō period. Her senses were more accustomed to sweet-smelling fragrances from the tropics, the smoothness of jewels, and objects in balanced, agreeable shapes. Even if it were for mercy, it would be unbearable to touch the leper with her lips. But if she were to refuse, her penance would be nothing more than a deception. She thought, "If I thought that the leper was filthy and was therefore unworthy of saving, I should have never imposed a penance on myself in the first place." Would the empress disavow her religious beliefs? Or violate her aesthetics taste? The empress had a choice between these two options. Now she could not stop. She pressed her most precious Tenpyō-era lips on the pox on the head of the leper. She sucked it and spit the puss out from her mouth that was lined with beautiful teeth. Then, she went from the shoulders to the chest, from the chest to the lower back, and finally to the leper's heels, everywhere there were poxes. Thus the lips of the noblest woman of all touched the filthy feet of a lowly, disfigured leper. The empress then implored, "I have sucked all the poxes clean; pray do not tell anyone about this." When the empress said these words, suddenly the leper transformed into a most solemn and serene shape and began to glow brightly. Then a voice said, **"You have cleaned the body of an *asura*.**[3] Do not tell anyone about it."

This is an inspiring story. We should be proud that there was an empress in Japan's history associated with this moving story, even if it is not all true. The monk Kokan, who authored *Genkō Shakusho*, commented that it was a good idea to build a bathhouse, but washing lepers and sucking poxes was unnecessary. There was no need for those trivial deeds. Further, he said that anyone with a true heart would get a glimpse of *asura*. I find his interpretation to be a bit objectionable. I would agree with Kokan if he were to say that the description of "cleaning the body and sucking the puss" and such was a concoction of Buddhist priests in later generations. However, I find it difficult to accept his opinion if Kokan **treated this story as true** and advanced the viewpoint that the empress' deeds were superfluous or that washing one thousand lepers was unbecoming of a woman. Such an interpretation would completely disregard the religious excitement embodied in this story. Only a woman with faultless convictions could have sucked the puss of a leper.

Of course, this is a legend. It is a legend that may be said to be a bit formulaic. Yes, if we assume that this legend was told on the basis of the knowledge about bathhouses, we may be able to make a guess about how steam baths were taken from the legend. It is impossible to think that the empress would go into the cramped, dark inner bathing room to wash the backs of common people, in the hot steamy heat. Thus I would think washing must have actually taken place outside of the inner bathing room. Bathers would come out of the bathing room after their bodies had been thoroughly heated to the point where they would feel as if all the grime on the skin had been washed out of the body. Because of the steamy heat, the bathers would be languid, drained of energy. As for cleaning, a tool like a Greek *strigil*, made of wood or copper, might have been used to remove sweat and the dirt from the body.[4] If we were to imagine that a tool like the *strigil* was used, we would not be surprised to think of the empress going into the bathhouse and cleaning the grime off the bodies of common people.

What is more important to consider here is the bathers' state of mind. If I had actually experienced steam baths, I would have a more concrete sense of what it must be like to take a bath in this way. If the bathing experience entails a peculiar type of intoxication, then an enormous complexity would be introduced to our discussion. I hear people say that the steam bath in Osaka today can give sensual pleasure, not unlike smoking opium, and if one frequents steam baths, one would not be able to go without it for any length of time. So, if a steam bath is capable of creating a physiological sensation of this sort, we must assume that the bather after emerging from the bath would be in a special state of mind. At this point, if Empress Kōmyō, intent on performing a penance of mercy, were to make a visit to the bathhouse with her ladies-in-waiting at a time like this and treated the sick as prescribed, it would not be unthinkable at all that a type of intoxication inherent in steam bathing and the joy of arising from performing a merciful act would combine, resulting in a fusion of religious ecstasy and sensual intoxication. The Tenpyō period was a time when people felt an affinity for this sort of phenomena, so my conjecture is not entirely absurd. If we were to allow ourselves this sort of fantasy, this legend of "administering bathing" could have arisen from the people themselves.

In order to "administer bathing" appropriately, larger-scale, more stately bathhouses, with larger rooms, must have been available in the Tenpyō period. Given the level of technology at that time, this would not have been very difficult. A building that may serve as a basis for this flight of imagination is the bathhouse at Tōdaiji, called *yuya*. Some time later after I had visited Hokkeji, Mr. Tsutsui Hidetoshi facilitated my visit to see a *yuya* situated in the northeast of the Great Hall of Buddha. This was not a very old structure but was a fairly large, stately building. The building was divided into a room in the front and a bathing area in back. The room could accommodate several dozen people and could be used as a changing room for the bathers or to administer bathing to people. Bathing was again steam bathing and, proportionate to the size of the building, the bathing area was quite sizeable. This, I would think, was in the old tradition of *yuya*. Judging from this building, it would have been possible for a large number of bathhouses to be in operation during the Tenpyō period.

THE TRADITION OF STEAM BATHING

The fact that the steam bath at Hokkeji continues to exist to the present day is not as remarkable as, for instance, the fact that the main image of worship at this temple still remains today without damage. The still existing steam bath, though minor in importance, is nonetheless fascinating to me, perhaps because bathing is much closer to the flesh or perhaps because the flesh is far more effective in making immediate ties between the present and the past. I would get a more concrete sense of steam bathing if I were to experience a steam bath firsthand and judge for myself how it would warm my body, how the skin would feel, how languid I would feel afterward, and what the pleasant sensation would be after sweating out every drop of moisture. It may not be tactful or even wise to imagine the past from these very physical sensations; however, it is the easiest way.

Later on, my friend Z told me about steam baths in the West. He told me about the smooth surface of a comfortably warm marble bench, the languid body from the heat and steam, running sweat, the tool to scrape off sweat from the body, and the refreshing shower—they all sounded wonderfully invigorating, in sharp contrast to the bathhouse at Hokkeji. This steam bath, also called the Turkish bath, originated in Asia, and it is conceivable that it shares the same origin as the steam bath of the Tenpyō period. These large differences may have come about from the way steam bathing was utilized in the life of an ethnic group, for example, depending on whether it was continual or with interruptions.

Notes

1. Empress Kōmyō was the wife of Emperor Shōmu and lived 701–760. She was a philanthropist and devout believer of Buddhism.
2. *Genkō Shakusho* is a book compiled by the monk Kokan Shiren (1278–1346) in 1322 and chronicles the history of Buddhism in Japan since its arrival in the sixth century. See *Genkō Shakusho* (Tokyo: Kyōikusha, 1980), translated into modern Japanese by Imahama Michitaka.
3. *Asura* (a.k.a. *shura, ashura*) is a member of the Hachibushū.
4. A *strigil* was a small tool used in ancient Greece and Rome while bathing. It had a handle and a hook and it was used to scrape off dirt and sweat after oil has been applied to the skin.

Pilgrimages to the Ancient Temples in Nara

Illustrations

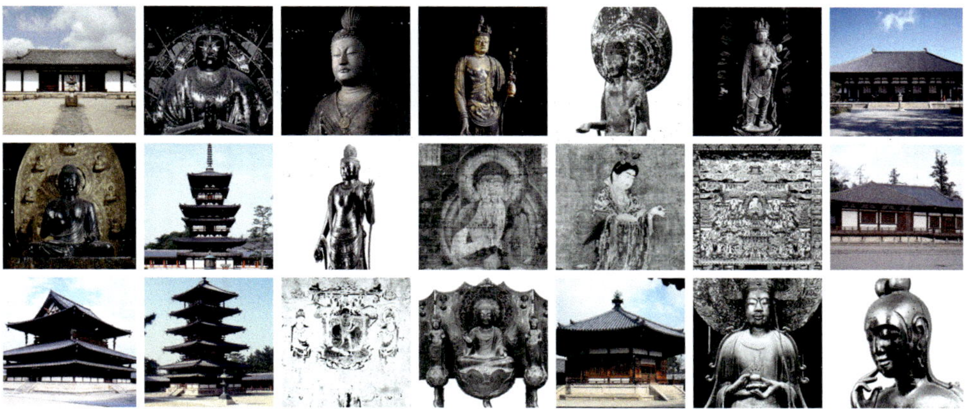

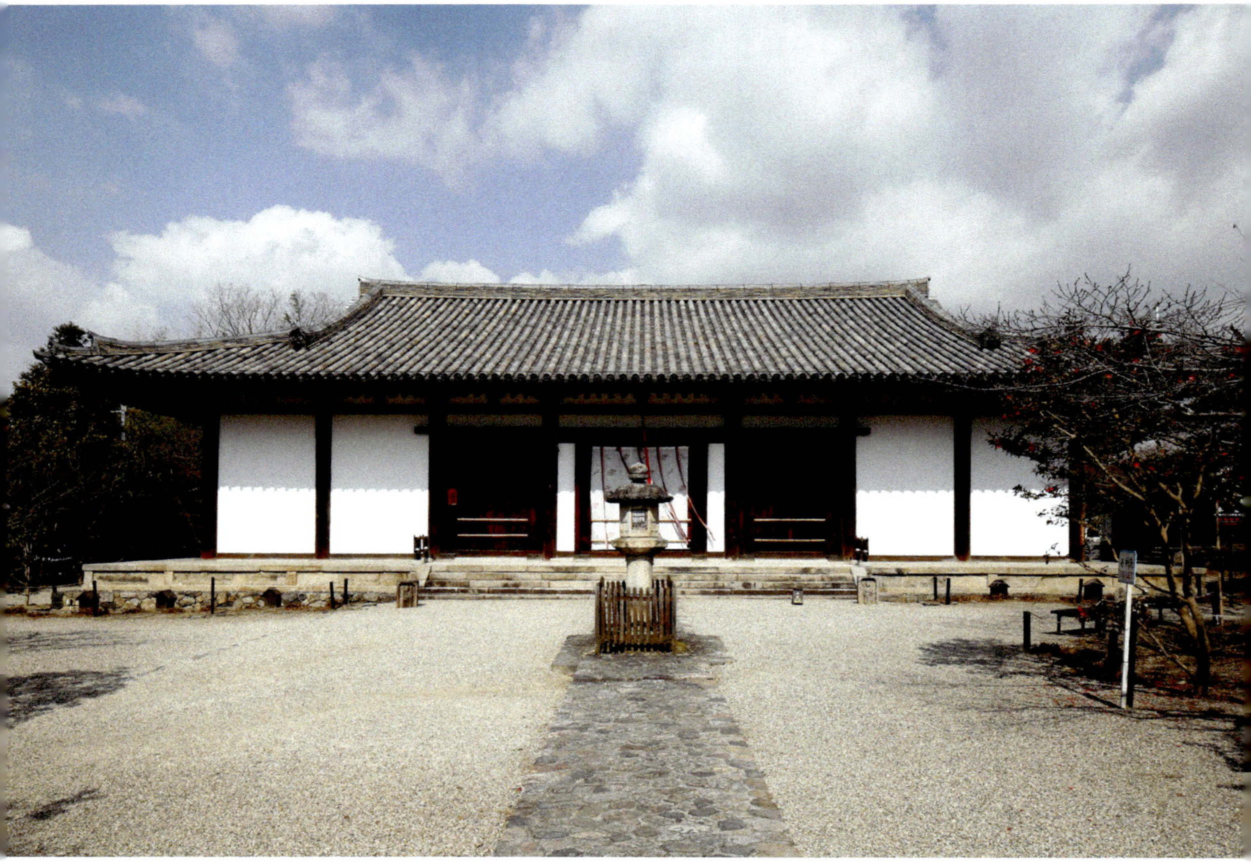

Fig. 1 (Above): Hondō (Main Hall of Worship), Shin Yakushiji. Photograph courtesy of Asukaen. *Fig. 2 (Opposite):* Fukū Kensaku Kannon, Sangatsudō, Tōdaiji. Photograph courtesy of the Nara National Museum.

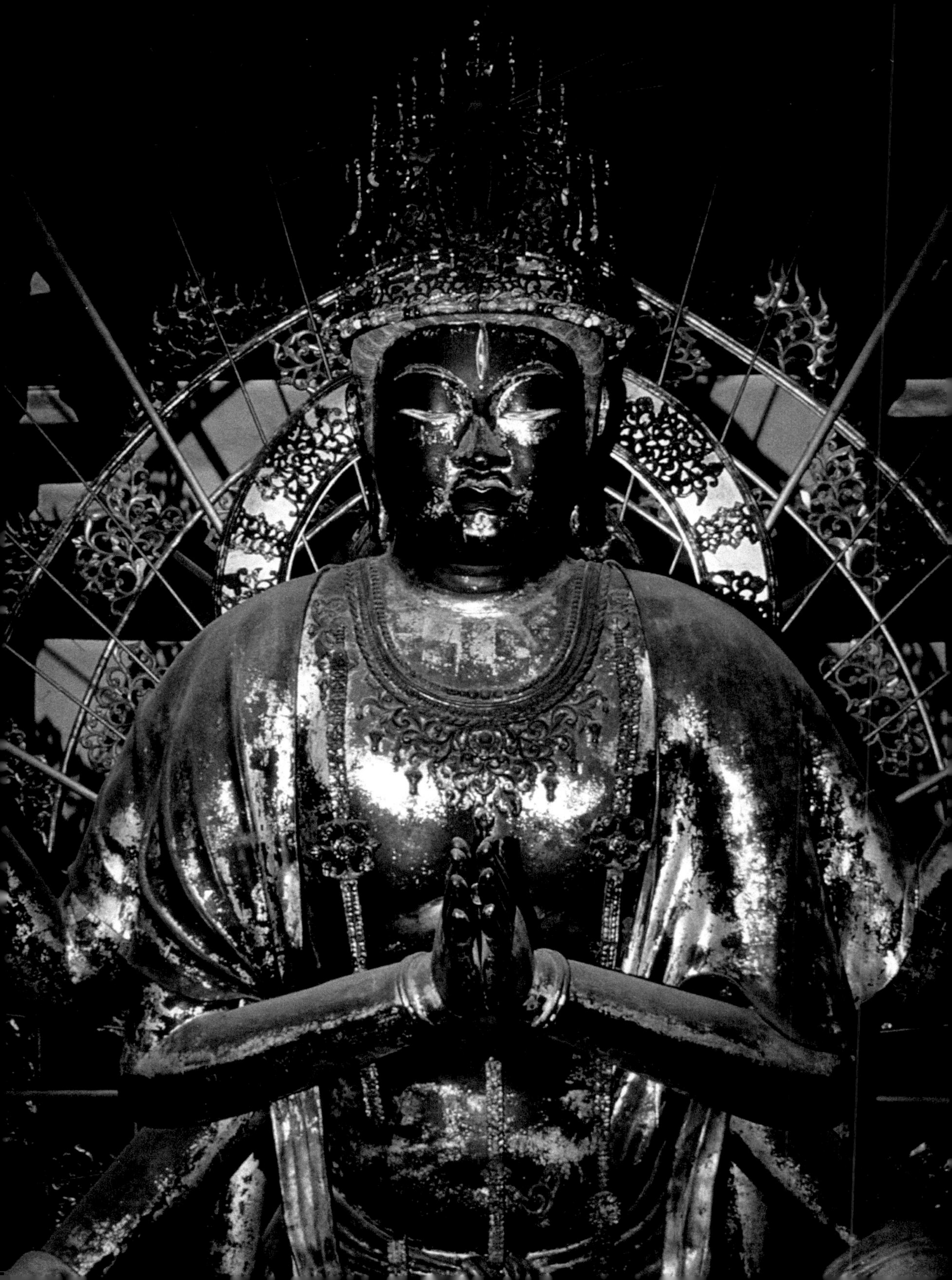

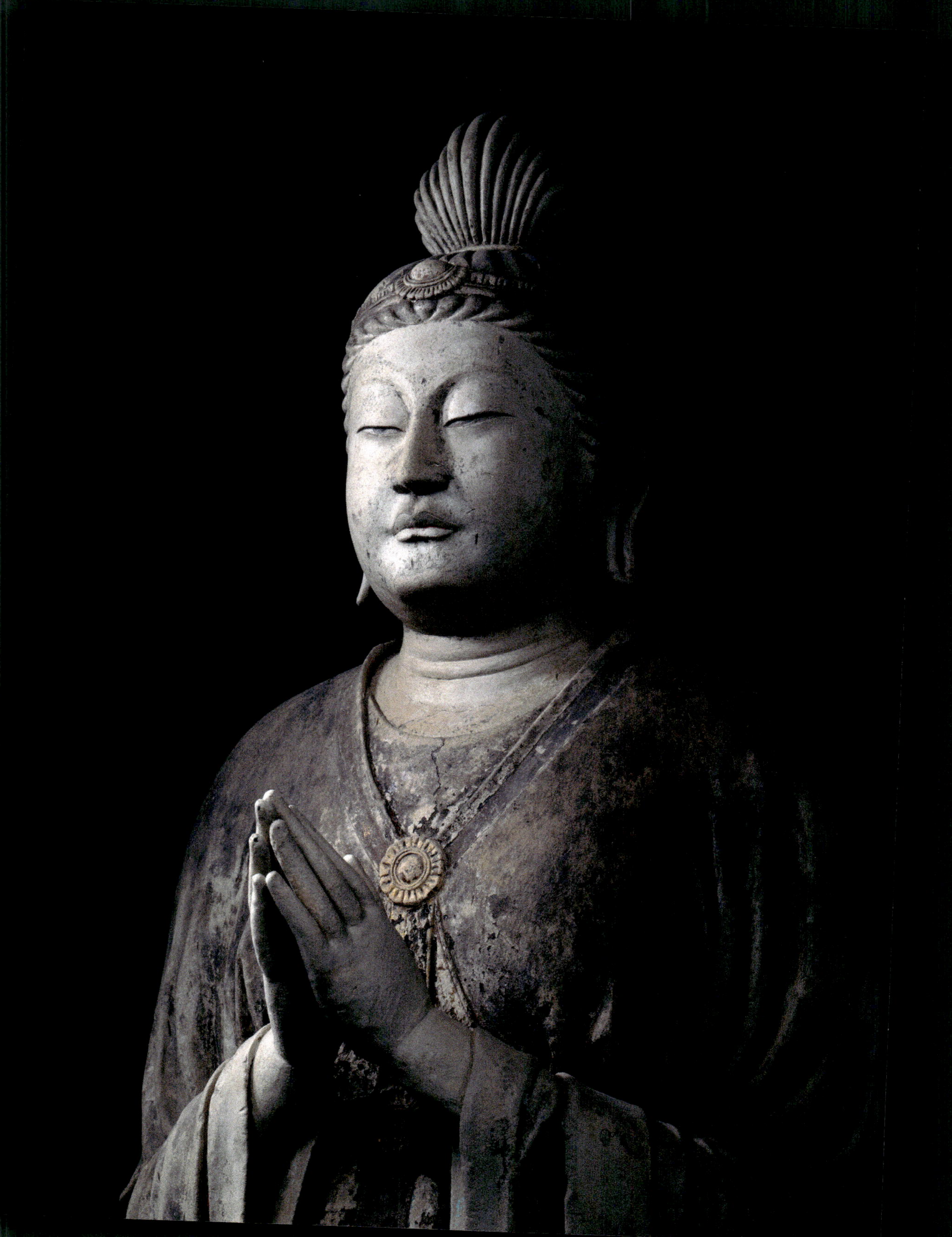

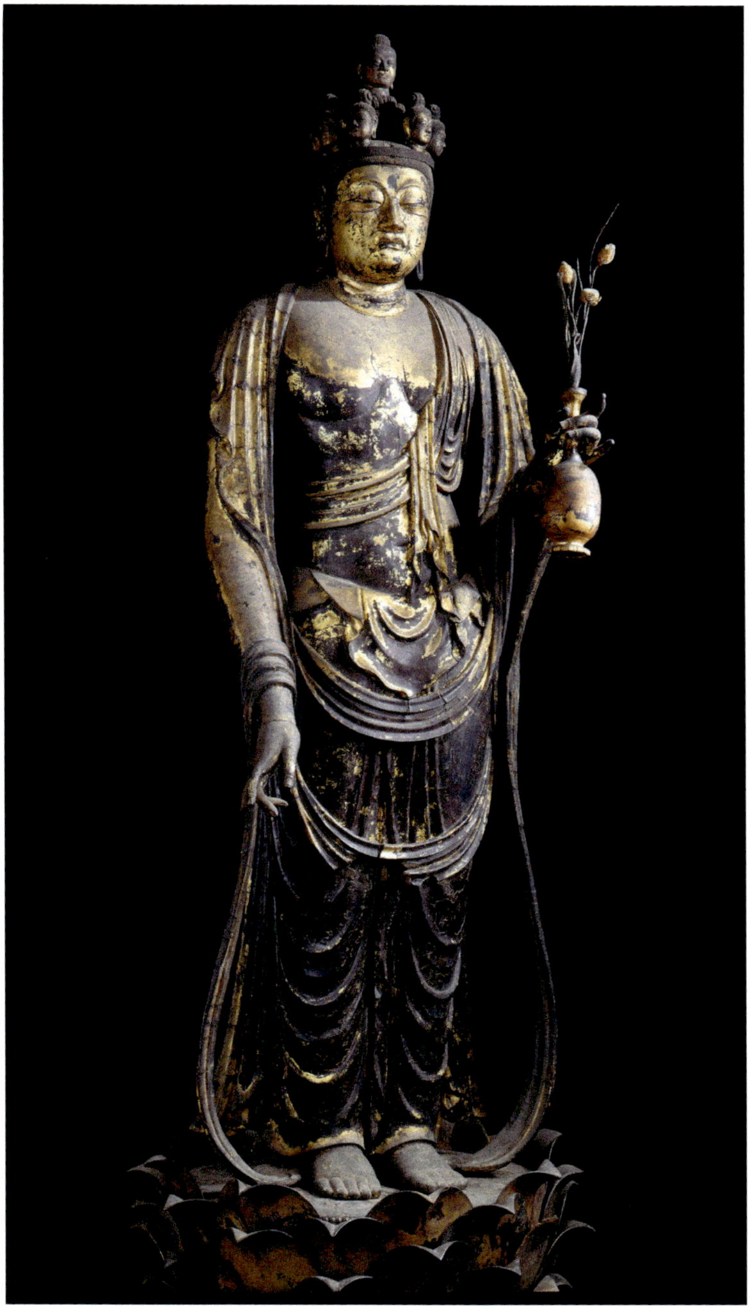

Fig. 3 (Opposite): Gakkō (Bonten), Sangatsudō, Tōdaiji. Photograph courtesy of Asukaen. *Fig. 4 (Above):* Eleven-headed Kannon, Shōrinji. Photograph courtesy of Asukaen.

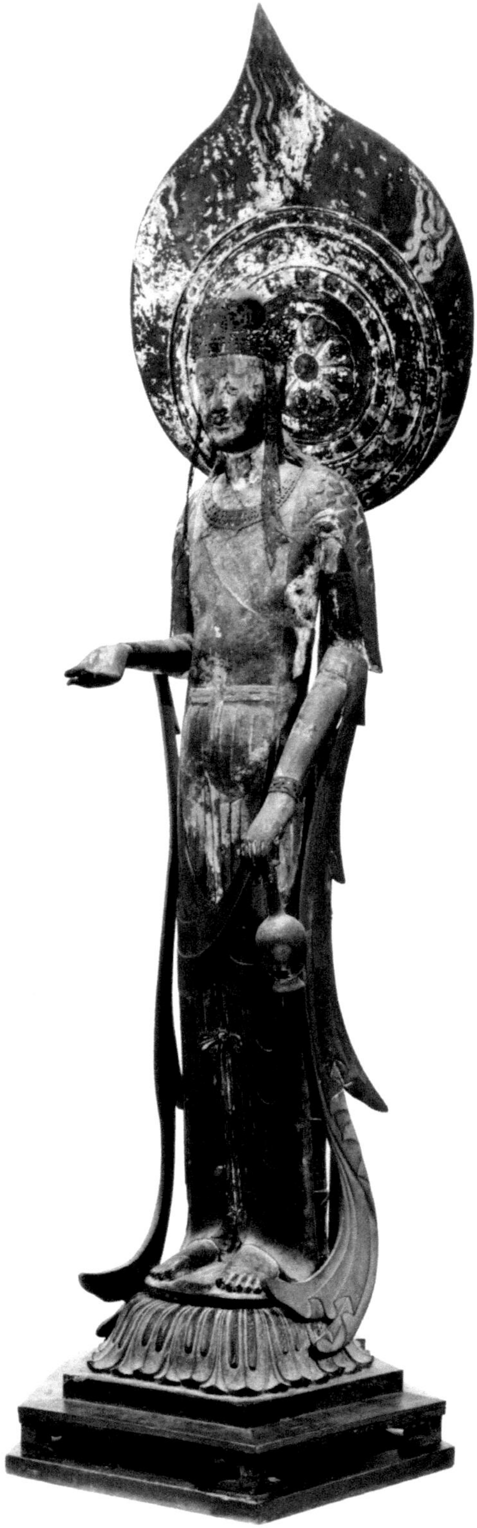

Fig. 5 (Right): Kudara Kannon, Hōryūji. Photograph courtesy of the Nara National Museum. Photograph courtesy of Asukaen.
Fig. 6 (Opposite): Eleven-headed Kannon, Hokkeji. Photograph courtesy of Asukaen.

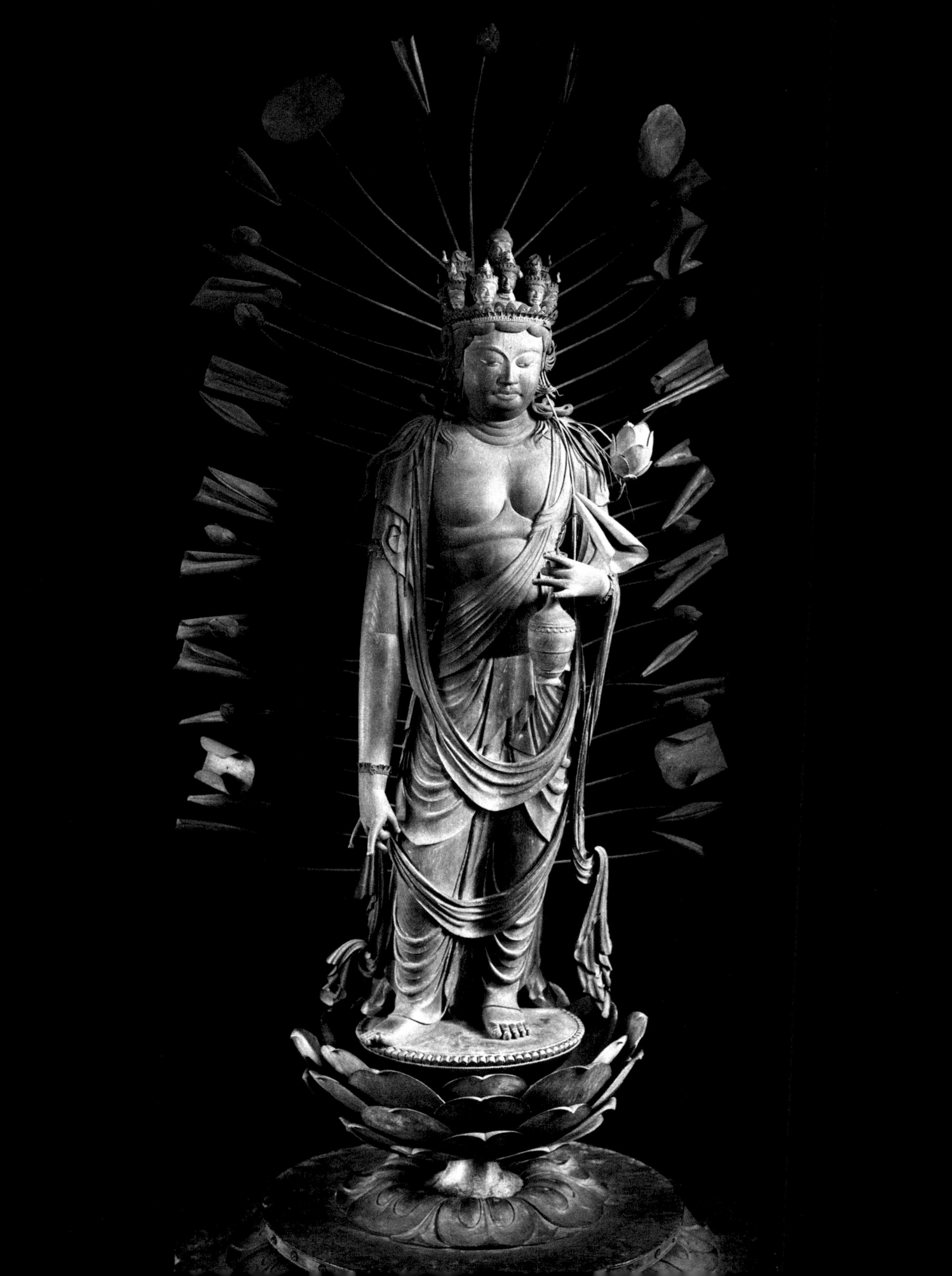

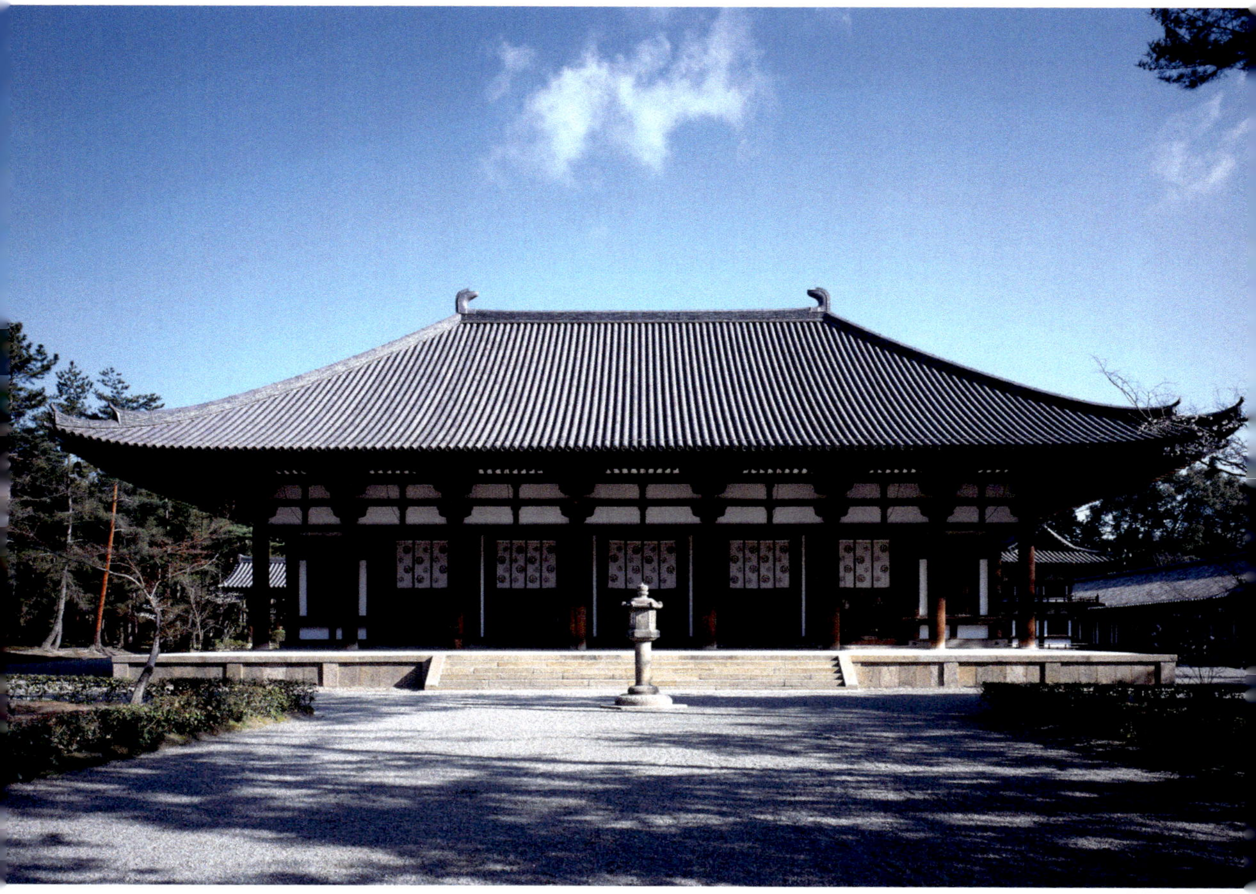

Fig. 7 (Above): Kondō (Golden Hall) of Tōshōdaiji. Photograph courtesy of Asukaen.
Fig. 8 (Opposite): Yakushi Nyorai Bodhisattva, Yakushiji. Photograph courtesy of Asukaen.

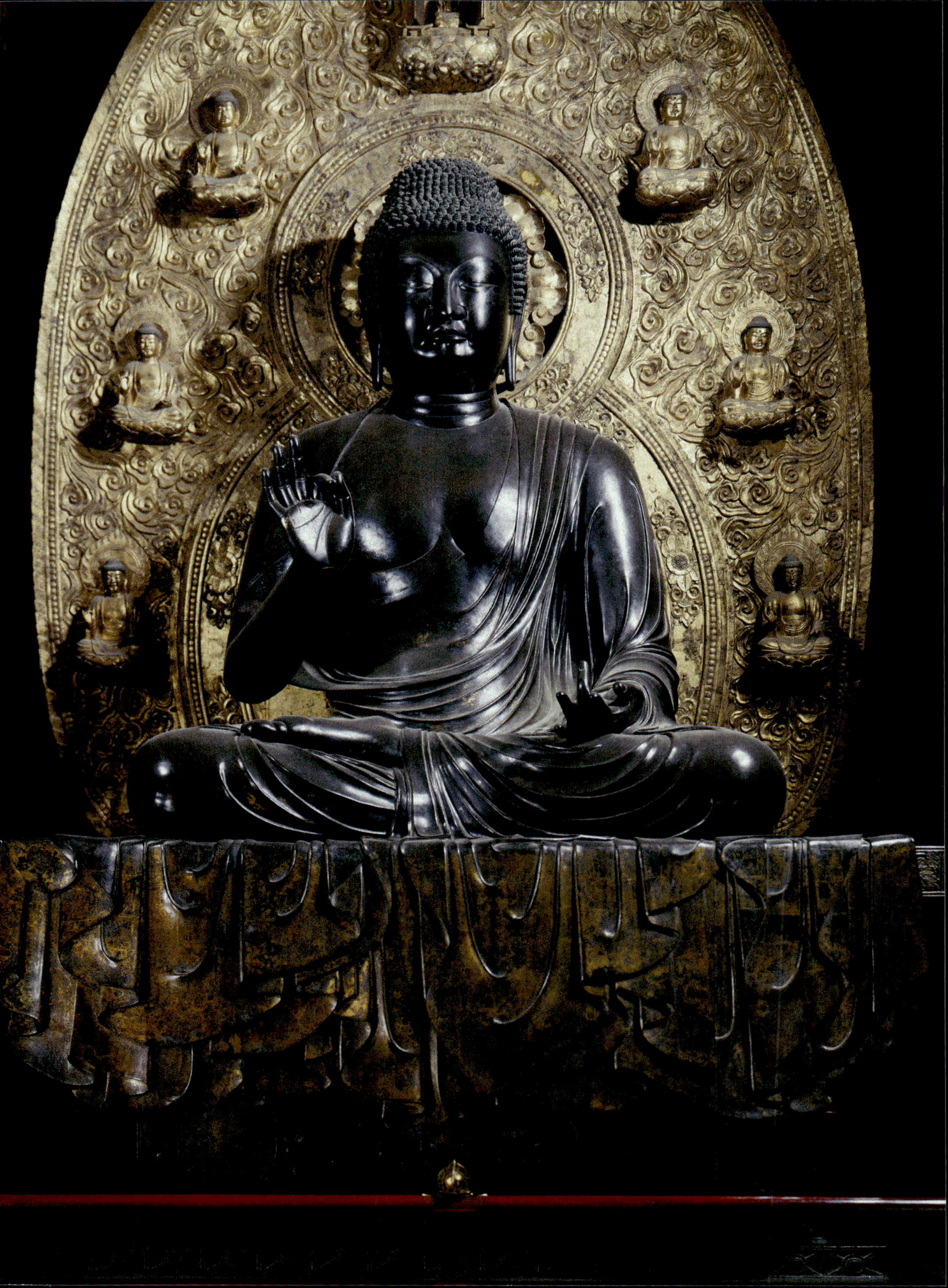

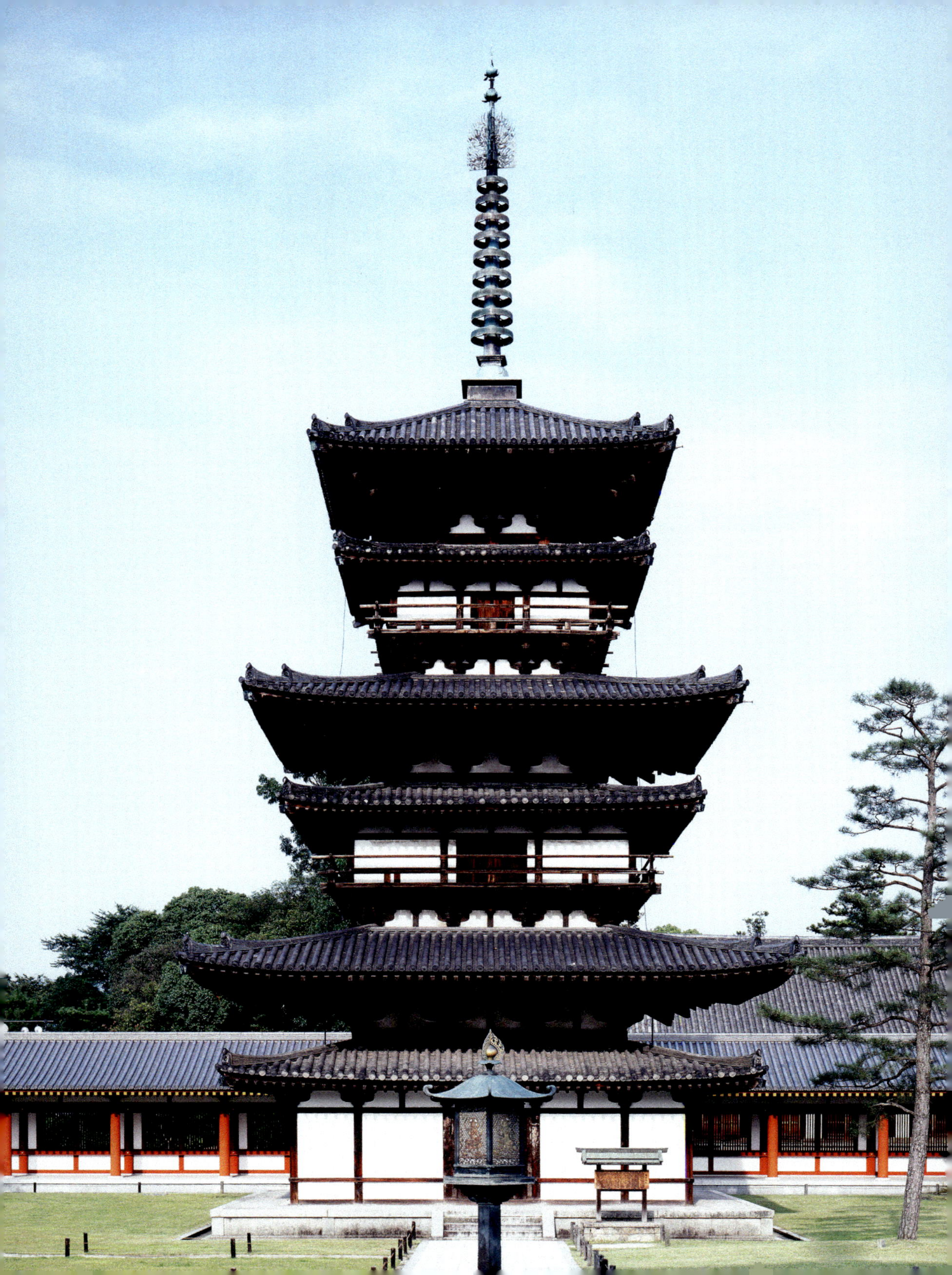

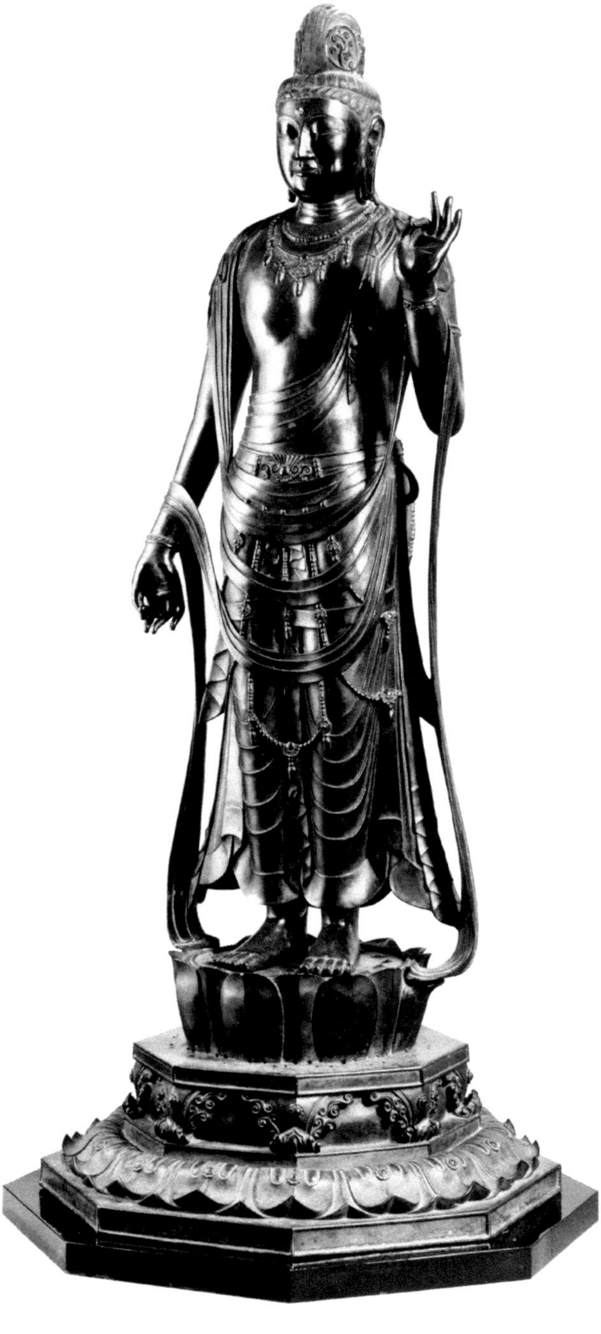

Fig. 9 (Opposite): East Tower of Yakushiji. Photograph courtesy of Asukaen.
Fig. 10 (Above): Shō Kannon, Tōindō, Yakushiji. Photograph courtesy of the Nara National Museum.

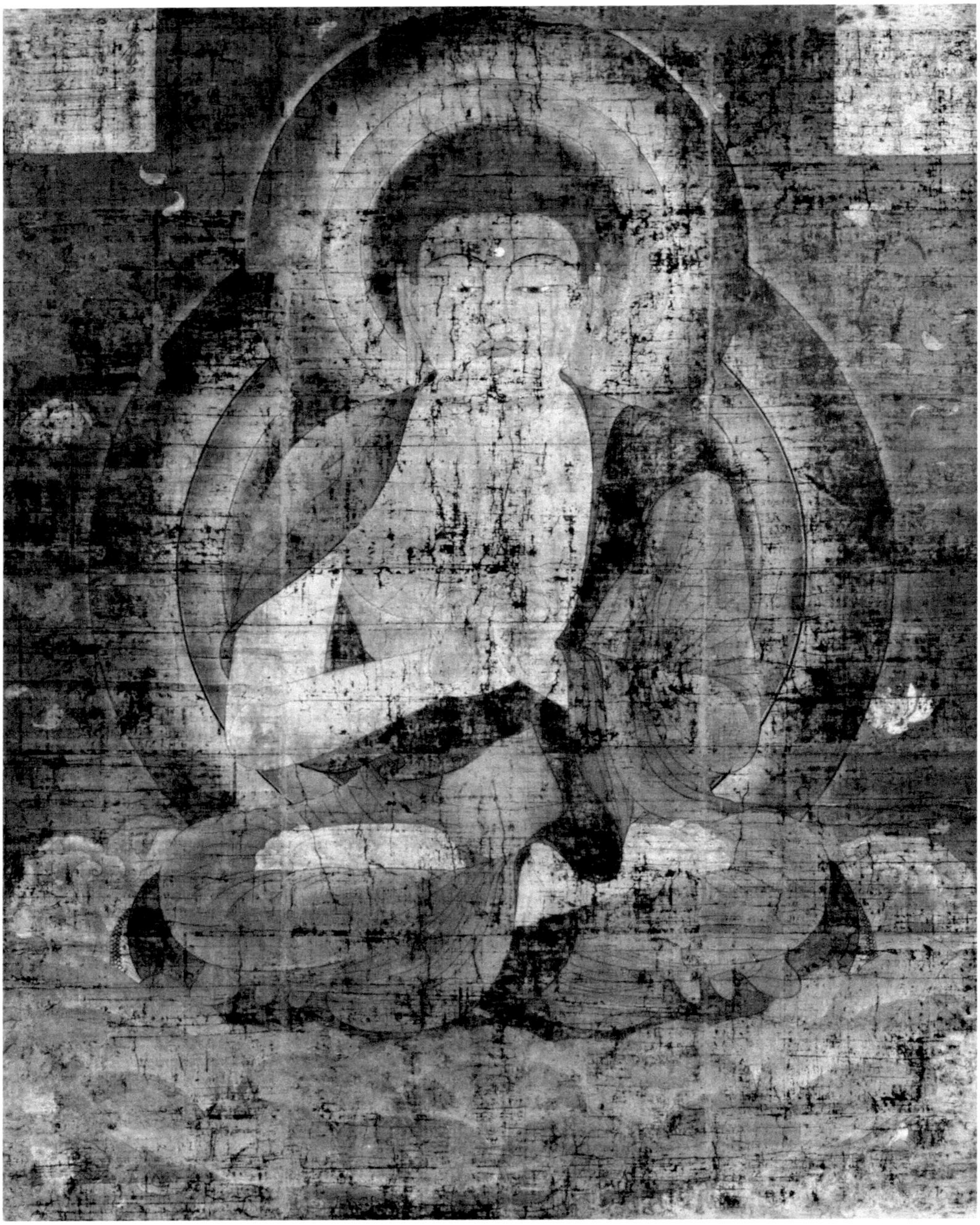

Fig. 11 (Above): Amida Buddha, from the Amida Buddha Triad, Hokkeji. Photograph courtesy of the Nara National Museum. *Fig. 12 (Opposite):* Kichijō Tennyo, Yakushiji. Photograph courtesy of the Nara National Museum.

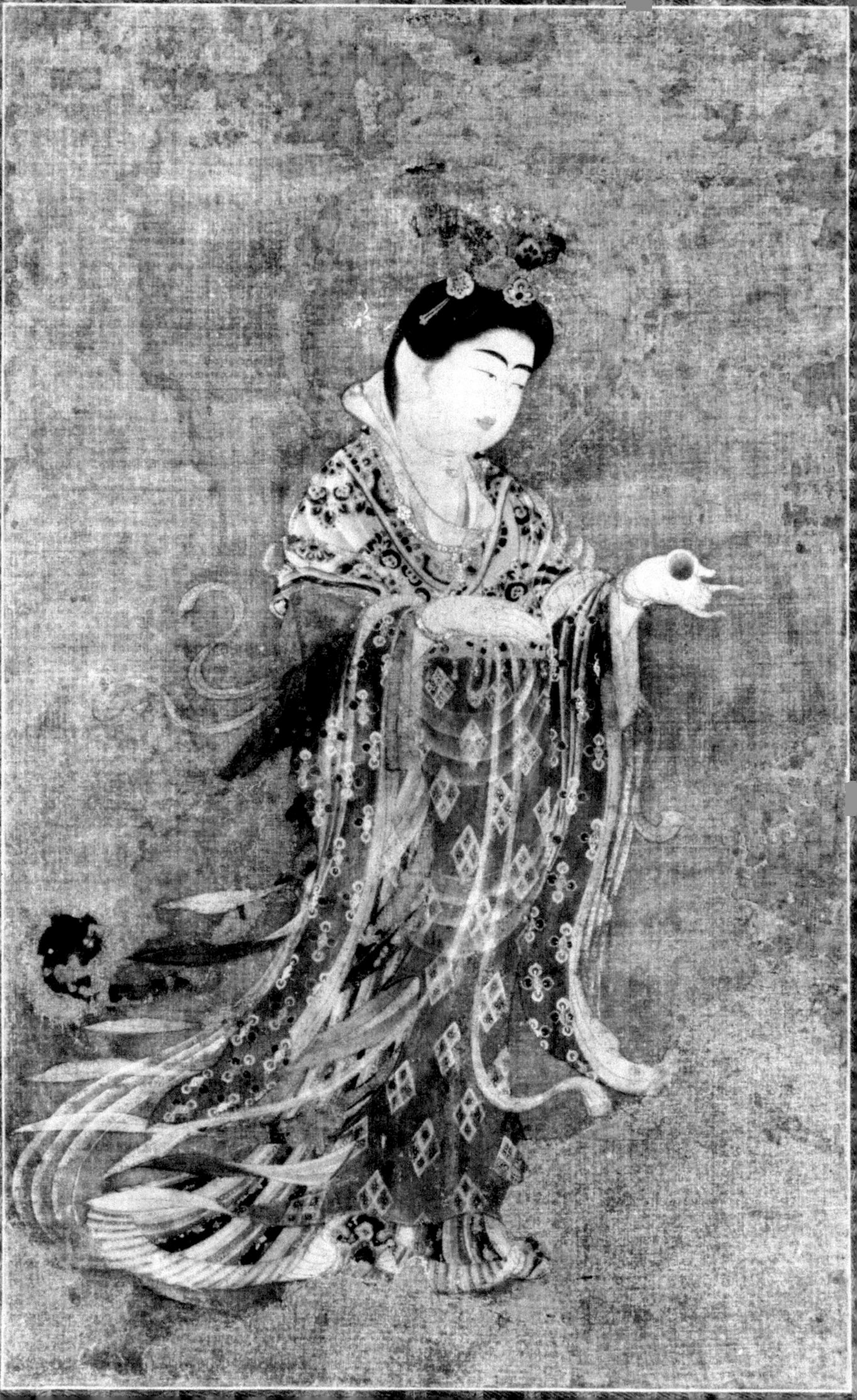

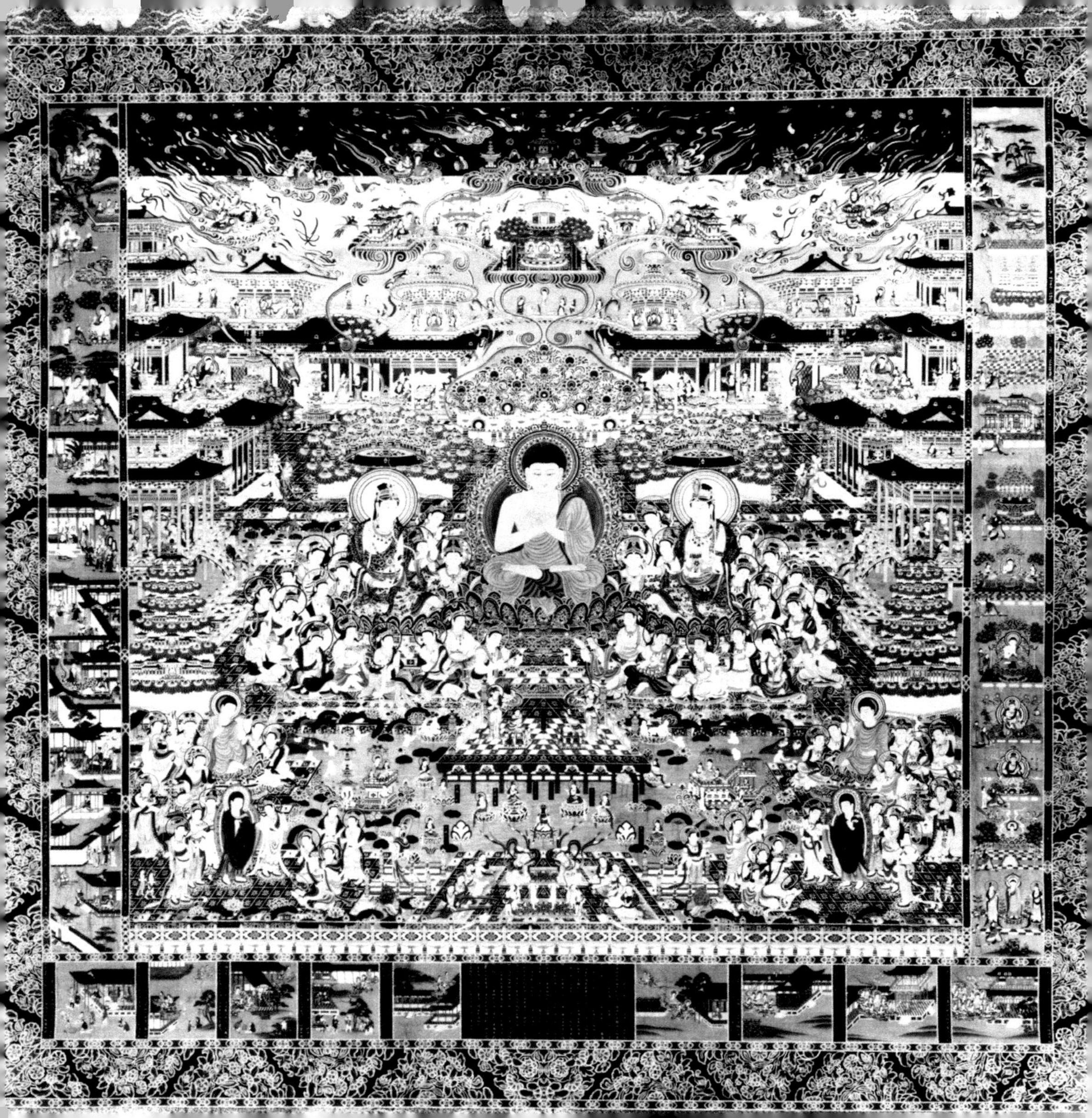

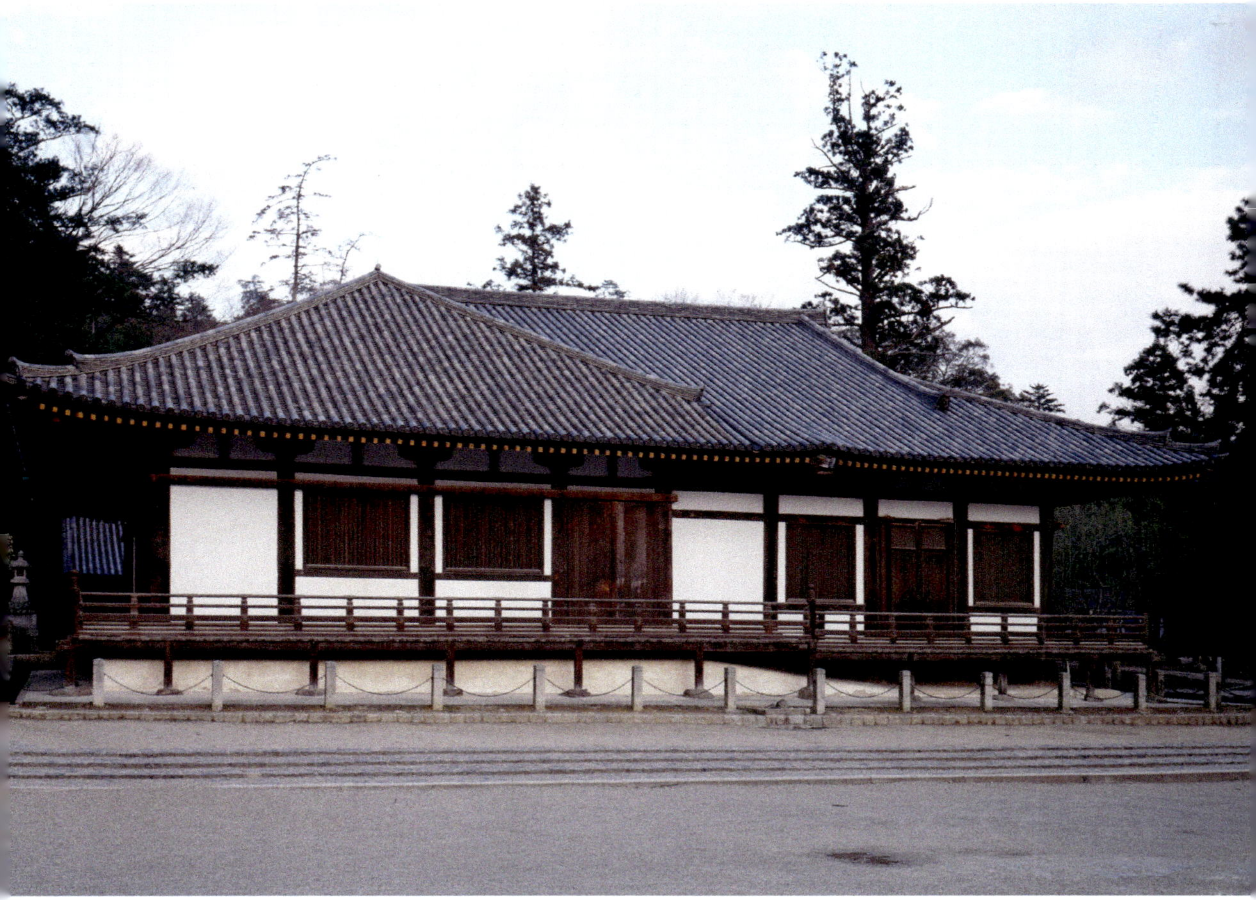

Fig. 13 (Opposite): Taima mandala, Taimadera. Reproduction made in the Bunki era (1501-1504). Photograph courtesy of the Nara National Museum.
Fig. 14 (Above): Sangatsudō, Tōdaiji. Photograph courtesy of Asukaen.

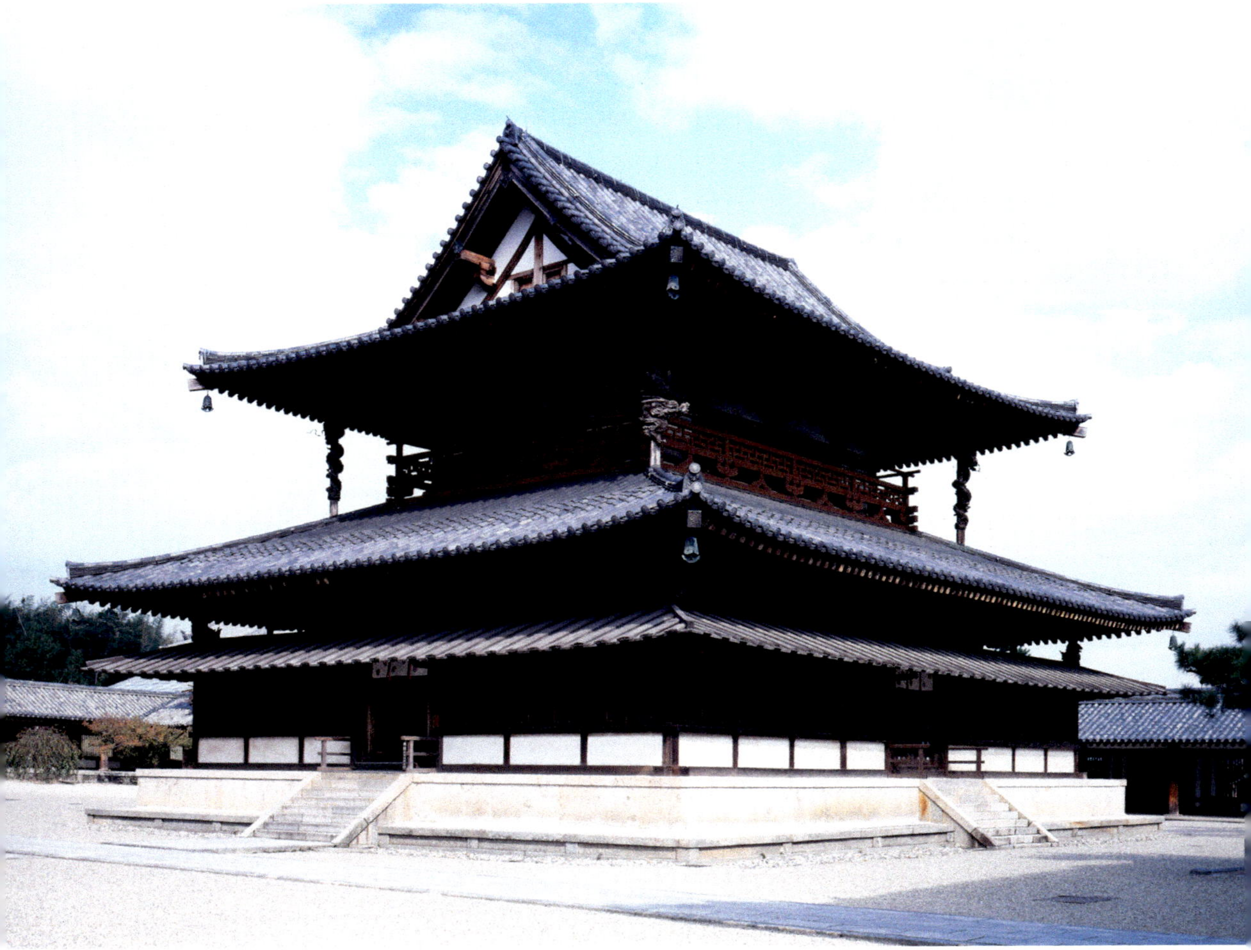

Fig. 15 (Above): Kondō (Golden Hall), Hōryūji. Photograph courtesy of Asukaen.
Fig. 16 (Opposite): Five-story tower, Hōryūji. Photograph courtesy of Asukaen.

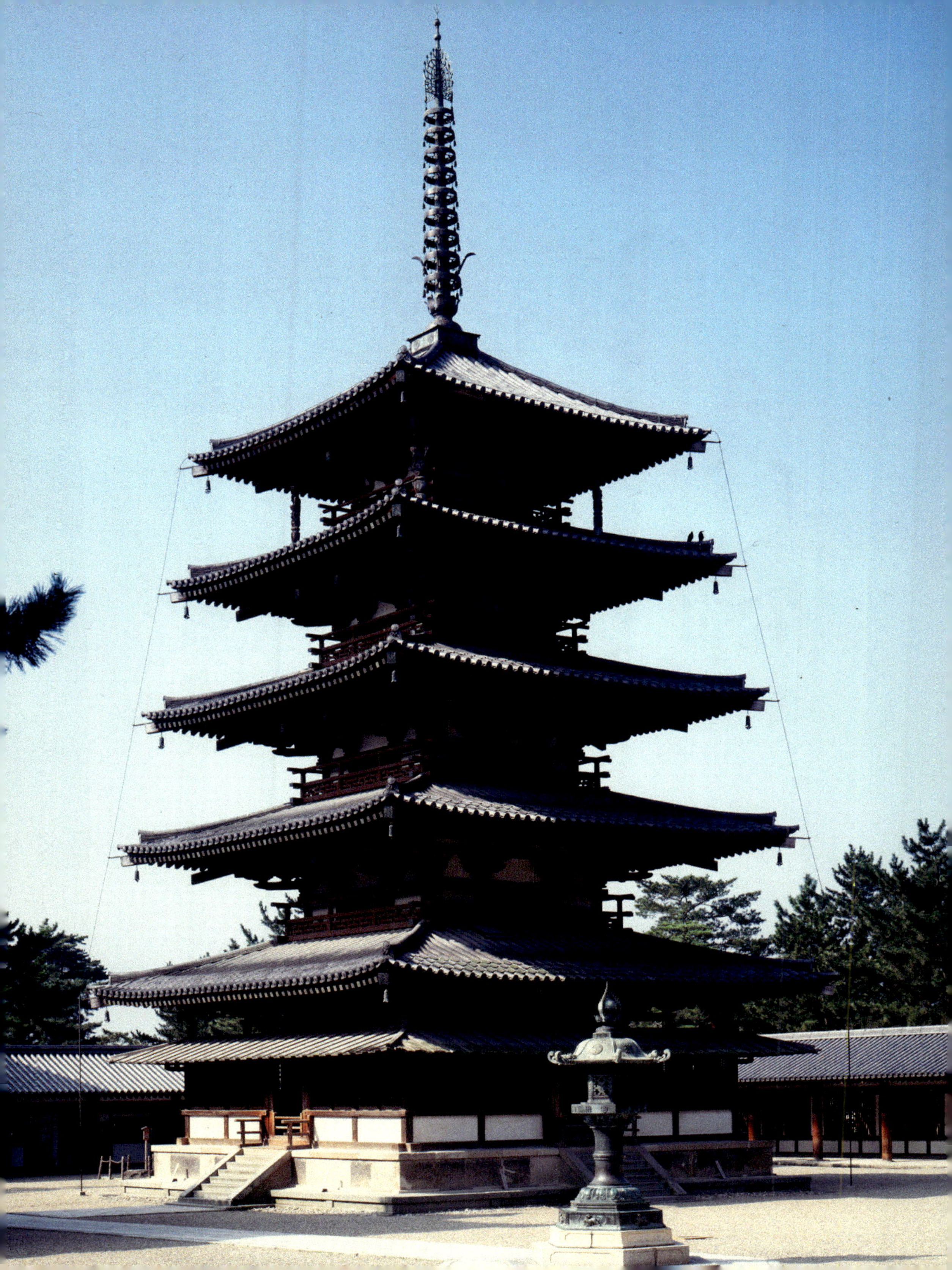

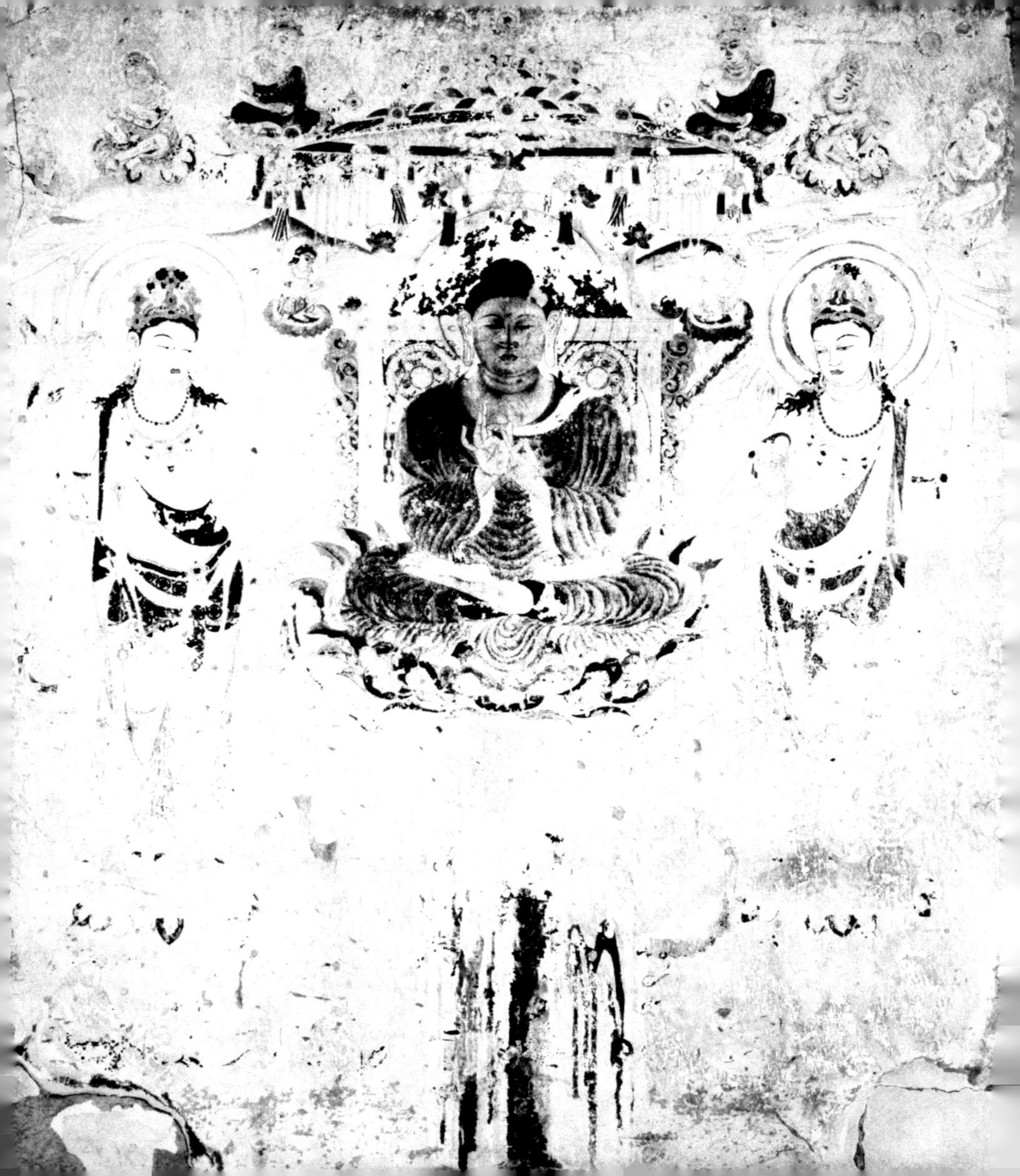

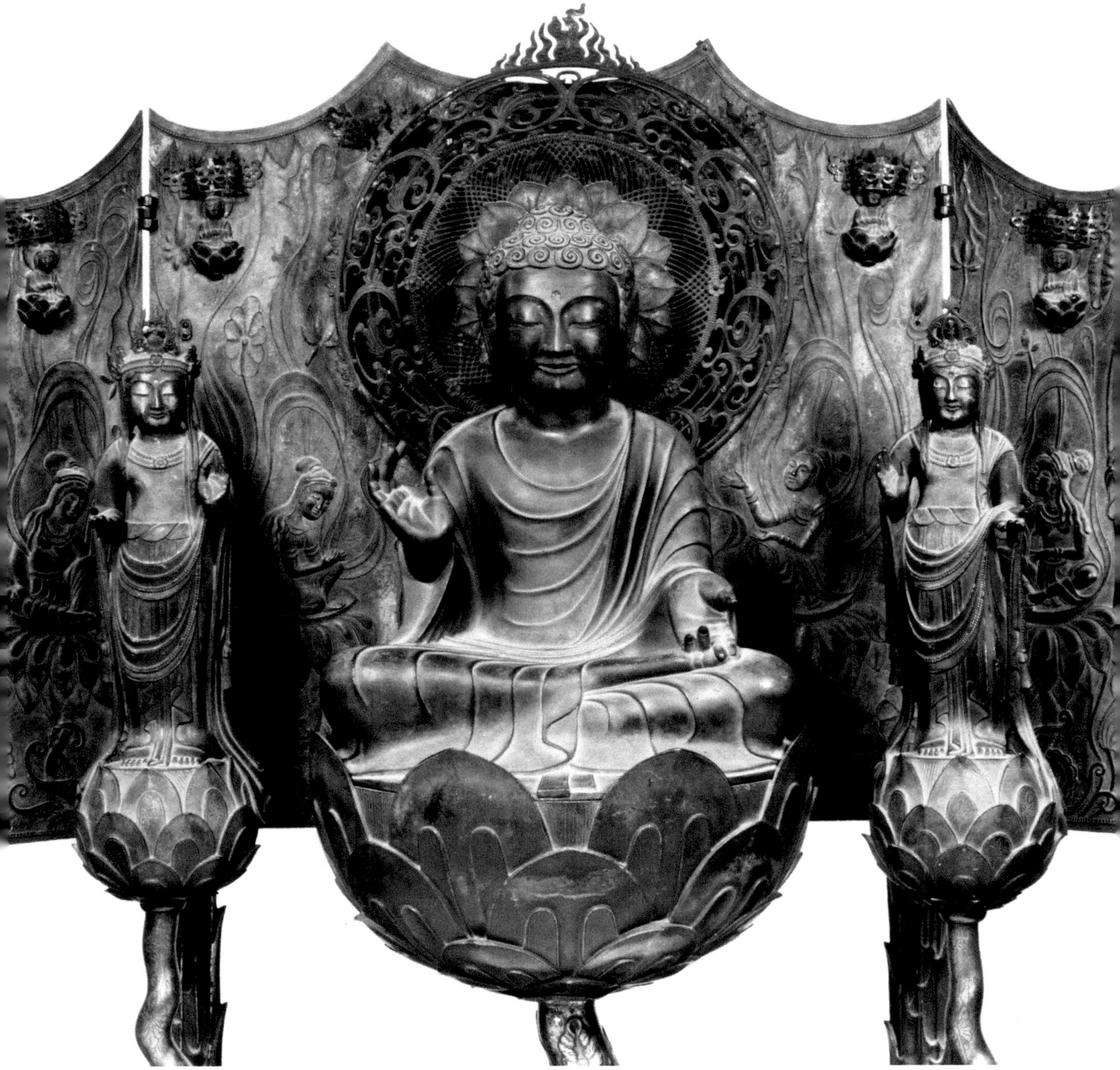

Fig. 17 (Opposite): Yakushi Nyorai and the attendants, Kondō (Golden Hall), Hōryūji. Reproduction. Photograph courtesy of the Nara National Museum. *Fig. 18 (Above):* Amida Buddha and the attendants in the Altar of Lady Tachibana, Hōryūji. Photograph courtesy of the Nara National Museum.

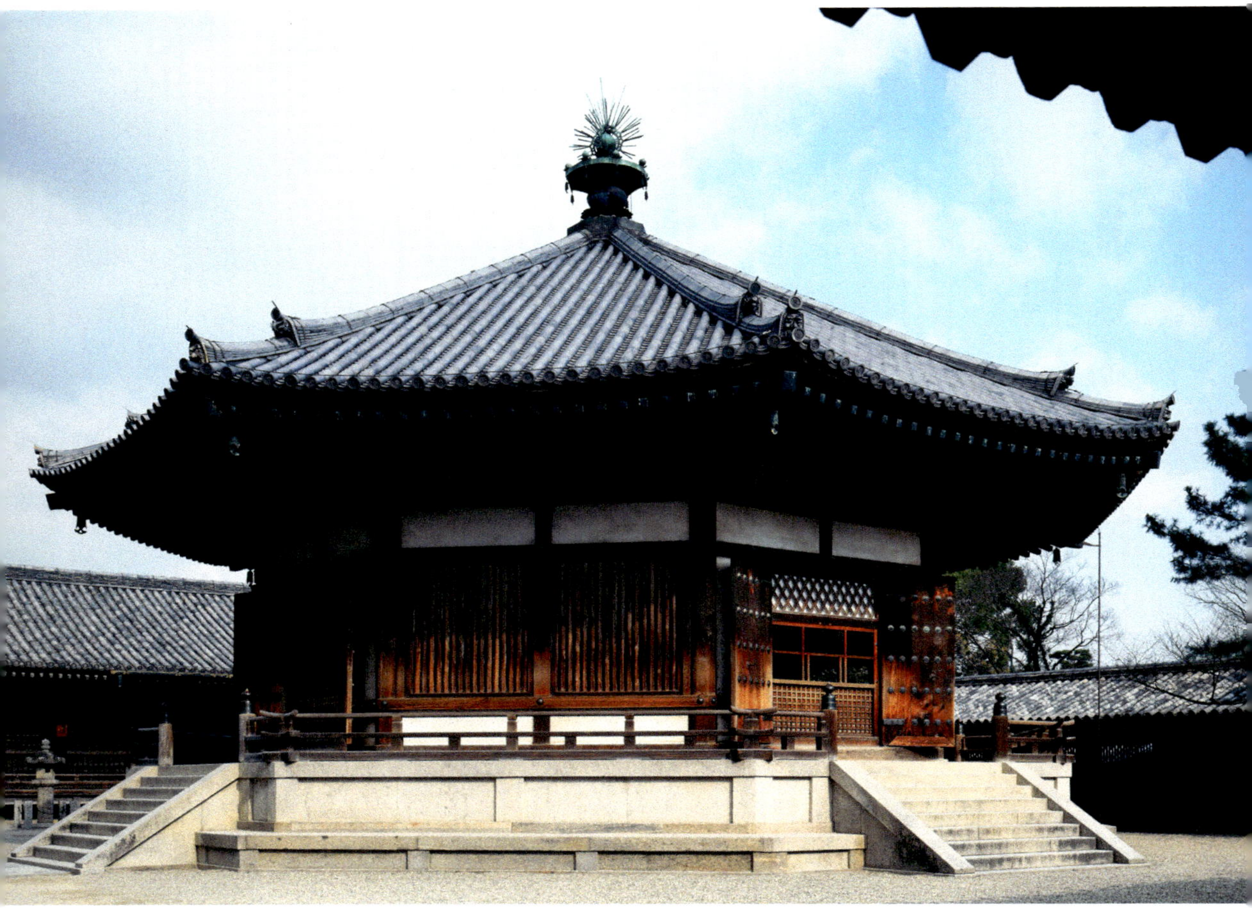

Fig. 19 (Above): Yumedono Hall, Hōryūji. Photograph courtesy of Asukaen. *Fig. 20 (Opposite):*Yumedono Kannon, Hōryūji. Photograph courtesy of the Nara National Museum. *Fig. 21 (Following page):* Kannon, Chūgūji. Photograph courtesy of the Nara National Museum.

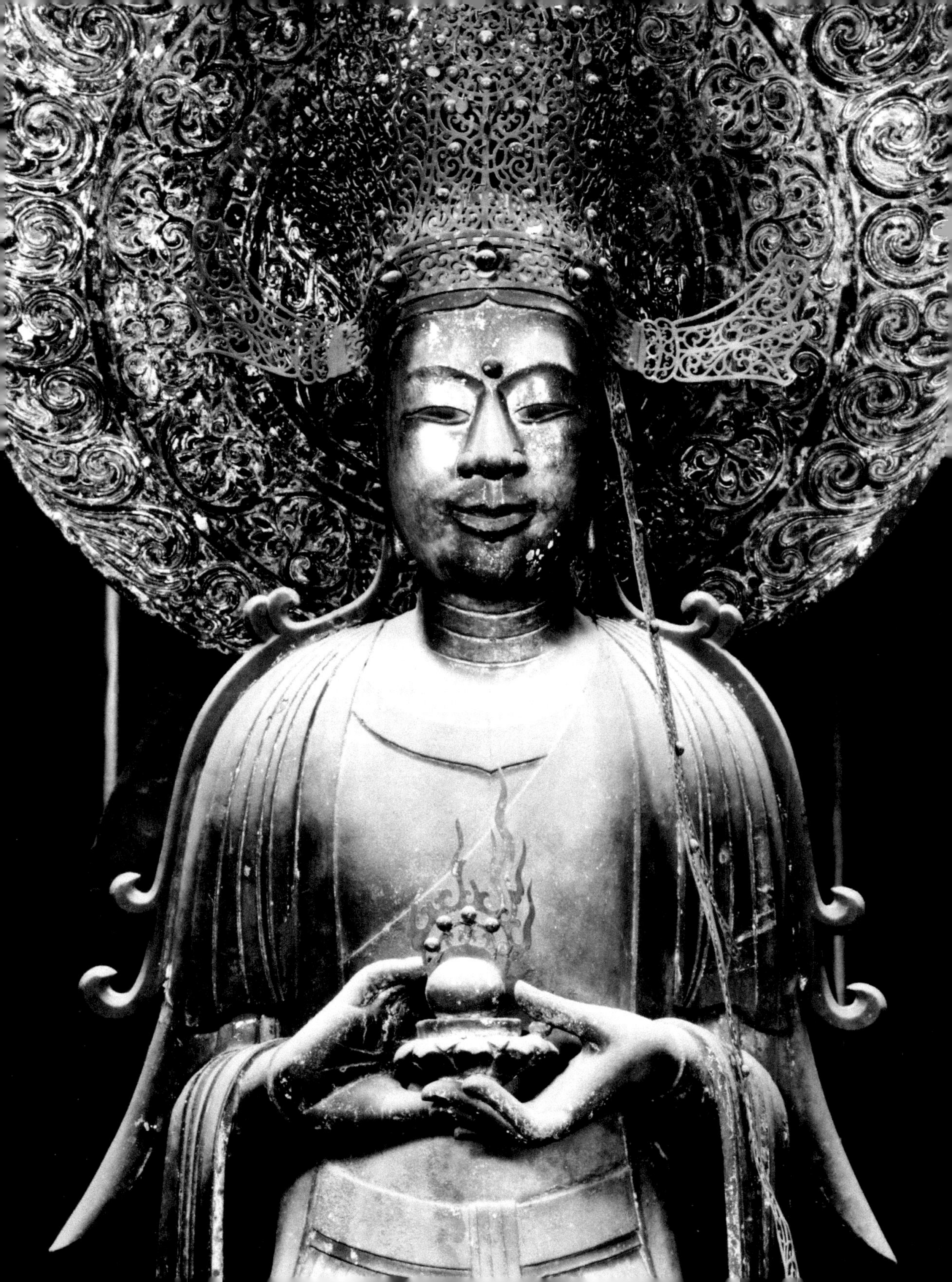

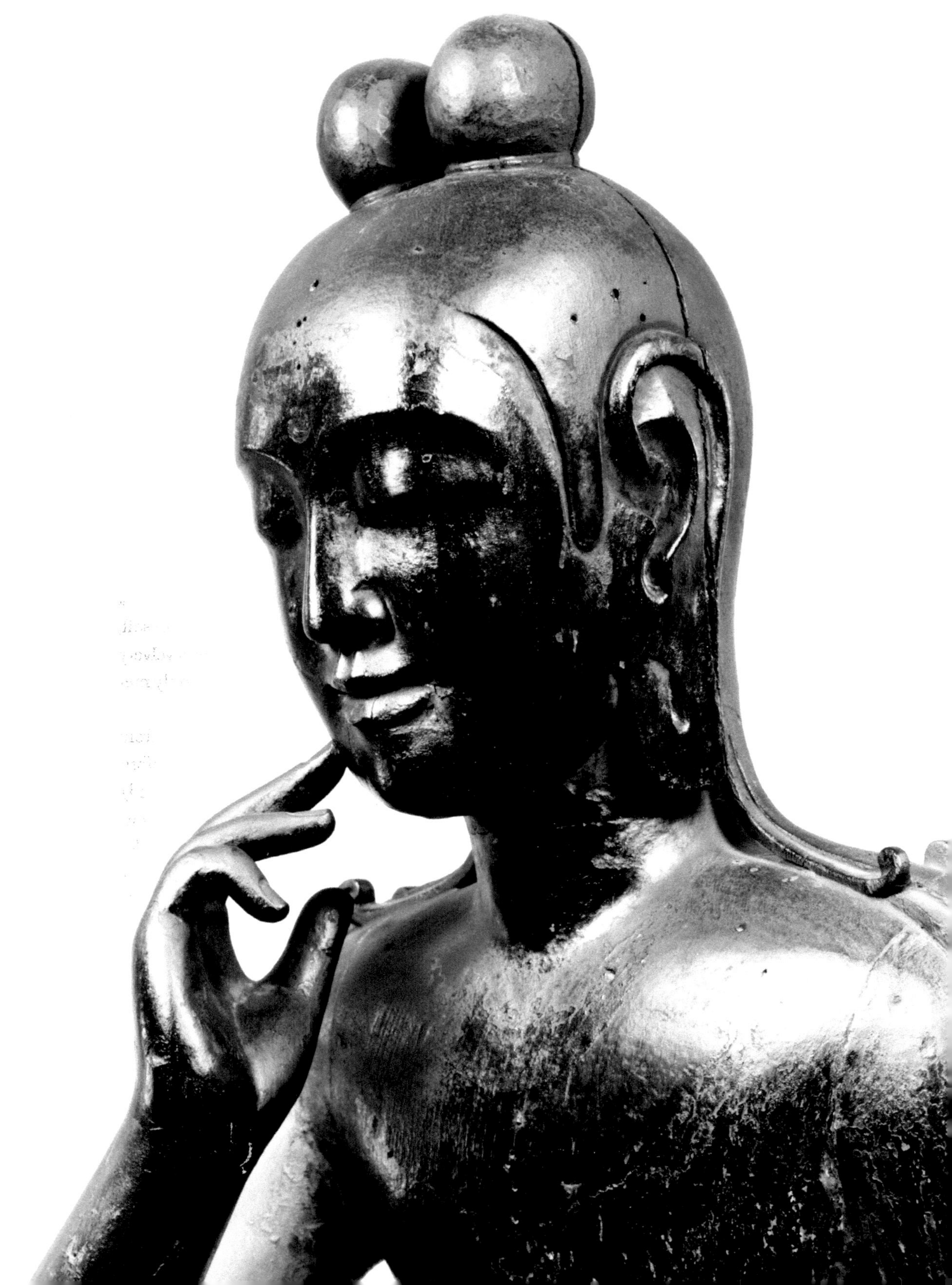

Chapter 12

VIEWING THE ANCIENT CAPITAL FROM HOKKEJI

If I looked east from the front yard of the bathhouse at Hokkeji, I could see the most peaceful scene of the mountains of the Mikasayama mountain range spread in front of me, with the rooftops of temples scattered throughout the mountains visible through the young green leaves of trees, as if they were floating on a sea of wheat fields that was now taking on a light golden color. I could also see a train pulled by a steam engine moving lazily across the wheat field. This scenery fills me with a tinge of melancholy, for I am once again recalling a childhood feeling. The grayish white sand of the front yard, mixed with reddish brown soil, and my feet treading on it both stir a whisper of nostalgia in me. Even in the nun's velvety and friendly words welcoming us, I find familiarity, which betrays the fact that we only met today for the first time.

Feeling somewhat dampened by emotion, I looked at the Great Hall of Buddha from across a wheat field, and an image of the Tenpyō era slowly overtook my imagination as before.

Hokkeji, or more precisely, Hokke Metsuzai no Tera (a temple where sins are destroyed), is an old nunnery established as a provincial temple by the state of Yamato. Apparently its existence is owed to Empress Kōmyō's ardent belief in Buddhism. The imperial decree for the building of the temple was issued in Tenpyō 13 (741), and even if we were to assume that the building of the temple began immediately after the decree, Empress Kōmyō would have been more than forty years of age. The empress's special affection was poured into this temple for the next twenty years. Accordingly, much interaction took place between the empress's palace and this nunnery. Later, the retired Emperor Kōken lived in the nunnery so it served as a palace for a retired emperor at least for the time being.[1] At this time, Ex-Emperor Kōken would have been forty-six or forty-seven years of age. Even after she returned to the throne, this temple again served as a palace.[2] Because of this, the temple underwent many renovations and additions. The position of *Zō Hokkeji Tsukasa*, or the supervisor of the Hokkeji renovation and additions, still existed as late as the Emperor Kōnin's rule.

If I had stood where we are now standing, I would have witnessed most major events of the latter half of the Tenpyō era unfolding in front of my eyes. There was a big ado about moving the capital, which caused all court nobles to move in droves to the north.[3] Then, in Ōmi, the bronze casting of a large Buddhas began. The old capital of Nara, with its roads covered with tall grass due to a lack of traffic and neglect, became dilapidated and desolate, making one feel the evanescence of the world. It was then that court nobles began to return to Nara. A hubbub soon followed this as people worked to make the mold for the large statue of Buddha. Thousands of carpenters, metalworkers and laborers began working busily. One would have been able to see workers carrying lumber and hunks of copper to the Narazaka area day after day. The mound of dirt where workers stood was created, and, just beyond it, one would have been able to see ferocious flames for copper founding. This would have continued for several years. Then the day of the Buddha's consecration ceremony would arrive. The night sky above the woods around Tōdaiji would light up with more than 15,000 lanterns. Several thousand monks' singing and chanting of praises to the Buddha would echo like waves of distant thunder. The east side of town would then become quiet, and then the activity would pick up again because the construction began for temples like Tōshōdaiji, Saidaiji, and Sairyūji on the west side of town. It was said that there were already as many as forty-eight temples by the time the capital moved to Nara and, by the time these temples on the west side of town began to be built, the number had doubled. The number would be quite fitting for a city that was known for Buddhism.

Imagine what it would have been like to listen to all the temple bells surrounding the capital being struck in unison. Today we are familiar with the sound of whistles signaling noon to factory workers, but what impressions would we receive if the whistle were replaced by the ringing of bells with the sound of their long, reverberating wavelengths? It would be a tranquil sound, and it would give a lively and cheerful sort of feeling because it is hard for me to think that the sound of temple bells in ancient Nara could symbolize something like the evanescence of all things.[4]

During Nara's heyday, *gigaku* and other similar forms of entertainment were all the rage. Where I am standing now, a place close to the imperial palace, I often would have been able to hear the sounds of *gigaku* and the like being performed. *Tōka*, or a mass step dance, and other similar types of dancing were also performed frequently for banquets in palace halls. I wonder what sort of actual sentiments the nuns felt on undoubtedly hearing all the commotion of pleasure outside. When a time period is filled with pleasure and decadence, we would expect women who demand living a truly pure life, to emerge. So, at Hokkeji, the temple where sins are destroyed, I wonder if nuns with this frame of mind actually lived there. Or, perhaps, did "new women" of the Tenpyō era, who had integrated both the religious ecstasy obtained from *gigaku*, chanting scriptures, and looking at Buddhist sculptures with another type of religious ecstasy attained from detaching themselves from worldly attachments, actually lived in the nunnery? These are all fascinating questions but it seems that we have very little to go on.

THE ELEVEN-HEADED KANNON OF HOKKEJI

The main object of worship at Hokkeji is a wooden image, no more than two feet and a few inches tall, called the Eleven-headed Kannon (Boddhisattva with Eleven Faces).[5] When we looked inside the miniature shrine in which the image was housed, lit by a small, faint light, we saw an image sooty from the burning of incense. Then, suddenly, the image's shining eyes and red lips jumped out at us. The face was plump and beautiful, and somehow creepy. Perhaps because of this first impression, I felt as if this image were somehow shrouded in a veil of "secrecy." The plumpness of the breast like a woman's, the voluptuous lines in the torso, its softness and pliability, the roundness of the right arm which is strangely long, a very special roundness of the right hand starting from the bracelet to the fingers that lift the heavenly garment—all these features were brilliantly and sharply carved out. Its beauty, at the same time, struck us with some hidden seductive power not observed in any other Tenpyō *kannon* statues (*see fig. 6, photo section*).

If one were to agree that the Nyoirin Kannon at Kanshinji embodies the mysteriousness of Esoteric Buddhism most unambiguously, this Eleven-headed Kannon, which imparts a similar sensation, would definitely be counted as among the best artworks of Esoteric Buddhism.[6] It seems to me that Esoteric Buddhist works very characteristically exhibit a type of sensuality, but from the standpoint of Esoteric Buddhism, which seeks to find expressions of sole truth in all things, it is to be expected that we should acknowledge the Buddha nature even in the carnal beauty of a woman's body. Yet, acknowledging the infinite depth at the bottom of this sort of beauty also resulted in lending a type of "darkness" to images of women. This Eleven-headed Kannon is an excellent example of this, for, in this statue, we find not only the awareness that carnality is an enemy, but also an awareness that this carnality at the same time possesses unfathomable power. In the voluptuous harmony of Tenpyō art, however, we do not see a split between these two types of awareness.

Because of the impressions above, I would agree with a recent hypothesis that this image was made in the Jōgan period (859–876). My friend Z, on the other hand, was never once willing to reconsider his own theory that the statue did not date any later than the last part of the Tenpyō era because in his view the statue imparted a thoroughly Tenpyō mood. Indeed, it's possible to see it that way if we wanted to do so. We may say that the plumpness of this Eleven-headed Kannon feels much more cheerful than those typical of Esoteric Buddhism. Most certainly, the formal features of this Eleven-headed Kannon are closer to such paintings as *Lady under a Tree* (Juka Bijin zu) in Shōsōin or *Celestial Woman of Wealth and Beauty* (Kichijō Tennyo) in Yakushiji, both of which date from the same period. The statue's unusually long right arm is particularly suspicious in that it hints of a connection to Esoteric Buddhism but the right arm of another very feminine Eleven-headed Kannon at Daianji are unusually long as well. This Eleven-headed Kannon's slight bend toward the front is not typical of Tenpyō statues, which are usually rigidly erect; however, its slight bending of the right leg, and also the fingers of the right hand lifting a part of the garment—none of these relaxed features can serve as evidence to show that this *kannon* is not from the Tenpyō era. For example, the aforementioned *Celestial Woman of Wealth and Beauty* (Kichijō Tennyo), also produced toward the end of the Tenpyō era, stands, maintaining a relaxed posture. As Mr. Sekino contends, the folds of the garment of this Eleven-headed Kannon certainly express the Tenpyō-style roundness, free of sharp edges.[7] Regardless of how the crown, the bracelets, the hair ornaments and such are carved, or even if the Jōgan period carving techniques might be evident in some places, these are not definitive factors in determining this statue's age. At the same time, it is too simplistic to conclude, as author and critic Takayama Chogyū did, that this gentle round face expressed the characteristics of the Tenpyō era. Having said that, it is also problematic to cut this off from the Tenpyō period altogether.

I would contend that this Eleven-headed Kannon was undoubtedly produced in the Jōgan period (859–876), but the fact that many specialists thought that this *kannon* dated from the Tenpyō period suggests that there is considerable basis for their opinion, and that is worthy of our consideration.

EMPRESS KŌMYŌ AND SCULPTOR MONDŌSHI

This Eleven-headed Kannon is associated with an interesting legend. *Kōfukuji Ranshōki* (Early Days of the Kōfukuji Temple), which may not be credible in every respect, tells of a story as follows. One day, King Kensei (Ch. *Jiansheng*, *Xianshen*) of Gandhara in northern India wished to see a live bodhisattva in person and went into a meditative contemplation for twenty-one days to realize this wish. The king then received a divine revelation in a dream that he should pray to "Empress Kōmyō, the wife of Emperor Shōmu, in the country of Japan." After he awakened, he thought to himself that it would be nearly impossible to travel to faraway Japan across the sea and land, whereupon he went into a meditative prayer for another seven days. Then the king received a second revelation, which advised him to send a skilled sculptor to Japan to make an image of the empress. The king would then see her with his own eyes and could bow down before the statue. Overjoyed, the king sent a sculptor to Japan. His name was Mondōshi, a descendant of the sculptor Bishukatsuma of India, separated by twenty-five generations. Mondōshi arrived in the port of Naniwazu and, through an official channel, tried to have an audience with the empress. Empress Kōmyō told the messenger that she was a daughter of a minister and the wife of Emperor Shōmu. "How could a person of this status consent to meet just any emissary from another country?"

she replied. She then had a change of mind, but only if Mondōshi could help her to realize a wish. Mondōshi agreed to do anything he could in his power to help her to make her wish come true. This was when the West Golden Hall was being built at Kōfukuji because Empress Kōmyō desired to commemorate her mother Tachibana no Michiyo. Empress Kōmyō thus requested of Mondōshi that the main statue of worship, an image of Amida Buddha, be created for the mother. In response to this request, Mondōshi suggested that perhaps a statue of Sakyamuni might be more appropriate if the empress would like to express her gratitude to her late mother, because, as he explained to the empress, during ancient times, there was the precedent of Sakyamuni expressing his gratitude to his mother Maya when he was visiting her in Tōriten.[8] Thus the decision was made to produce a statue of Sakyamuni. Thirty Japanese sculptors were selected to assist Mondōshi. Attendant figures flanking the main image were also created by Mondōshi. The empress visited the workshop. When Mondōshi observed the empress' body carefully, it was not that of a woman, but that of an Eleven-headed Kannon. Mondōshi produced three *kannon* statues. He took one to his home country. One was placed in the palace and is now enshrined in Hokkeji. The third is at Seganji.

There is little doubt that this story does not tell the truth, but what is more interesting is such questions as why this legend that the statues were modeled after Empress Kōmyō came into being and why Mondōshi was chosen as the sculptor.

Mondōshi is said to have been the maker of the statues of the Eight Deities that protect the laws of Buddhism (Hachibushū) and of the Ten Principal Disciples of Sakyamuni now located at Kōfukuji. Putting aside the question of whether his name was actually Mondōshi for the time being, there is no doubt that these images were made by a man of extraordinary talent. I would think everyone who has seen these images would immediately agree that the man was extremely skilled at carving statues. Are we equally sure that he participated in the production of statues for the West Golden Hall of Kōfukuji? The existing statues have been credited to Mondōshi, as were the images in the West Golden Hall, but the latter images no longer exist.[9] That is, there is no way of determining if the hands of Mondōshi made these images. According to such historical documents as *Fusō Ryakuki* (Brief History of Japan), *Genkō Shakusho* (History of Buddhism after Its Arrival in Japan) and others, the images of the Ten Principal Disciples and those of the Eight Deities were enshrined in the West Golden Hall.[10] Contradicting this account, *Kōfukuji Ranshōki* (Chronicle of the Early Days of Kōfukuji) also states that these statues were moved to the Kōfukuji location from a temple called Gakuanji where they were originally enshrined and that these are not the original statues that were placed in Kōfukuji's West Golden Hall. In another document, called *Shichidaiji Junreiki* (Record of a Pilgrimage to Seven Great Temples in Kyoto), it is stated that these protector images were those that were originally placed in the Nukatabe temple and were moved to West Golden Hall of Kōfukuji.[11] Every year after this move, disturbances began to be observed within the temple compound, whereupon the statues were supposed to have been returned to the home temple in the Chōshō era during Emperor Sutoku's reign.[12] The description ends by saying that finding these statues at Kōfukuji, therefore, is a mystery. In any case, there is no way to determine if the images now at Kōfukuji were made by the man who created the statues that adorned the interior of the West Golden Hall at its beginning. The legend, however, demands that we believe that Mondōshi created the most important Buddhist images at Kōfukuji. In other words, the most important of all extant Buddhist images must necessarily be those produced by Mondōshi. That is to say, Mondōshi simply refers to the best sculptor at Kōfukuji during the Tenpyō period. This, in turn, means that Mondōshi was the man who produced the main object of worship for the West Golden Hall. Empress Kōmyō must have given passionate attention to the building of the West Golden Hall because of her devotion to her mother Tachibana no Michiyo. Hence, as the legend has it, it is not impossible to imagine that Empress Kōmyō stepped into the workshop of the sculptors. And it is equally possible to entertain a hypothesis that the sculptor received creative inspiration from her majesty's personal appearance. Empress Kōmyō, who was then about thirty-two or -three years of age, could have been perfect for a model of the *kannon* statue. If we were to think in this way, then the Kōfukuji legend would seem to be rewarded with a breath of life, though tenuously. At least it was possible. Instead of discussing whether it was or was not, this flight of imagination is perhaps more meaningful to a person interested in thinking about whether it was possible or not possible.

STATUS OF A SCULPTOR

However, we wonder if an idea such as using Empress Kōmyō as a model for the statue would be allowed in society then. Carvers of Buddhist images then were a type of laborers and worked for a man in charge of constructing a temple, who held the title *Zōbutsu Tsukasa*. As such, they could have been totally different from the image of artists we hold today. In fact, they might have been people with an entirely different status. Though this is possible, I do not think so. Indeed, in old records we see that work assignments for the carvers were counted just like those for other laborers. On the other hand, it is not impossible to find records of a famous artist receiving special treatment from emperors and kings; the case of a man like Kuratsukuri no Tori comes to one's mind.[13] The beginning of Tenpyō was a time when the admiration of Tang culture reached its peak, so much so that the more a person was able to embody its culture, the more he was idolized. Japanese poet Abe no Nakamaro (701–770), for example, received special favors from Emperor Xuanzong (685–762) of the Tang and became friends with the poets Wang Wei (701–760) and Li Bai (701–762). I would think that the facility of those few to digest Tang culture, and Nakamaro was one of them, was not by any means underdeveloped for these elite few. When the men who accompanied Nakamaro to China, such as Kibi no Makibi and the monk Genbō, returned to Japan carrying a great deal of artwork and books on art, religion, and other branches of scholarship after nineteen years of study there, the Japanese imperial court received them back with extraordinary enthusiasm. Overnight, under the influence of Namamaro and others, the spiritual lives of court nobles underwent a complete transformation. It is also reported that Miyako, the birth mother of Emperor Shōmu, who was then on the throne, was suffering from depression, and that she made a complete recovery owing to the care given by Kibi no Makibi and Genbō. Then it was decided that Makibi would supervise the education of Princess Abe no Himemiko, who was then destined to ascend to the throne.[14] These phenomena cannot be explained solely by the desire of these court officials to emulate Tang culture superficially. I would think that the courtiers satisfied the voids in their hearts by interacting with these new people. Their hearts were filled with admiration for that wide world of Tang, which was so full of life. I cannot find a reason why these very people with such sensitivity could not have been emotionally taken by the man from Gandhara (or perhaps an anonymous Japanese carver who the legend made into the man from Gandhara), who created the masterfully executed works of sculpture only a year or two before the return of Kibi no Makibi and Genbō. It is my guess that courtiers granted the sculptor an audience with them any number of times. It is, as I said before, "quite possible." If this were indeed the case, the man undoubtedly saw a number of female courtiers, that is, true women among all women. The sculptor's desire for creation was stirred and fired his imagination. Then he made an Eleven-headed Kannon, not too large or small, as he was filled with joy as he created it for creation's sake. This is also "quite possible." We do not know who these statues were given to, but the legend that the sculptor took at least one of the three *kannon* statues **back to his home country** gives us a clue about his motivation for producing these works. That motivation for producing them, just for the sake of creating them, is also "possible."

VESTIGES OF EMPRESS KŌMYŌ

What I have been talking about thus far is an extension of my own interest about the idea that the image might have been modeled after Empress Kōmyō. I certainly do not mean to imply that we see vestiges of the empress in Hokkeji's *kannon* figure. We would expect refined flashes of emotion on the face of the empress, an intelligent sparkle in her eyes, rhythmical movement of her heart on the lips, tender shades of undying passion on her cheeks. Unfortunately, the face of this Eleven-headed Kannon does not meet these parameters. It is voluptuous but does not exude refinement. It is passionate but not soft and tender; it is rough. The vestiges of the empress that the legend of the maker Mondōshi leads us to expect, judging from the image of the Naga dragon king credited to Mondōshi, must be much purer and more beautiful.[15] So, it would be far more pleasing to me to hold dear to my heart the theory that this Eleven-headed Kannon was made in the Jōgan period and not modeled after Empress Kōmyō.

Now, then, what evidence is there to conclude that this statue holds a certain relationship to the Tenpyō era? **It was possible** for a *kannon* image to be modeled after Empress Kōmyō, but this Eleven-headed Kannon was not. Thus, there is no hint of a connection between the empress and a *kannon* statue . . .

The only tie between them remains no more than a product of my imagination. If it was possible that a *kannon* statue could have been modeled after Empress Kōmyō, I would say that it could have been enshrined in her majesty's palace quarters. If it is possible that the statue was indeed placed in the palace, then we may say that Hokkeji, which enjoyed a special relationship with the palace, came to develop a special relationship with the *kannon* statue. In this connection, *Shoku Nihongi* tells that, when Empress Kōmyō passed away in 760, temples around the country held memorial services and had painters produce paintings of the Pure Land of Amida. For the first anniversary of her death, it was determined that state-built nunneries should commission an image of Amida Buddha measuring 16 feet tall and two attendant bodhisattvas.[16] In addition, it was determined that a new sub-temple at Kōfukuji called Amida Jōdoin (Temple of the Pure Land of Amida Buddha) should be built and that it would be used for anniversary ceremonies of her death. For this purpose, I would say, it is quite possible that a *kannon* that resembled the empress played some very significant role. If that was the case, then, the statue had to be transported to Hokkeji.

Since it was not impossible for this statue to be housed in Hokkeji, I would say that it was also possible that it received special reverence from the nuns at the temple because of the special respect they had for the late empress. And when, for some unknown reason, a new statue had to be built, the nuns might have naturally wanted the new image to resemble the old image. There were no known instances of producing copies during the Jōgan period, so the maker of this new statue no doubt went about the work with a resolve to produce a statue that was better than the original. What he produced, I must contend, would have been thought of as a statue that bore the vestiges of Empress Kōmyō.

Thus I arrive at the hypothesis, perhaps fantastic, that the present Eleven-headed Kannon was a new creation by someone in a later generation who was mindful of the original modeled after Empress Kōmyō. That legend was not smoke where there was no fire. I therefore conclude that finding traces of the Tenpyō era in the Eleven-headed Kannon is not without basis in fact.

Notes

1. Emperor Kōken lived 718–770 and reigned 749–758.
2. Ex-Emperor Kōken returned to the imperial throne as Emperor Shōtoku and reigned until her death in 770.
3. The capital was moved to Nagaoka in 784, then to Kyoto in 794.
4. Watsuji is alluding to the beginning sentence of *The Tale of the Heike*, "The sound of Gion Shōja bells echoes the impermanence of all things." See *The Tale of the Heike*, translated, with an introduction, by Helen Craig McCullough, Stanford, CA: Stanford University Press, 1988.
5. Elsewhere, this image is given the height of 100 cm or three feet and four inches.
6. Kanshinji is a temple of the Shingon Sect of Buddhism in the city of Kawachinagano, Osaka Prefecture. This seated image is about 42.5 inches high and six-armed. It was produced using the dry lacquer technique.
7. Sekino Tadasu (1868–1935) was an architectural historian at the Tokyo Imperial University. When he worked for the Interior Ministry, he was put in charge of surveying and dating old buildings in Nara Prefecture.
8. Tōriten (Skt. *Trayastrimsa*) is the second highest heaven in the Buddhist universe.
9. The West Golden Hall, along with the Lecture Hall and the South Gate of the temple, was destroyed in a 1717 fire and never rebuilt.
10. *Fusō Ryakuki* (Brief History of Japan) is a history of Japanese Buddhism and culture written around 1094. The work is attributed to the monk Kōen.
11. *Shichidaiji Junreiki* (Record of Pilgrimage to Seven Great Temples in Kyoto) is a book written about the author's pilgrimages to seven great temples in southern Kyoto (Tōdaiji, Gengōji, Saidaiji, Yakushiji, Daianji, Kōfukuji, and Hōryūji). It was written by Ōe Chikamichi in the first half of the twelfth century.
12. Emperor Sutoku lived 1119–1164 and reigned 1123–1241.
13. Kuratsukuri no Tori was a sculptor, probably of non-Japanese decent, who was active in the early seventh century (Asuka period). He is credited with producing the images of the Sakyamuni and his two attendants triad (Jp. *Shaka Sanzonzō*) at Hōryūji.
14. The princess lived 661–721. As emperor, she ruled 707–715.
15. Naga is one group of the eight minor Indian deities that protect Buddha's teachings. It is also called Ryūō. Naga is one of the eight statues in Hōryūji attributed to Mondōshi.
16. "State-built nunneries" refers to *kokubunniji*.

Chapter 13

THE WOMEN OF THE TENPYŌ ERA

It is indeed a misfortune that we do not have a portrait of the most representative lady of the Tenpyō era. Because of this misfortune, we are forced to go back and forth, wandering aimlessly between clinical, unsympathetic opinions about women of Tenpyō and equally idealistic opinions.

However, we can make a guess about women's status and quality from studying the situation for men. During a time when there were such men as Rōben, who was both efficient and energetic, it is unthinkable to imagine that there weren't women with high sensibilities fitting our dreams. The activities of women described in *Shoku Nihongi* are merely superficial, and this book does nothing to support our contention, but we may very well find credible evidence if we consult *Man'yōshū*. Even so, when we think about the state of culture at the particular time when *Man'yōshū* was being compiled, we must admit that art and literature may not accurately reflect people's sentiments. Due to the growth of new culture, the people became more sophisticated quickly and remarkably, but their own language to express this maturing process was still in its infancy. Yet, at this same time, achieving enough proficiency in a foreign language like Chinese for self-expression was no easy task. Synthesizing these Chinese and native Japanese cultures and creating a new style was a difficult task during the Tenpyō period, as any similar task would be today. Thus it would have been the case that even a person of complex emotions could only produce simple, uncomplicated art and literature. Added to this, we notice that the *Man'yōshū* poems tend to be poems of romantic love exchanged between lovers. Those poems were aimed at moving the other person emotionally and were hardly meant to express objective descriptions. It makes sense then to think that *Man'yōshū* poems do not perfectly express women's minds. If we were to try to explain people's minds only by means of *Man'yōshū* poems, we would lose almost all the meaning of Buddhism and Buddhist art.

Though the contents of love poems in *Man'yōshū* may be simple, there is some evidence to show that the context in which the poems were situated was not by any means simplistic.

Ladies of the day were impatient when revealing their passions in poetry and did not take the time to analyze the complexity of emotion and describe it, but this fact does not mean that the women did not experience any complicated entanglement of emotions. Even under the overwhelming influence of newly arrived culture, the center of their lives was romantic love affairs. It was the kind of unbridled love that consumed both the mind and the body simultaneously. At the same time, in those days, romantic love meant immediate marriage, and a lover straightforwardly became a de facto wife. There was little interest in separating the two. I would imagine that when love was waning, lovers naturally separated from each other. Furthermore, life was stable when it was supported by romantic love. Consequently, women of these times had the freedom to change husbands as love dictated, but they also suffered from the danger of being thrown away like old socks by the men with whom they became intimate. Though tragedies did not take place which can be attributed to some institutional barriers that prevented lovers from being attracted to each other, all sorts of tragedies did occur stemming from the crisscrossing of attractions and rejections. In these situations, women could not simply rely on the attraction of the senses in order to hold on to the happiness of love. We cannot rule out the idea that women's poems in *Man'yōshū* are equal to or better than the men's owing to these situations in which women found themselves.

During the Tenpyō era (and this can be generalized for other periods as well), polygyny was not looked upon with suspicion. Emperor Shōmu, whose main wife was Empress Kōmyō, had other consorts. Women might have been conditioned to accept such cases. For example, one of the *Man'yōshū* poems is composed by a woman in eastern Japan who tells her husband, stationed in western Japan, not to forget her even when he rests his head on another woman's lap.[1] But I would think that the immortal truth, whether now or in ancient Japan, is that romantic love demands monopoly. Men surely wanted it, as did women. In situations common in the old days, in which the husband and wife lived in separate residences and saw each other only infrequently, I think undoubtedly this feeling of wanting to monopolize the other must have been particularly prone to intensifying. The emotion of a woman, in the longing for her husband and even anticipating deathly collapse without him escalating by the hour, can only be understood in this way. Ōtomo no Sakanoue no Iratsume, a woman poet in the Nara period, once wrote: "Only I say I love you. You say you love me but I know you say it just to ease my mind."[2] These hateful words make sense only in this context. If men's romantic love was less constrained than women's, women must have suffered far more intensely.

Though it is true that this was a time when one could behave as love dictated, some restrictions still existed. One was, for example, a fear of "whispers." "I was avoiding seeing you because there were words going around" or "if you're so serious about our love culminating, let us see each other regardless of what others might say" (Takata no Ōkimi) typify this.

Ōtomo no Sakanoue no Ōiratsume wrote, "We could have met on a different night. Why did we see each other on that fateful night and suffer from all manner of gossip?" and so forth.[3] Clearly romantic love was very much constrained in this way. But, what were these "whispers"? Romantic love between a man and his sister or between a man and a married woman should be shunned, and it was, but it is difficult to fathom the idea that romantic love should be seen in a disapproving light, especially during the time when romantic love was not considered to be dirty or uncultured. I would say that, perhaps unexpectedly, there was the authoritative presence of parental love that gazed upon the future of a daughter. There is a poem with a phrase that reads, "I entrust my heart to you, which I have not revealed **even to my mother**."[4] In this case, if a woman was afraid of "whispers," the mother's authority must be at the bottom of her fear. Another poem goes "If the unthinkable were to occur, let us be buried together at the graveyard on Ohatsuseyama Mountain; I will never leave you and pray do not worry."[5] If we were to take this to mean, as one accepted interpretation has it, that a woman in love wrote this poem and sent it to the man, who was afraid of **being rebuked by his parents** for being in love without their knowledge, we must acknowledge that parental authority was quite far-reaching. (I admit that understanding this sort of background for this poem is perhaps unneeded.) That is not enough, however. During the time when romantic love weighed on people's minds a great deal, we must naturally think that jealousy wielded a great deal of power as well. A man who monopolized a beautiful woman no doubt attracted all manner of hostility from men who had any feelings toward her. A woman intoxicated by the wine of blissful love would likewise become the target of hostility of women in less fortunate circumstances. This feeling then turns into hatred and then to an evil curse. People would pray for misfortune to befall on happy lovers. Being humans of natural inclinations, I would not think it was in any way unexpected that feeling the people of Tenpyō would feel like this. Thus, love became persecuted because of the heart that took it seriously. There were likely other reasons why whispers stirred fear in people's minds. Whatever might have been the case, rumors were feared and avoided at any cost. Love affairs had to be cloaked in deepest secrecy. And this secrecy was the educator of a woman's mind at the most profound level.

Women of the Tenpyō era were not always passive in affairs of romantic love. Many poems in *Man'yōshū*, such as those by Kasa no Iratsume, are about pressuring men into love affairs.[6] Certainly Tenpyō women were a good match for their men. In poetry, politics, and religion, Tenpyō women, more so than in any other periods, took an enormously active part in these activities. Likewise, they were brave in matters of love as well. Just as men were polygynous, women too did not refuse to have many husbands, often one at a time. The woman poet Kagami no Ōkimi, whose poems are included in *Man'yōshū*, reputedly had the three most desirable men of Hakuhō as husbands, assuming that this woman was the same woman as the woman known as Princess Nukata. Tachibana no Michiyo, the mother of Tachibana no Moroe, a politician of considerable power during the time when the Great Buddha of Nara was being cast, later became a wife of Fujiwara no Fuhito and gave birth to Empress Kōmyō.

Thus it is impossible to think that these Tenpyō women would spend their days idly and feeling simply lyrical. If the men of this period were endowed with the ability to look out across the expansive ocean of life and culture, I have no doubt that women would possess this ability too. As the fully matured cultural life originating in India and China was infecting the men of Tenpyō, it was also infecting the women of Tenpyō.

Our insight in this area is not helped at all by any evidence in *Man'yōshū*. We are surprised by the fact that Empress Kōmyō's poem, which she composed for the Yuimakō prayer meeting (to read the Vimalakirti Sutra) to be sung in praise of the Buddha, reads as follows:

Shigure no ame ma nakuna furi so
kurenai ni nioeru yama no
chiramaku oshimo[7]

This poem is remarkable in that it is entirely devoid of expression of any feeling whatsoever toward the Buddha. The world of *Man'yōshū* and the world of Buddhist art are clearly distinct. The difference does not merely exist in the gap between lyrical poetry and plastic art. It is a difference in taste, demands, and desires. In other words, a difference in the roots of human emotion. The fact that there were two worlds like these in one era is not surprising at all to us today as we see with our own eyes a number of independent worlds. Simply because we cannot see a digestion of foreign culture in *Man'yōshū*, it is premature to conclude that the people of the Tenpyō period did not digest and assimilate it. Though perhaps limited to a small number of specialists, the understanding of Buddhist philosophy had already begun by this time. The casting of the immense Buddha and the building of towers and a huge hall to house the Buddha, to say the least, were major social events of enormous significance that could not have left the people's minds unaffected. It is unthinkable that these events did not reach the very depth of people's souls. It was true that producing Buddhist art and making use of it habitually was copying China, not indigenous to the Japanese. From that perspective, the *Man'yōshū* exudes characteristics specific to Japan. But if we recall that *yōga* or oil paintings produced by the Japanese who studied Western art in the beginning of Meiji was a form of Japanese art, and some of these *yōga* were arguably better than traditional Japanese painting (*nihonga*), isn't it possible to think that Buddhist statues and pagodas fashioned in the Chinese style are art of Japan proper and hold more value than the poems in *Man'yōshū*? There is no reason, it seems to me, to obsess over the meaning of "creativity" specific to the Japanese people. Even if we were to concede and admit that Tenpyō culture was a collaborative creation of Japanese and foreigners, it shouldn't be any different from other ancestral cultures of Japan, so long as the foreigners became part of Japan's ancestors. *Man'yōshū* poems are certainly a valuable art form, but they are only a small representation of Tenpyō culture and do not speak for the whole. Thus we can feel confident that we are able to read the souls of the Tenpyō people by studying their Buddhist art.

BUDDHIST MONKS AND NUNS IN THE TENPYŌ PERIOD

How did nuns in the Tenpyō period live their daily life? I wonder about this because I would imagine their inner life must have had considerable depth.

Asserting that Buddhism has little to do with people's inner lives because the *Man'yōshū* offers little evidence for it seems to be a one-sided view, as I indicated above. Equally unbalanced is the idea that the Japanese people's inherent optimism could not have assimilated the pessimism that underlies Buddhism, an idea does not have any currency with the Six Schools of Buddhism in ancient Nara, namely Sanrinshū, Jōjitsushū, Ritsushū, Kegonshū, Hossōshū, Kushashū, for it is not only through pessimism that one can find a path to approach this artistic and philosophical religion. Was the experience of human suffering essential for religion? If that was the case, we can unequivocally answer this question by noting that life in Tenpyō, with frequent famines and epidemics, had no shortage of human suffering.

The authorities had no sympathy for monk Gyōki's (668–749) religious movement to promote social causes. Criticism of his activity was pointed:

> The deceitful **apprentice monk** Gyōki and his apprentices **recklessly** told the townsmen in the streets of the retributions for deeds in their previous existence. Moving in groups, Gyōki and his men promoted self-immolation by burning fingers and arms as part of religious devotion, visited homes of people, deceived them and pressed them to give them things other than food, **falsely represented** themselves as followers of the sacred path, and **seduced and corrupted** a multitude of people. Because of this, the morals of the people were greatly disturbed, resulting in people of all ranks deserting their work. Not only were the man's teachings about Buddhism wrong but his conduct was in violation of law.[8]

Such was the criticism levied against Gyōki in Yōrō 1 (717) when he was nearing fifty years of age. This is the same Gyōki who was later considered to be synonymous with a **bodhisattva.** This social movement continued despite the authorities' numerous attempts to stop it. An official account of the movement reported to the emperor, five years after the above criticism, in Yōrō 6 (722), stated,

> Recently, it has been reported that **monks and nuns living on the west side of the capital city** have failed to cultivate religious precepts and, instead, using their superficial knowledge, have seduced the public by speaking of the retributions for their sins in their later

> existences. Owing to this, **some women and children** even abandoned their parents and husbands and left home. Some followers carry scriptures on their persons and beg for food on the roadside. Some of the people have accepted heresy and falsely promoted it as the Buddhist law among villagers. These people may at first appear to follow the Buddhist way of life, but it is certain that they will cause wicked social disturbances later.[9]

Nine years after this, there was a turn of events. The authorities officially recognized Gyōki's work as being socially beneficial and permitted male followers who were sixty-one and older and women of fifty-five and older to be officially recognized as monks and nuns.[10] Other followers who wandered about in the streets with begging bowls had to be taken into official custody (Imperial Decree of Tenpyō 3 [731]).[11] At that time, the authorities believed that monks and nuns should normally reside in temples and receive teachings, so Gyōki's religious activities must have appeared to be a radical departure from the accepted way. But it is problematic for us to regard this movement straightaway as an insignificant, superstitious movement just because the authorities did not approve of it. Gyōki's followers preached to people about the impact of the retribution for deeds in this life on their future existences. This was the correct thing to do for any follower of Buddhism. They went about begging and relied on donated food. This was also correct. These acts were certainly not enough to accuse them of misrepresenting the sacred path. People in all walks of life abandoned their work and left home, apparently excited by Gyōki's teachings. This may be evidence that Gyōki was able to reach people's souls through his teachings. This could hardly be thought of as seducing or leading farmers astray. Also, the fact that people who embraced Buddhism renounced carnal desire could be taken as evidence that their belief in Buddhism arose from their inner needs. Authorities, however, did not welcome this sort of thoroughgoing religious fervor.

I would think that common people at that time, at least some of them, probably felt a much stronger need for religion than those in the upper classes. But if the teachings of Buddhism were carried out literally by the people, no social structure could continue to exist. This is because, if everyone became Buddhists, there would be no one producing food, as everyone would be begging for food. Because of this vexed situation, regulating **the process of becoming Buddhist monks and nuns** became a necessity. The authorities mandated that for a person to become a monk or nun, they must lead three years of a pure life, free from any violation of Buddhist precepts, and memorize the Lotus Sutra. This was tantamount to limiting people's religious desire.

The authorities soon had to find a resolution to this conundrum. As Gyōki became recognized as the hero of the time, the promotion of Buddhist temples became one way of solving social problems. That is, it was thought that natural phenomena that create social instabilities had to be overcome by Buddhism teachings. Accordingly, a large number of temples, especially *kokubunji* temples in provinces, began to be built. This was followed by an increased demand for monks and nuns. Many followers of Gyōki, who wandered in the streets and begged with food bowls, were taken care of quite expediently by this new need. For instance, when the emperor fell ill, 3,800 monks and nuns were ordained.[12] On the occasion of the emperor's memorial service at his imperial grave, one thousand monks and one thousand nuns were newly ordained.[13] When the Great Buddha of Nara was completed, one thousand monks and nuns received their precepts in a ceremony in the imperial palace.[14] No doubt some of these were from the nobility, but most of them were those from middle and lower classes seeking religious truth.

This was as if vagabonds were being transformed into one of the revered Three Jewels of Buddhism. Thus the seeds of social activity that Gyōki planted among the people became one of the most powerful supports of Tenpyō culture.

At least one-third of the people who received the Buddhist precepts were nuns. Among those were surely old women who expected nothing more in the present world. It is also clear that, as indicated in the imperial report mentioned above, there were quite a few wives and their daughters. Did these nuns actually abandon their attachments to the world and lead a pure life?

Most certainly among these nuns were pious believers who chose to become true Buddhists, stimulated by the suffering in their own lives. Yet, it is also possible to say that many women chose to become nuns because they couldn't be satisfied by their present lives and felt compelled to do so by the strong attachments to their present lives, because, paradoxically, they held an unceasing desire to live better lives in their present existences. These women sought a life that was worth living, and perhaps not all of them denounced the world. Some of these women may have become nuns without much forethought because their parents forced them to, or they might have been taken in by the craze of the day. It may be that these women held no **religious conviction** in the true sense of the word. What did these nuns who renounced the world feel when the initial enthusiasm waned? These women were guaranteed a certain level of material comfort by the state, and their hearts were nourished by religious art. But it is difficult to think that their carnal desires were satisfied. Some undoubtedly violated the pledge of abstention and some returned to the secular world after several years. That was as nature intended. Without this assumption, how can we conceive of Tenpyō women behaving bravely in matters of love?

The foregoing may serve as evidence that these women's inner demand to renounce the world was not as strong as it could have been, but this fact certainly does not support the notion that they were unmoved by Buddhist culture. Cutting oneself off from lust is possible for only a selected few. But it is not impossible for everyone, and this includes those who committed the sin of satisfying their lust, who might have felt the mercy of the absolute being Buddha and were bathed in the religious ecstasy brought about by beautiful idols and music. These women may have broken the nunneries' religious precepts, but I am certain they were still emotionally moved and cried in the presence of Buddha.

Yet, there is no indisputable evidence that the behavior of the Tenpyō nuns was unbecoming of their profession. Many imperial directives issued to monks and nuns by the authorities were meant to warn them of their lax, declining academic standards. For instance, one such directive issued in Yōrō 4 (720) admonished:

> Chanting and singing should follow established rules. Monks and nuns of late, however, do so only according to their own rules. This should not be allowed to become accepted as the custom. From this point on, chanting and singing should conform to the rules established by Tang priest Dōei and Buddhism scholar Shōgyō.[15]

Beginning when the number of nuns and monks increased abruptly, around the time of the casting of the Great Buddha, it is conceivable that a new mode of thinking gradually set in, and with it, a type of decadence as well. Directives aiming to curve the lustful behavior of monks and nuns began to be issued beginning in the Enryaku period (782–806). One such directive, issued in Kōnin 9 (818), was reportedly particularly vehement, according to *Nihon Isshi* (History of Japan).[16] This directive may have resulted from Esoteric Buddhism's practice of secluding its followers in a mountain retreat. Whatever the case may have been, one can see a good deal of difference in character between monks and nuns in mid-Tenpyō and those in Kōnin.

No other book is more useful in telling us the character of monks and nuns in the Kōnin period than *Nihon Ryōiki*. Most of the stories date from the Tenpyō period but if one looks at the book as literature, the prose style is typical of the Kōnin period. So it is difficult to see through *Nihon Ryōiki*, as it were, and make an educated guess at Tenpyō. But perhaps the sentiment of a nun affiliated with the Okamoto temple who felt strong attachment to a *kannon*, or the mercy of a maiden follower of Gyōki by the name of Taime, who was a daughter of a high-ranking nun at a nunnery in Tomi and almost sacrificed her maidenhood to save a frog, may represent some aspects of nuns during the Tenpyō era.[17] Though the ethos of Kōnin is that it is simple, it has an element of decadence. The character of Tenpyō on the other hand is much more cheerful and irreproachable.

MEETING A NUN

The nun we met was rare in her beautiful complexion. According to a younger nun who attended to this nun, she regularly rises around 4 am, goes to the main hall of worship and reads scriptures. "She is totally absorbed in the scriptures until young children have dressed themselves and walk to the main worship hall," the attending nun said. In winter, when she is almost finished reading the scripture in the morning, the day would finally dawn. She retires to bed early. Her beautiful complexion no doubt comes from this daily routine.

Then, the high-ranking nun opened a box and took out a small toy figurine in the shape of a dog. She placed it on paper and pushed it toward us. The dog stood on its front legs, kicking the hind legs high. Finger marks where she used her fingers to fashion the chest or the legs of the dogs were still plainly visible on the clay, lending it a sense of immediacy and charm.

"If a child hangs this from the waist, it somehow protects the child from bugs and such; that's what I hear. They keep asking me for it so I have given it away to a lot of people. I have almost none left. But take it, if you'd like," she said.

This was a handmade dog charm made by the nun herself. Then she told us about the history of this charm, how to make it, and so forth. I noticed a doll displayed in a glass box on the *tokonoma* alcove to the right of her. The freshness in the cheeks of this nun was just like a baby's. The overall feel of her face, however, was not unlike the Mokukenren, which is one of the images of the Ten Principal Disciples of Buddha at Kōfukuji.[18]

Notes

1. See *Man'yōshū* 14.3457, which reads, *Uchihi sasu miya no waga se wa yamatome no hizamakugoto ni a o wasura su na*. "Though you have just been called back to the Capital City, where you will rest your head on the lap of a woman there, do think of me from time to time."
2. A total of eighty-four poems by Ōtomo no Sakanoue no Iratsume were collected in *Man'yōshū*. She was one of the most respected poetesses of the time. For the quoted passage, see *Man'yōshū* 4.656. *Ware nomi zo kimi ni wa kouru waga seko ga kou to iu koto wa koto no nagusa zo.*
3. Takata no Ōkimi, 4.539, which reads, *Waga seko shi togemu to iwaba hitogoto wa shigeku ari tomo idete awamashi o* and *Ōtomo no Sakanoue no Ōiratsume*, 4.730, which reads *Awamu yo wa itsumo aramu o nani su to ka sono yoi aite koto no shigeki mo.*
4. See *Man'yōshū*, 11.2537. *Tarachine no haha ni shiraezu wa ga moteru kokoro wa yoshie kimi ga mani mani.* "I haven't even told my own mother but my mind is already made up. Yes! You can do with me whatever your heart pleases."
5. *Man'yōshū*, 16.3806, *Kotoshi araba Ohatsuseyama no iwaki ni mo komoraba tomo ni naomo hiso waga se.*
6. A total of twenty-nine love poems by Kasa no Iratsume are included in *Man'yōshū*, all of which were sent to Ōtomo no Yakamochi.
7. See *Man'yōshū*, 8.1594. "O autumn rain, when will you let up? What a pity it will be if the trees were to lose their golden leaves on account of the rain."
8. See the entry for the twenty-third day of the fourth month in Yōrō 1 (717) in *Shoku Nihongi*, vol. 7. Self-immolation did not mean death by burning but was a religious act to show one's devotion to the teachings of Buddha. At the end of the Heian period, the monk Ōshō is said to have burned himself to death, an act that was inspired by a Buddhist story of Kiken Bosatsu, who had killed himself by fire in his previous life. See *Ōjōden Hokekyō Genki* (Tokyo: Iwanami Shoten, 1995). Empahsis added by Watsuji.
9. This description is found for the tenth day of the seventh month in Yōrō 6 (722). See *Shoku Nihongi*, vol. 9. *SNKBT* 13:120–123.
10. *Shoku Nihongi*, vol. 11, entry for the seventh day of the eighth month of Tenpyō 3 (731). *SNKBT* 13: 246–247.

11. Ibid.

12. *Shoku Nihongi*, vol. 16, the entry for the nineteenth day of the ninth month of Tenpyō 17 (745). *SNKBT* 14:16–17.

13. *Shoku Nihongi*, vol. 17, the entry for the eighteenth day of the twelfth month of Tenpyō 20 (748). *SNKBT* 14:60–61.

14. See the *Shoku Nihongi* entry for the ninth day of the fifth month, Tenpyōshōhō 1 (749) in *SNKBT* 14:79–79.

15. See *Shoku Nihongi* entry for the twenty-fifth day of the twelfth month of Yōrō 4 (720) in *SNKBT* 13:80–83.

16. *Nihon Isshi* is a history book dealing with events between 792 and 833, compiled by Kamo no Sukeyuki in 1692. See *Nihon Isshi* in *Kokushi Taikei*, vol. 8 (Tokyo: Yoshikawa Kōbunkan, 1932), reissued in 1965 and 1997.

17. Okisome no omi Taime was a daughter of nun Hōni. According to the story, Taime came upon a snake trying to swallow a frog. Taime pleaded for its life in exchange for becoming the snake's wife. See *Nihon Ryōiki* in *SNKBT* 30:74–75.

18. Mokukenren (a.k.a. Mokuren, Skt. *Maudgalyāyana*) was a disciple of Sakyamuni.

Chapter 14

THE WESTERN SIDE OF THE CAPITAL CITY

We had stayed too long at Hokkeji, so we tried to make up some time by taking a rickshaw. We headed west. Leaving the village in which Hokkeji is located, we soon found ourselves in an old area called Miyashiro. Miyashiro is a locality with abundant cultivated fields on a hill from which we could overlook, to a limited extent, the Sahogawa river basin, where the old capital of Nara once stood and where the cities of Nara and Kōriyama are now located. Far in the distance to the south, one could make out mountains like Miwayama, Tō no Mine, the Yoshino Mountains, and Kongōzan. In the mist, we could even pick out Unebiyama and Kaguyama. To the east, we could see the Mikasayama Mountains and the forest surrounding the Kasuga Taisha Shrine. To the west, we could see Ikomayama rising above layers of small hills. These hills all majestically rise above the ground in their own gentle way. They are majestic but they are also demure as if to invite a tinge of sorrow. No wonder a place like this would charm someone like me into living here.

The road we were on led us toward the western side of Miyashiro and continued south on the old Ichibō Ōji road on the west side of the ancient capital of Nara. We passed the ancient villages of Amagatsuji, Yokoryō, and such. Then we came upon a forested area that enveloped Tōshōdaiji.

The rickshaw took a right turn from the main road. We got off in front of a precarious-looking small bridge that spanned the Akishinogawa, which was more like a stream than a river. We walked on a narrow sandy, tree-lined pathway. The texture and sounds of walking on the sand gave us a fresh, lighthearted feeling. On the right side of the path, there was a low, earthen wall, parts of which were collapsing to the ground. From a broken opening, we could see the ruins of a worship hall or some such building in a tangled growth of weeds.

Rays of sunshine shone through the tunnel of trees diagonally toward us, suggesting that dusk was near. In a bright spot, bathed in the late afternoon sun, stood Tōshōdaiji.

We entered the compound from the side entrance. We should have walked around to the main entrance on the south side for my friend T, who was visiting the temple for the first time, to see the Golden Hall. But, by this time, everyone was a bit weary, and we couldn't muster the energy to make a circuitous route to the south entrance; so we ended up willy-nilly at the side entrance to the Golden Hall. Entering the compound, the large pillars that comfortably hold up the roof on the backside of the hall came into view, giving me a start, as I anticipated from my last visit. The line of the eaves reminded me of ocean waves, which, when I looked at it diagonally from below, exuded strength and power. I could sense an entirely new beauty, even though this was not my first visit.

THE GOLDEN HALL OF TŌSHŌDAIJI

It wasn't as if I did not know the beauty of this hall when it is viewed from the side. Some time ago, I had stood in the pine forest on the west side of the hall and looked at the building diagonally from behind, like today. I was completely taken then by the classic, commanding presence of the hall. The power of the roofline as well as its lightness, the solid nature of the pillars as well as their serenity made a strong impression on me. But I did not notice then that a harmony of disparate elements, powerful grace, cheerful solemnness, and other characteristics were so deeply dependent on the delicate balance of the roof and pillars. The eave line that curled up ever so slightly as it neared a roof corner embodied a powerful significance that expressed the stable balance between the weight of the roof and the support of the pillars. At no time during the Tenpyō period could a building with a roofline this delicate have been built. Clearly, here at the Golden Hall we were in the presence of the embodiment of the intuition of a talented artist, not the formulaic technique of a carpenter whose work can be easily copied (*see fig. 7, photo section*).

Thinking these thoughts, I made my way to the front of the hall. When looking at the entire hall from the front, though I find it hardly necessary to say this, I could not help but be struck by its extraordinary beauty. As I have said before, this hall was born no doubt out of the sharp, refined intuition of an artist. The delicate way the lines and planes curve as the roof sweeps down from a hipped roof in four directions, just the right balance between the roof areas and the lengths of lines—these are achieved by a delicate battle of force between them (here I do not mean the actual battle of structural forces but the relationship between these elements that is expressed). And we could see how this uncanny balance was achieved in the fact that the entire architectural composition is firmly tightened by the ornamental tiles that were set tilting up slightly at an angle at either end of the top ridge and by the tiles placed at each of the four ends of the roof ridges, which are also slightly curled upward, lending it a sharp finish. One of these ornamental tiles at the end of the top roof ridge is a rather poor copy of the original made during the reign of Emperor Godaigo, which results in diminishing the focus on the top roofline to tighten it and bring it to the center as the architect had planned.[1] This sort of visual sensation is enough to make us realize how organically all the elements are brought into harmony. One could also see that no small amount of delicate attention was given to the relationship between each element, namely, the roof, the pillars that support it, and the complicated set of bracket arms around the eaves. The balance between the size of the pillars and the size of the hall itself, the harmony of spaces between the pillars with the structural support the pillars could give—none of these could be changed even the slightest. As the roof of the structure sweeps down to the sides, the roof fans out and seems to increase its weight. In order to support this increase and give it the necessary push up from below to counteract it, the eight pillars were set widest apart in the center with the span gradually narrowing toward the end. The gradual narrowing of the span matches very precisely the gradual increase of the weight of the roof. Of course this relates inextricably to the curvature of the plane of the roof and ridgelines. Because of the slight curve of the eave line, even the pillars farthest apart in the center of the structure share the weight of a given corner of the roof. Thus, the weight of the roof and the bottom that supports it are beautifully balanced without straining each other, resulting in an exquisite harmony.

All these facts may be revealed by exact mathematical calculations. For instance, the rate at which the distance between pillars becomes narrower toward either end of the structure as well as the rate of increase of weight on a pillar as it nears either end can be computed mathematically. Corresponding to this, the roof ridgelines as well as the roof planes bend up as they near the end. I would think that there exists a relationship between the increasing weight born by the pillars and the rates of curvature of the roof ridge and roof plane. Here, however, I am not speaking of actual structural forces. Regardless of whether the roof curls up or bends down like willow branches, the weight of the roof remains the same. But if there is a strong pillar underneath a roof that curls up, the curvature itself serves as an expression of the strength of the pillar's support. At issue is whether or not an intricate structural relationship that we do not expect may be hidden behind this architectural rendition.

Strolling in the area in front of the Golden Hall, I passed a short period of blissful time. The tall pine trees that surround this hall caused in me a sense of intimacy that was hard to describe. A pine grove and this building, for some reason, certainly go together perfectly. It is hardly possible to find any work of Western architecture, regardless of what style it is built in, that goes well with pine trees. It is not possible to place the Parthenon in a pine forest. Likewise, no Gothic cathedral would look right surrounded by those gently curving pine boughs. We should associate these buildings only with the cities, open fields, and forests of the countries in which they are found. Therefore, temples and shrines in Japan, too, are endowed with those intrinsic connections with the Japanese climate and customs. If we agree that Gothic buildings have vestiges of northern European forests, can we not also assume that our temples and shrines have the fragrances of pine and Japanese cypress trees? I wonder if the roof of this hall hints at the bowing boughs of pine and cypress trees. Does the hall as a whole not suggest a feeling of vigorous pine trees or even perhaps old, craggy, and gnarled cypress trees? The fact that wooden structures in the East have these roots is enormously interesting to consider when we ponder about how we might reduce cultural differences down to climate differences.

When we look at this Golden Hall from the front, what impresses me most is its handsome beauty. This could be so because the pillars visible in front of the building stand as pillars, just like a portico in Greek architecture. But the long and quiet eave line surely owes its strength to the pillars. This sort of curvature is not observed in any Greek architecture, neither can we detect a hint of this quiet composure in the curved lines of Roman architecture. All curved lines of Gothic architecture seem to conspire to form acute angles, and they represent a different type of beauty. The singular beauty of this eave line is specific to Eastern architecture. In that sense, the Golden Hall is the masterpiece among all extant buildings in the East.

At the same time, it is impossible to appreciate the building's beauty without paying due regard to its colors. The old vermilion paint on the pillars has gradually faded to gray and seems to disappear toward the bottom of the pillars, close to the ground. The gray—around the pillars, doors, beams, details in the eaves—looks as if it is embraced gently and warmly by the ancient color of the roof, forming a quiet harmony with the white of the walls. These dull and indistinct colors seemed to exert a subtle force that most certainly couldn't but evoke a sad, quiet sentiment. This could be called the force of *sabi*, created by centuries of the interaction of the atmosphere with the sun. This doesn't mean that the colors of all halls that embodied *sabi* would give the same impression as this hall did. I would say that the particular shape of this hall, which serves as a base for an arrangement of colors, gives increased power to the colors. At the same time, the thought occurred to me that the old, elegant colors endowed the entire building with the profound and mysterious fragrance of life.

INTERIOR OF THE GOLDEN HALL

We walked into the hall itself guided by Mr. S., who was a member of the crew that was repairing the large dry lacquer statue in the Golden Hall. The impression of the interior was no less substantial than the outside. It was simple yet powerful. Two large round columns standing on either side of the dais for the Buddhist image hold up the high ceiling in the center of the building and seem as if they suppress any movement of air inside of the hall. The pillars also seemed to skillfully mitigate the simple harmony of the red and white colors on the side and back walls with the complex impression of the inner sanctuary that is profusely decorated. Weaving through the pillars, we walked around to the front of the main image of worship, which measures sixteen feet high. The sharp smell of the repair materials hit our nostrils. The main object of worship, a statue of Vairocana, which developed open areas of damage, had been moved off the lotus-shaped pedestal and been positioned on a roughly woven straw mat on the dais. I approached the Buddha and felt the wavy clothing of the knee of Vairocana. Mr. S. commented on the high quality the ancient lacquer. In the area where we were standing, bits of old dry lacquer, lacquer containers, and such were strewn about in disorder and, among all this clutter, a worker, clad in old, dingy work clothes, squatted and worked silently. This sight triggered in me a flight of imagination about the emotional state of makers of Buddhist images in ancient times. I wondered if they weren't feeling a deep happiness in the act itself of creating Buddhist images.

To be perfectly frank, I must say that I had never been moved by this statue of Vairocana. I had felt that it was an unexciting, ordinary work and not becoming of this grand hall of worship. Perhaps because I was able to come close and touch the details of the statue on this occasion, I came to have a great deal of affection toward the statue as a whole. Indeed, though it seemed that it still had a certain amount of dullness, this shortcoming did not amount to unskilled awkwardness. This piece was certainly inconspicuous, overshadowed by the beautiful grandeur of the building, but quite good for an ordinary late Tenpyō statue. At the very least, the statue certainly contributes to the integrated beauty of the hall, which I suppose means that the statue has a powerful presence.

SENJU KANNON, A *KANNON* WITH ONE THOUSAND ARMS

With these new thoughts, I again looked at the statue. As I did so, I began to feel a stronger love toward this and other statues in the hall. In particular, the Senju Kannon (Bodhisattva with One Thousand Arms), standing to the right of the Vairocana, surprised me because I found myself so attracted to it. In this statue, one can clearly see the full effect of the strange beauty of arms. Any number of arms, each perhaps slightly larger than a human arm, with the fingers extended toward the front of the image, lined up and, amidst these arms, the sixteen-foot *kannon* sits with its large, faintly gold, gilded body. It was a symphony of arms. From these hands, with no warning, one could almost hear high-pitched tones of flutes or trumpets bursting forth as if they were heavenly revelations. The sensation of sound comes from a few, large arms that stick out from among five thousand fingers rushing out toward the viewer like ocean waves. This symphony, with its individual sounds that awaken people's souls and the harmonies of these sounds—in other words, with individual hands that each suggests a certain sentiment and the strange impression that this group of hands together give—brings this bodhisattva's beauty to the fore. The sharpness of impression one receives from this statue is far more intense than that of either the main Vairocana image or the Yakushi Nyorai (Healing Buddha) statue on the left of the dais.

I wondered why I did not expect to receive this sensation from the Senju Kannon, for I had experienced the sensation from these "hands" as much as a year earlier. A year ago, there was scaffolding around the *kannon*, and the *kannon* itself was wrapped in white cloth. These one thousand arms were each tagged with an identifying number and were lined up in the work area on the west side of the Lecture Hall. I went up close to the arms and looked at two or three of them very closely. I thought they were very well made, all realistically produced, so much so that the sight of these arms lying around as if they had been cut off from the shoulder had a sort of strange, eerie effect on me. Seeing the arms together as a part of a standing statue in one coherent composition did not make me have a ghastly feeling, but the sheer number was impressive when I looked at them all lying in an area larger than a 100-*tatami* mat room (approximately 1800 square feet). At that time, I was quite aware of myself in trying to appreciate Tenpyō art, but the sight did nothing but give me an other-worldly, grisly feeling. I should have realized what sort of strange impression these life-like arms, when put together into a statue, would give me. Now I looked at the Senju Kannon with my own eyes, I realized that it took this long to notice it. Each of these arms, which had given me that weird feeling, was used very effectively and came alive artistically. When I saw the *kannon* myself, I could not help but feel a sense of respect toward the ancients who imagined it and produced this composition.

I have once seen a photograph of a scene of a play called Kiseki (The Miracle), which a man by the name of Reinhardt directed.[2] It was a photograph of several hundred—or perhaps more than one thousand—arms outstretched towards the female protagonist standing on a high pedestal in the center of the stage. I was quite impressed by the effect of these arms, but, if I had thought about it a little more, I would have thought about the Senju Kannon as an art form that strictly took advantage of the pure effects of a multitude of hands and arms.

Mr. S. told us about the work it took to put the arms back to where they belonged after finishing repairs. He said that though each one was numbered, it was unimaginably difficult to refit each one back to the exact original position. And there were many arms that did not quite fit. Mr. S. related to us how much hard work it took to make these arms fit back into their sockets without error.

LECTURE HALL

We left the Golden Hall and moved to the Lecture Hall. This hall used to be called Chōshūden, when Nara was the capital city.[3] That is to say, this is a building constructed during the Wadō era (708–715) when the capital was moved to Nara. But the building as it stands now does not even give a hint of being a building dating from the Tenpyō period. After the building was remodeled during the Kamakura period (1185–1333), the feel of the current building is probably a great deal different from the original. The interior pillars and the ceiling, however, date from the original Tenpyō building. The exterior of the hall gave an impression of the typical delicate beauty of a building erected in the Fujiwara era.

It is quite meaningful, I think, that the Golden Hall and the Lecture Hall were built in two completely different architectural styles. The artistic interest that compelled the ancients to express the difference in mood between these two buildings, which may be likened to one between a worship hall and a research institute, is, I think, quite deserving of our respect.

Among all the various statues that lined the Lecture Hall, I thought that a head of the Buddha and a head of a bodhisattva, reputedly made by Tang dynasty sculptor Gun Hōriki, were particularly beautiful.[4] These heads once belonged to large statues, but the bodies have been lost and only the heads remain. The head of the Buddha even lacked a complete nose. As I looked closely at the head of the Buddha, paying attention especially to the eyes, mouth, cheeks, and how they were carved in broad strokes, I began to sense a feeling of comfort that was difficult to put into words. The face of the bodhisattva was complete, save a few flakes of paint that had come off, so the head retained its original form perfectly. Thus, we could see the dreamy eyes, narrowed by heavy eyelids, refined nose, the beautiful, full lips, as if to attract us unimpeded. It is certain that these heads are superior to those of the statues in the Golden Hall. If these heads were in fact produced by Hōriki, as recorded in the temple history, I have no doubt that the original main object of worship in the Lecture Hall, a sixteen-foot statue of Sakyamuni, would have been magnificent.

Notes

1. Emperor Godaigo lived 1288–1339 and reigned 1318–1339.
2. Watsuji is probably referring to Jewish Austrian actor and theater director Max Reinhardt (1873–1943). The play was based on a medieval legend. The production was based on Karl Vollmoeller's *The Miracle*.
3. Chōshūden was a hall in which administrators of the capital came together in the morning to change their clothes before setting to work.
4. As Watsuji explains in Chapter 15, Gun Hōriki was probably from Konron (a country in present-day Vietnam), not strictly from Tang China, but who followed the Tang monk Ganjin to Japan.

Chapter 15

THE TANG DYNASTY MONK GANJIN

The Tang dynasty monk Ganjin and his disciples arrived in Kyūshū after a difficult voyage at the end of the year 753, which was the year after the Great Buddha of Nara was consecrated, in 752.[1] The welcome they received at the capital city of Nara was extraordinary. All high-ranking officials and Buddhist monks did their utmost to welcome them and meet their needs. Emperor Shōmu (701–756, r. 724–749), by this time retired, issued an imperial order appointing Ganjin to oversee all aspects of Buddhist education and ordination. Soon thereafter, a platform was built in front of Tōdaiji, where Ganjin himself presided over a ceremony of ordination for Ex-Emperor Shōmu, Empress Kōmyō, Emperor Kōken, and many others.

This open-armed welcome is not surprising when we consider Ganjin's impeccable reputation and the exceedingly difficult trip he endured to come to Japan. The *Ganjin Tōseiden* (Chronicle of Ganjin's Trip to the East) may not be perfectly trusted as to its veracity in every detail, but according to this record, both officials and the general populace had revered Ganjin in China.[2] In the area of northern China that is bordered by the Huai River to the north and the Yangtze River to the south, there was no Buddhist monk more respected than Ganjin when he was around forty-six years of age (this would have been around Tenpyō 5 [733]). Ganjin gave official ordination to common people as well as to monks. He was referred to as Jukaidaishi (Great Teacher Who Gives Ordination). Around this time Ganjin is said to have lectured on Buddhist canons and commentaries on scriptures forty times, on shorter versions of Buddhist precepts seventy times, on various righteous deeds and faith ten times, and protocols for ordination more than ten times. Ganjin was well versed in all three essential areas of Buddhist scholarship.[3] He never once stopped the pursuit of truth. In his free time between these lectures, Ganjin erected Buddhist temples, conducted memorial ceremonies for 100,000 monks, and produced sculpted images of the Buddha and bodhisattvas. At other times, he held large meetings attended by people from all walks of life, including commoners as well as the aristocracy, with the aim of reducing the difference in wealth between them, and he tried to give a helping hand to the sick and afflicted. It is impossible to enumerate all his deeds. He is said to have made copies of the complete corpus of the Buddhist scriptures, amounting to 33,000 volumes. Moreover, Ganjin gave ordination to more than 40,000 Buddhists. As many as thirty-five of his disciples are known to us today by name. This was his reputation in China. He was such an important person that people tried to dissuade him from traveling to Japan and, when he did set out on a trip, he had to maneuver to escape the pursuers. At one time, when all preparations were made and he was ready to set sail to Japan, a storm made it impossible, destroying almost everything. Subsequently, after more than ten years and five more attempts, he was not able to reach Japan. During this time, he suffered many tribulations but never gave up the desire to travel to Japan.

In the autumn of Tenpyōshōhō 5 (753), Fujiwara no Kiyokawa, Japanese ambassador to the Tang dynasty, along with Ōtomo no Komaro, deputy ambassador, Kibi no Makibi, and others traveled to Enkōji (Ch. *Yanguang* temple) in Yangzhou, which was located at the mouth of the Yangtze River and where Ganjin was. The Japanese diplomats asked Ganjin if he would join them on the emissary ship to Japan. Ganjin consented immediately. But as the rumor spread in the temple that he was secretly traveling to Japan, the temple barricaded all exits and did not allow him to go outside. Enlisting help from a Zen monk, Ganjin managed to slip out and boarded a boat on the Yangtze and, joining the disciples, then boarded the waiting ship for Fujiwara no Kiyokawa, which was moored at Huangsi port in Suzhou. The Japanese ambassador, fearing that authorities might search the ship, eventually had Ganjin and his men removed from his ship. On learning this, the deputy ambassador Ōtomo no Komaro, under cover of darkness, had Ganjin and his men board his ship and stay in hidden quarters. Thus, finally, Ganjin's long desired hope was realized.

According to the description in the chronicle *Ganjin Tōseiden*, the monks who accompanied Ganjin included: Monk Hōshin (Ch. *Fajin*) of the Hakutōji (Ch. *Baita*) in the Chinese province of Yōshū (Ch. *Yangzhou*), Monk Donsei (Ch. *Tanjing*) of the Chōkōji (Ch. *Chaogong*) in the province of Senshū (Ch. *Quanzhou*), Monk Shitaku (Ch. *Situo*) of Kaigenji (Ch. *Kaiyuan*) in the province of Taishū (Ch. *Taizhou*), Monk Gisei (Ch. *Yijing*) of Kōunji (Ch. *Xingyun*) in the province of Yōshū (Ch. *Yangzhou*), Monk Hōsai (Ch. *Fasai*) of Reiyōji (Ch. *Lingyao*) in the province of Kushū (Ch. *Quzhou*), Monk Hōsei (Ch. *Facheng*) of Kaigenji (Ch. *Kaiyuan*) in the province of Tōshū (Ch. *Douzhou*), and eight other monks. The party also included Nun Chishu (Ch. *Zhishou*) of Tsūzenji (Ch. *Tongshan*) of Tōshū Province (Ch. *Tengzhou*), and two nuns. Others in the party included monk Ban Sendō (Ch. *Pan Xiantong*) of Yōshū province (Ch. *Yangzhou*), An Nyohō (Ch. *An Rubao*), **a man from Kokoku**, Gun Hōriki (Ch. *Jun Fali*) of **Konron**, Zenchō (Ch. *Shanting*) from the country of Senba, and others.[4] The entire party consisted of twenty-four people. The province of Senshū (Ch. *Quanzhou*) was then located in present-day Fujian Province; Daishū (Ch. *Taizhou*) and Kushū (Ch. *Quzhou*), in Zhejiang Province; and Kushū (Ch. *Quzhou*) and Tōshū (Ch. *Douzhou*), in present-day Guangxi Province. The word Kokuku then referred generally to the western region of China; the country of Konron to Cochinchina, that is, present-day southern Vietnam (or Indo-China now under the control of France); and Senba (a.k.a. Chanpa, Ch. *Zhanbo*) to a part of Cochinchina. These people can be considered to be mostly Southern Chinese.

Of the people listed above, **Nyohō**, a man from Kokoku, is said to have been the architect for the Golden Hall of Tōshōdaiji. We do not know how or why this man, who was only about twenty years of age when he arrived in Japan, could become the architect of that grand hall of Tōshōdaiji. It is unknown when the Golden Hall of Tōshōdaiji was built, but if we were to believe the description in *Shōdai Senzai Denki* (Perpetual Chronicle of Tōshōdaiji), it would have been when Nyohō was twenty-five or twenty-six. One scholar contends that the building was built after Ganjin's death, thus Nyohō would have been more than thirty years of age then and had spent more than ten years in Japan. During this time, Nyohō received ordination from Ganjin on the platform built in front of Tōdaiji and became a full-fledged monk. When an ordination platform was built at Yakushiji in Shimotsuke Province (in present-day Tochigi Prefecture), Nyohō was appointed to serve there as the priest for ordination. If we were to assume that Nyohō had a god-given talent for architecture, I wonder when this talent was nurtured. According to the *Shōdai Senzai Denki*, Nyohō was a Korean and had been a disciple of Ganjin since childhood. If we suppose that he acquired various architectural skills in his teens while serving Ganjin, then there is no doubt that the *Shōdai Senzai Denki* description that Nyohō was "a man of extraordinary talent, better than any known man" is indisputable. If he had that much talent, it is inconceivable that Nyohō would spend those five or ten years of his formative early twenties idle. In other words, we must assume that those five or ten years were spent on the grand Tōdaiji, which was just then being completed or had just been completed. The reason I say this is that the Great Hall of Buddha was built before the consecration of the Buddha, but we know that the temple complex itself was not yet complete. When we think about this in this way, it is not impossible to think that the commotion of the construction of Tōdaiji somehow nurtured Nyohō.

When Ganjin died, Nyohō was only about thirty years old. Before his death, he and the two other more senior disciples Hōsai and Gisei were entrusted with the responsibility of overseeing the remaining tasks. It is thought that for the next forty or fifty years, from the end of the Tenpyō period to the Kōnin period, Nyohō was active as the highest-ranking monk of Tōshōdaiji. It is also recorded that he was very close to monk Kōbō Daishi.[5]

Gun Hōriki, the man from Konron, was the person who reputedly sculpted those beautiful heads of Buddha. The fact that there was Konron man with a deep connection to India among the sculptors of Tōshōdaiji seems to explain, in an interesting way, why there is a carved wooden statue of a figure at the temple with thick thighs and the garment clinging to them in a typical southern Indian manner. The *Shōdai Senzai Denki* does not describe Hōriki's personal history, but it is interesting to note that, in Ganjin's second attempt to travel to Japan in Tenpyō 15 (743), the following list of passengers appears: seventeen priests, a jewel carver, a painter, sculptors of Buddhist images, a specialist of inlay work, a specialist of metal casting, an embroidery worker, a learned man in the arts, and engravers of stone—eighty-five people altogether.[6] Judging from this list, it is clear that Ganjin wanted to bring artists and it is then natural to guess that Hōriki was also an artistic person. In the many buildings of the Tōshōdaiji, each building enshrines several statues of the Buddha or bodhisattvas. Hōriki no doubt supervised Japanese workers to produce these images. I would imagine that he or his disciples produced many of the wooden statues at Tōshōdaiji.

The people responsible for making the main image of worship enshrined in the Golden Hall are said to be Shitaku and Donsei. Some say that Gisei produced it. These monks were all Tang priests who accompanied Ganjin to Japan. In particular, Shitaku learned the highly technical skill of producing Buddhist images and produced, in addition to the main object of worship, the Yakushi (medicine Buddha) that stands to the left of that main image, the seated statue of Ganjin in the Kaisandō, and many other statues of the Buddha and bodhisattvas.[7] Furthermore, Shitaku wrote the three-volume *Tōseiden*, which is now lost, on which the extant *Tōseiden* is based, as well as the one-volume *Enryaku Sōroku* (A Catalogue of Monks in the Enryaku period [782–806]). No doubt Shitaku was a man of superior abilities among Ganjin's men. There must be some reason that Shitaku was assigned to produce the main image of worship, going over the head, as it were, of Hōriki, who was a talented artist. What I suggest is that Hōriki was not accustomed to producing dry-lacquer sculptures. It was very difficult to carve a statue measuring 16-feet high out of wood, and dry-lacquer was in fashion, so it was decided that the main image would be made of dry-lacquer. Many workers of dry-lacquer were available in Japan at that time. So, under Shitaku's supervision, the production began. Hōriki learned from this process, and he was later able to produce the 16-foot image of Buddha, which now sits in the lecture hall. The foregoing is my hypothesis, which is also convenient if we want to link Hōriki with India.

As for the sculptor of the Senju Kannon (Bodhisattva with One Thousand Arms), there is an interesting story associated with it. According to the *Shōdai Senzaiki* (Record of One Thousand Years of Tōshōdaiji), the maker was a celestial being. The story goes that, for seven days and nights, a heavy fog covered a small densely wooded hill about two blocks northwest of the temple and no one could see what was taking place inside.[8] During this time, a celestial being produced this statue. According to another account, recorded in the *Shichidaiji Junreiki* (Record of a Pilgrimage to Seven Great Temples in Kyoto), a spirit in the form of a human being is said to have produced it.[9] The account relates that Takeda no Sakome produced it but that this person was a spirit in human form. In any case, it seems that there was an event that startled the people of the time. If one can visualize the workshop scene in which those numerous arms of the Senju Kannon were made one by one, it would quite naturally give birth to any number of myths.

CATALOGUE OF ITEMS GANJIN BROUGHT

There were only a few foreigners who came with Ganjin, but they brought a large number of items.[10] In order to get a sense how the work that Maruzen Bookstore does now would have been done in the old days, let me quote an excerpt from the *Tōseiden*.[11]

3,000 pieces of Buddha's bone

An embroidered image of Divine Blessing mandala

One painted image of the Amida Nyorai

One carved image of Senju Kannon (Bodhisattva with One Thousand Arms) in white sandalwood

One embroidered image of Senju Kannon (Bodhisattva with One Thousand Arms)

One painted image of Kuse Kanzeon Bosatsu (Savior Bodhisattva)[12]

One statue each of Yakushi Nyorai, Amida Buddha, and Miroku Bosatsu (Maitreya)

Painted screens for same.

Daihōkōbutsu Kegonkyō Sutra (Flower Garland Sutra), 80 volumes.

Daibutsumyōkyō Sutra (Great Names of Buddhist Deities Sutra), 16 volumes.[13]

A portion of the *Daibonkyō Sutra* (Great Wisdom of Perfection Sutra), copied in gold ink.

A portion of the *Daijikkyō Sutra* (Sutra of the Great Assembly), copied in gold ink.

A portion of *Nehangyō* (Nirvana Sutra), 40 volumes, copy made in China's Southern Dynasties.

A portion of *Shibunritsu* (Monastic Rules) in 60 volumes.

Hōreishi Shibunso (Chinese monk Fali (569–635)'s Commentaries on the Monastic Rules), 5 books, each book consisting of 10 volumes.

Kōtō Ritsushi Shibunso (Commentaries on the Monastic Rules by the Chinese monk Guang Tong [487–536]), 120 sheets of paper. *Kyōchūki* (Records of Southern China), two books.[14]

Chishūshi Bosatsukaiso (Commentaries on the Bodhisattva Precepts by the Chinese monk Zhizhou [668–723]), in five volumes.*Reiken Shakushi Bosatsukaiso* (Commentaries on the Bodhisattva Precepts by the Chinese monk Lingxi Shizi) in two volumes.

Tendai Shikan Hōmon, Gengi, Mongu (The Tendai Method of Concentration and Insight), Commentaries on the Lotus Sutra, and a line-by-line commentary on the Lotus Sutra)

of the Tendai sect of Buddhism. Each book in ten volumes.

Shikyōgi (The Four Doctrines of Tendai Buddhism, written by the Chinese monk Zhi-yi), in twelve volumes.

Shidai Zenmon (The Gradual Dhyana Gateways), in eleven volumes.

Gyōhokke Senbō (Conducting a Ceremony to Repent All Human Sins to the Buddhist Deities), in one volume.

Shōshikan (The Rudiments of Concentration and Insight), in one volume.

Rokumyōmon (Six Steps to Samadhi), in one volume.

Myōryōron (Commentaries on Precepts, Rules, and Regulations) in one volume.

Teihin Ritsushi Shokusōgiki (Commentaries on the Monastic Rules by the Chinese monk Dingpin [d. after 741]), in nine volumes.[15]

Additional explanations of the aforementioned work, one volume.

Kaiso (Commentaries on Buddhist Precepts), two books, one volume each.

Kannonji Kōritsushi Giki (Commentaries on the Monastic Rules by the Chinese monk Daliang of the Guanyinsi temple), two books, ten volumes in total.

Nanzan Senritsushi Gan Chūkaibon (Supplementary Notes in one volume and Commentaries on the Monastic Rules by Master Daoxuan (596–667) of Zhongnan Mountain).

Gyōjishō (Book on Annual Events), five books.

Katsumaso (Commentaries on Karma) and others, two books in all.

Kaiso Ritsushi Kaihonso (Commentaries on the Monastic Rules by the Chinese monk Master Huaisu [625–698]), in four volumes.

Daikaku Ritsushi Hiki (Critical Comments by Master Dajue on Daoxuan (596–667)'s Commentaries), in fourteen volumes.

Onkun (Explanation of Character Sounds), two books.

Bikuni Den (Biographies of Buddhist Nuns), two books in four volumes.

Genjō Hōshi Saiikiki (The Great Tang Records on the Western Regions of the Monk Xuanzang), one book in twelve volumes.

Shūnanzan Senritsushi Kanchū Sōkai Kaidanzu (Diagram for the Ordination Platform by the Chinese monk Daoxuan of the Zhongnan Mountains), in one volume.

Hōsenritsushi Nikaibon (Monastic Rules for Buddhist Nuns by the Chinese monk Faxian), one book and commentaries on same in two volumes.

Jade ring, three **hand-held banners made of crystal**.

[missing text]

Three jars filled with **seedlings of the bodhi tree**.

Twenty seedlings of **blue lotus**.

Eight bowls made of **tortoiseshell.**

Two pairs of **leather sandals from India.**

An original piece of calligraphy by General Wang Xizhi (303–361).

Three pieces of calligraphy by Wang's son Wang Xianzhi (344–386).

Fifty writings with different scripts from India, including Zhuli.

The records show that the jade ring, three hand-held, crystal banners, and as well as all the items listed in the list after the flags, were presented to the imperial household. The first item, 3,000 pieces of Buddha's bones, was also presented to Ex-Emperor Shōmu when Ganjin and others had an audience with him for the first time. Among these items, we note only a few works of art, including two embroideries, two paintings, three paintings produced on screens, and four sculptures. No doubt the screens and sculptures were small in size. As for Buddhist scriptures, we notice that many of these are commentaries. We don't know immediately until we make a more thorough investigation if they brought these works to fill a void in Japan's collection of scriptures at this time. Even if they did not, I would say that the importation of these commentaries influenced Japan's Buddhist world considerably.

NARA PERIOD AND THE BEGINNING OF THE HEIAN PERIOD

I think all of us would like to separate rather clearly the Nara period from the Heian period that followed it. I would say that this impulse is misled by our desire to follow a historical period distinction that was created merely for convenience. I do admit that there is a great deal of difference in mood between the Tenpyō (710–794) and Kōnin periods (ca. 800–ca. 900) but the transformation from the end of Tenpyō to the beginning of Kōnin was gradual, with no crisp demarcation line between the two. In the Kōnin period, we notice a reaction against decadence evident at the end of Tenpyō, as well as a continuation of decadence. In comparison to the transformation between Tenpyō and Kōnin, there was far more change and transformation in the one hundred years after monk Kūkai's death in 835. In terms of public manners and customs, Heian style formal court clothing called *ikan sokutai* became the official attire. Women courtiers walked with their long hair trailing down behind them. Women's clothing, which, up until this point in time, was contoured around their bodies closely like today's Western clothing, changed to elaborate, multilayered court clothing, called *jūni hitoe*, which deprived the wearer of freedom of movement. In architecture, the *shinden* palace architectural style typical of the Fujiwara period was established around this time.[16] In literature, the poetic tradition of the *Man'yōshū* changed to *waka*, which was amply characterized in the *Kokinshū*. *Kanji* were simplified to kana and prose written in this writing system began to be produced. In other words, the Japanese began writing in Japanese for the first time. In art, a delicately beautiful style was born, and this style of art began to be accepted as quintessentially Japanese by people in the succeeding generations. In religion, a new type of religious fervor, called *kūya nenbutsu* and thought to have begun with monk Kūya, came into vogue. These believers chanted prayers as they danced while banging feverishly on gourds and gongs. All these things suggested that the times were changing.

Ordinarily, this period is seen as a time in which foreign culture **became indigenized.** If we were to use this criterion for defining a period, we must say that the Kōnin period was a time when foreign culture was brought into Japan. We have to be careful to note that the point here does not relate simply to importing and digesting foreign culture. Changes in taste, such as *ikan sokutai*, *jūni hitoe* and long hair, as mentioned above, are not simply evidence to show that copying changed to creating. The *shinden* architectural style and the invention of *kana* are generally thought to be evidence for a change from making copies to creating something new, but this view is not entirely correct. That is, *kana* is not **an indigenization of *kanji*** but is an invention of the Japanese writing system using *kanji*. Also, *shinden*-style architecture is not a Japanization of Han architecture but should be thought of as a formation of Japanese residential housing, which made use of the architectural techniques the Japanese learned from China. Hence, we should regard these changes and developments as uniquely Japanese developments, which **were based on the foundation of** foreign culture. In other words, it is not that a culture specific to Japan embraced foreign culture, but that peculiarities of the Japanese people developed in this particular way in a society where the air was thick with foreign culture. This point of view is different from the one that contends that foreign culture was simply inserted into existing Japanese culture in that, I argue, that foreign culture provided the soil for the development of native Japanese culture. If one takes this point of view, we may say that Japanese creativity is not something that stands as the opposite of foreign culture but that it was actually born out of foreign culture.

We can recognize that a good deal of progress was made between the time when the Japanese could not write in their own native language and the time when they could. But we should notice that this progress did not come about because the people made an effort **to gain cultural independence.** The Japanese people, living in a society where the great Tang dynasty culture came flooding into Japan, were fervently devising a way to use the Chinese language. The use of the Japanese language was, until then, limited to *senmyō*, which was a type of writing used for imperial decrees, and the *waka*. This in turn means that the language was acknowledged to be useless for new ideas and systems from abroad. Even after the time when the Japanese language obtained a modicum of refined character, Chinese prose (*kanbun*) was always thought to be more prestigious. Setting aside the period when only women wrote in Japanese, *kanbun* was very highly regarded even after such famous native writers as Chikamatsu Monzaemon (1653–1724) and Ihara Saikaku (1642–1693) emerged. Further, being able to write *kanbun* was a necessary skill for any scholar. The same attitude pervades even today—any scholar who can publish his scholarly effort in a foreign language earns a certain type of respect precisely because he could do so in a foreign language. So, at the time when the Japanese did not have a writing system truly of their own, we have no reason to fault the Japanese for never thinking twice about *kanbun* as their own native writing system. The Japanese writing system was born out of necessity—to supplement people's lack of learning. In other words, Japanese prose writing was born from the women, who had few opportunities to study Chinese. Similarly, Japanese prose written in a mixture of *kanji* and *kana* in later times originated in the *samurai* class who were unable to write in Chinese. Further, the colloquial language was born from the common people who were incapable of understanding even the written form of the language. As we can plainly see, the written language was born not out of the people's desire for the independence of Japan's own culture, but **out of unavoidable necessity**. Therein lies the significance of the writing system as a product of Japanese creation.

Even if we admit the *Nihon Shoki* was written in Chinese, it was still a work of the Japanese. Thus we must regard the *kanbun* written during the Nara period as a product of the Japanese, just like the *kanbun* during the Edo period. According to the opinion of one specialist, *kanbun* written during the Nara era was virtually free of Japanese influence and serves as a fine example of *kanbun* writing. This is an interesting view, since it considers something to be of fine quality when it does not have any hint of Japanese flavor. We can say the same thing about visual art. Regardless of how unabashedly foreign every artistic element in a work of art may be, it is still Japanese art if it is created by a Japanese. It is by no means shameful in itself, then, to follow a foreign artistic style. The only important thing is to create something great in that style.

It is certain that the people in the Tenpyō period produced some great things. Without this foundation, the Fujiwara culture that followed it could not have arisen.

Notes

1. Ganjin, Jianzhen in Chinese, lived 688–763. Ganjin's arrival in Nara is chronicled in the *Tōdaiji Yōroku*, *Shoku Nihongi*, and *Tō Daiwajō Tōseiden* (Trip to the East of the Great Tang Monk Ganjin).
2. See *Tō Daiwajō Tōseiden* in Komatsu Shigemi, Kikutake Jun'ichi, and Ono Katsutoshi, *Tōseiden Emaki* (Picture Scrolls of Tōseiden) Tokyo: Chūōkōronsha, 1978, 113–118, for Ganjin's background and details of events leading up to his trip to Japan.
3. The three essential areas consisted of monastic rules, meditation and seeing truth, and wisdom to forgo attachments.
4. Ban Sendō is described in this document as a male Buddhist who was yet to enter priesthood officially.
5. Kōbō Daishi was also known as Kūkai (774–835).
6. There are various interpretations for the Chinese term 修文, which is rendered here as "a learned person in the arts." It could be a person learned in rhetoric or in rules and protocols of, perhaps, monastic life. For the original text, see *TSD*, T51.p0989b.
7. Kaisandō is part of Tōshōdaiji that commemorates the person who opened the temple, that is, Ganjin.

8. This record is known today as the *Shōdai Senzai Denki*, compiled by Sekiguchi Shizuo and Yamamoto Hiroya. Tokyo: Shōwa Joshi Daigaku Kindai Bunka Kenkyūjo, 2004.

9. See *Shichidaiji Junreiki* in *Dainippon Bukkyō Zensho*, vol. 83. Tokyo: Kōdansha, 1972.

10. By stating "There were only a few foreigners who came with Ganjin," Watsuji seems to mean that there were only few non-Chinese people who traveled to Japan with Ganjin.

11. Apparently the original *Tōseiden* is now lost, but each of the four extant copies gives a slightly varying account, e.g., the lists of sutras brought by Ganjin to Japan are not consistent with each other. Maruzen is a chain of large, comprehensive bookstores in Japan. Underlines and emphases, appearing as four types of *bōten* in the original texts, are Watsuji's own.

12. Kuse Kanzeon Bosatsu may be known as Kuze Kanzeon Bosatsu or Guze Kanzeon Bosatsu.

13. Butsumyōkyō contains a list of names of Buddhist deities that are chanted out loud in a Buddhist ceremony called *butsumyōe*, the purpose of which is to pray for forgiveness for sins committed during the year.

14. This book is a record of the area from present-day southern China (from Zhejiang Province) to northern Vietnam.

15. This is a commentary on Fali's Commentaries on the Monastic Rules.

16. The *shinden* style refers to a domestic architectural style used for building aristocrat's mansions during the Heian period (794–1185), consisting of a main building to which other smaller structures were connected by corridors.

Chapter 16

YAKUSHIJI AND THE THREE IMAGES IN THE LECTURE HALL

We arrived at Yakushiji close to dusk. We all knew the pinnacles of Asian art were at this temple.

Although we arrived after closing time, Mr. Y. worked hard to persuade the temple to let us in. As a result, shortly, a young apprentice monk stood before us with giant keys. We entered through the small back gate, and there we found the Lecture Hall. Its doors, covered with dust, were falling apart in a sad state of disrepair. On the other side of an old pond, the back of the temple's Golden Hall was visible, which looked a bit like an abandoned building. The open area surrounding these buildings was full of tall weeds, which made the whole temple give us a sense befitting an ancient, abandoned temple.

The monk stopped by the door to the Lecture Hall. Z asked the rest of us if we wanted to see inside. "Sure," we chimed in. "After all, we came all this way. It will give us something to talk about later." After this short exchange, the large keys made a huge clanking sound and the monk opened the dusty old doors. Inside we found ourselves in an area encircled by a striped black and white curtain. We lifted this curtain, walked into the Lecture Hall itself, and found a statue of Yakushi Nyorai Bodhisattva, 16-feet tall, with two statues flanking the main image. The images looked down on us quietly in the semi-dark, empty hall. I just casually looked up at them and something caught my eye. They were copper statues, major works of art filled with classical majesty, totally different from insignificant, poorly crafted figures that weren't worthy of viewing. I remembered that there are some who praise the quality of these works, and I thought that they could be right about that. As this thought occurred to me, I moved to one side of the statues. The profile of the main image's head was beautiful and couldn't be taken lightly. The statues flanking the main image were not badly rendered either. Here, too, we can recognize an artist at work.

It made me feel happy to find beauty in these images. The surface of the main statue, though, was rough and pitted, giving it a lusterless, ugly copper color. If this statue were smooth with fresh color and luster, it would capture people's hearts more readily. The statue, as it is now, somehow makes it look cheap; this is influenced undoubtedly by the surface texture and color. When I saw these images for the first time, I could not believe judging from the condition of the surface that they were only one thousand years old. But, I heard later that they were found not too far away from the temple, buried deep in the ground for several hundred years, before they were excavated during the Tokugawa period. They were then moved to this temple. The condition of the surface bore the traces of "buried art." If that was really true, then these three images are a source of mystery. The temple which originally enshrined these images should have been of considerable significance. If that were the case, how would we explain the fact that we know nothing about how the temple was reduced to complete dust? These three images compel us to find an answer to this mystery.

YAKUSHI NYORAI BODHISATTVA IN THE GOLDEN HALL

We entered through the back door into the Golden Hall. As we walked to the side of the hall, I found myself a bit excited about being able to see the image once more. First, the shiny, half-naked body of an image that flanks the main statue jumped into view. Then, as we surveyed this huge body from head to toe, our eyes followed a sight line between this guardian deity's right hand—gently bent at the wrist—and the large thighs and, then, in an instant, led our eyes to the profile of Yakushi Nyorai Bodhisattva, with that "enrapturing beauty," in a seated position just beyond the flanking deity. We hurried around to the front of the Yakushi Nyorai. There we stood transfixed. Then we found seating and so we sat there, completely captivated by the Yakushi. The late afternoon light was just about perfect today. The smooth, shiny skin of the Yakushi Nyorai was quite sensitive to how the light rays fell on it, and I knew that it did not show up to its best advantage unless there was just the right amount of light shining on it.

The beauty of this figure is indescribable. It can only be understood when one sees it in person. The statue is majestic, rich, and splendid. Its beauty is harmony itself, an embrace of both gentleness and strength. The gentle lustrous light reflecting off the right hand, palm open in front of the chest, is enough to move our souls. The voluptuous yet elegant body—featuring the wide, delineated, holy chest that is as clear and pure as the blue sky, the delicate and soft robe that flows from the strong shoulders to the chest and then to the arms, and the lotus sitting position that places the entire upper body in a tranquil harmony—seems to be an unceasing source of beauty, springing from the entire being of the image's lines and planes. This beauty is different from the beauty of the human body that we feel from Greek sculpture. Greek sculpture no doubt expresses ideal beauty as a reflection of a pinnacle of human desire, but in this Buddhist statue, we see something else, that is, a transcendent being in human form, which reflects our desire for reaching the "Other Shore."[1] If we suppose that we had to find a concrete symbol of the absolute world in religious sentiment that assumes that the present world is only temporary and sought true life in the world beyond it, it would be unavoidable, it seems to me, that a statue such as this would be imbued with superhumanness. This mood is especially noticeable in the head and its beauty. Though the face features heavy eyelids, a broad nose, and a bone structure that displays other characteristics specific to Mongoloids, such as under-defined facial contours, it is not inferior to any human race with respect to refinement and dignity. A Greek once commented that the facial features of some Asian race resembled a meatball, which I suppose may have a ring of truth to it, but I would say that the Greeks would not have imagined that these meatballs would actually be able to produce an example of such shining beauty. The cheeks and their unusual roundness, the voluptuousness, which in places indescribably becomes more tightly defined—these facial features of a supposed meatball show infinite mercy, wisdom, and dignity. Don't the long, narrow, slightly open eyes well with tears of great mercy? In the cheeks, lips, and the chin that glisten from soft reflected light, do we not sense immeasurable intelligence and willpower? Certainly it is not a face of a human being. Its beauty is beyond human (*see fig. 8, photo section*).

What produced this beauty was undoubtedly the spirit of artists who believed in realism so much as to be able to go beyond it. They first perfected the technique of forming a statue of a human body from the feet up and, only then, learned the process of forming a supernatural being from the head down. If the artists were not able to grasp the essence of natural beauty or unable to express the grasped beauty with sharpness and sensitivity, they would not have been able to crystallize the swirling inner ideas and give them appropriate shape. Of course, this statue did not just appear out of nowhere; that is, it was not built without any model. Certainly, this was definitely not the first time that artists conceived of this type of crystallization of ideas. Yet, at the same time, this is not to say that even if there were a model, a masterpiece such as this could easily be constructed. Artists who were able to produce a masterpiece like this may have had access to hundreds, nay, thousands of models to study from, but they would have still used their own eyes to grasp beauty and their own passions to reduce their ideas to form. Copies of Greek sculptures produced during Roman times, however superb they were technically, lost the essential life force and the freshness on the surface. But here, not a hint of dullness of that sort can be detected in the Yakushi Nyorai image. The statue is fresh as if it were born yesterday.

I continued to study this image closely. The black luster of the surface was enough to make it impossible to look away from it. The luster had yet another effect. The amazing way the surface of the statue was created made this effect of luster possible. The special stretching characteristics of copper, which I might call its "soft hardness," met with the artists' inspired use and crystallized in that beautiful skin and the robe's indescribable, robust smoothness, giving me, in the end, a strange visual sensation of skin that looks so stretched yet, at the same time, so soft as if to melt at any moment, and which appears to possess a hardness and coldness of something eternally indestructible but is also warm to the touch and pliable if one were to squeeze it. This use of copper would not have been possible unless the artists had possessed this amazing understanding of the beauty of the human body. Look at the open right hand. Look at the garment flow from the shoulder to the elbow, enveloping the left arm. That's only one part of the entire image, but taking notice of these minor details, one can come to realize what the artist's eyes were trained on. But that was not the full extent of observation the maker of this image made of human beauty, as it still does not reach the true profundity of this work. What I think is significant is the choice and idealization the artist made. In order to serve his ideas, the artist brought some types of beauty to the fore and relegated other sorts of beauty to the background. In order to lead those crystals of ideas to a perfect harmony, some were emphasized and some were deemphasized. As a result, the beauty of the parts coming to life is due to the beauty of the whole, which allows the entire image to express an immeasurable life energy and charm. In short, then, at the very bottom of this beauty lies the artistic spirit of the maker.

We do not have the faintest idea who this artist was. We don't know if he was Japanese or Tang Chinese. He was, however, an ancestor of ours. And a rare, true genius. If a genius were to represent an entire ethnic group, our ancestors 1,200 years ago would be represented by this genius. It is correct to trace this work to the early Tang dynasty by examining its stylistic features. It is not unthinkable, also, to make a guess about copper statues during the Tang period, of which so few remain. But if we can compare and contrast the spirit embodied in this work to that in Tang works, I would say it would be immeasurably meaningful for understanding of our ancestors. I think I can detect a certain fleeting characteristic not seen in the Tang dynasty's carved stone Buddhas and India's copper statues in the greatness and flexibility in this work. Is it not possible to get a grip on this fleeting thought? Solving this puzzle, I believe, will be a key to understanding the times, that is, the so-called Hakuhō period in art history, when the nation of Japan came into genuinely concrete existence.

ATTENDANT IMAGES

In comparison to the main image, the flanking statues, called Nikkō and Gakkō, were not as outstanding. The faces and the rest of the bodies of these two statues were fashioned in a very similar manner and this similarity lends a kind of harmony to the three Buddhist statues. My sense is that the makers of these two lesser deities are different from the artist (or artists) who created the main image. The artist responsible for making the robe that clings to the lower half of the body of the main image so superbly could not possibly be satisfied with the insipid treatment of the robe covering the lower half of these lesser deities. I think the same observation applies to the faces and hands as well as to their shoulders. Of the two, the one on the right (Nikkō) is superior. Different artists could have made these deities. It is quite conceivable for the master artist of the caliber who produced the main image to have had two or three assistants who were skilled enough to produce these images.

DATE OF PRODUCTION OF THE IMAGES AND EMPEROR TENMU

As to when these images were produced, it would have been some time during the seventeen years between the last years of Emperor Tenmu (631?–686, r. 673–686) and the retirement of Emperor Jitō (645–703, r. 690–697) from the throne. Emperor Tenmu first commissioned these images in part to pray for his empress's recovery from an eye ailment. After the emperor died, the empress, who succeeded him as Emperor Jitō, fulfilled his initial wish after spending more than ten years on the project. The consecration ceremony of the main image was conducted during the last years of Emperor Jitō. The Yakushiji complex was completed shortly thereafter, in the first year of Emperor Monmu's (683–707, r. 697–707) ascent to the throne. The casting of the main Yakushi Nyorai image, as detailed in the *Yakushiji Engi* (The Chronicle of Yakushiji), was reportedly done **before the death of Emperor Tenmu.** The evidence for this is that there is an inscription found at the base of the pinnacle of the East Tower, which reads, "**Before plating (of the main image) could be done**, the emperor died."[2] If this was the case, then the main years spent on the production of these images could be pinned down to the period **during the last years of Emperor Monmu**. Then the last five or six years of **the great capital city of Asuka in Nara** would have been indeed remarkable.

Emperor Tenmu ascended to the throne after the Jinshin War of 672, and this fact has begot numerous debates that center around him. To us, Emperor Tenmu is a person of high interest in a different sense. First of all, he is famous as a poet whose work has been collected in the *Man'yōshū*. A well-known romantic verse of his that reads, "If I did not love you, who is as beautiful as violet flowers that cover these hills? How could I be so madly in love with you, even though you're now another man's wife." This was sent by the emperor to Nukata no Ōkimi, a well-known poetess, after which it became a focus of controversy.[3] This poem tells very well of the emperor's passionate personality. This same passion also showed up in his belief in Buddhism. He decided to adhere to the precept against eating red meat and decreed that it be banned. From this point on, the culture of meat eating in Japan never again flourished. This is to say that both in terms of character and culture, the Japanese have been strongly influenced by Emperor Tenmu. The emperor also decreed that all provinces in Japan follow the rule that each household should build a Buddhist altar and equip it with a statue of Buddha and a copy of the scriptures. This became a powerful tradition that continues until today. In any case, such a policy had a truly significant meaning, at least in the beginning, in that it strongly promoted Buddhism as the national religion of Japan. No one can dispute that under this emperor Buddhism grew dramatically and flourished. The custom of emperors' frequently visiting temples or permitting numerous monks and nuns to live within the imperial grounds and the like began during the last years of this emperor's reign. Monks and nuns of various temples as well as high officials in his administration all put forth a concerted effort to chant scriptures, produce Buddhist images, conduct rites of ordination, offer prayers and and so on, so that the emperor might recover from ailments—these events never took place before his time. Right before the death of Emperor Tenji, one hundred images of Buddha were consecrated in the imperial palace and rare jewels were presented to Hōkōji to help him recover, but these actions paled in comparison to Emperor Tenmu's passion for relying on Buddhism. Emperor Tenmu died as everyone chanted a Buddhist prayer; in comparison, Emperor Tenji died during a dispute concerning imperial succession. The main person who directly laid a foundation of Tenpyō culture was not Emperor Tenji but Emperor Tenmu.

THE ASUKA CULTURE DURING EMPEROR TENMU'S REIGN

The engine of culture at that time was undoubtedly the new returnees from Tang China. Some of them were **scholars who were knowledgeable about the Chinese language and Chinese classics**. These seem to have become the professors and assistant professors of national studies in universities, which were established around this time. The Code of Taihō, issued in 701, a decade and a half after the death of the emperor, mandated that a university have an enrollment limit of 430 students, taught by seven professors and two assistant professors. In addition there were to be five administrative officials, including the head of the university. There were courses in **national studies for each country, like China**, headed up by one professor and twenty to fifty students. In addition, there were students who studied medicine under medical doctors. As for courses, these were primarily for the study of Chinese classics. In addition, there were courses for **calligraphy** and **phonetic studies**. Phonetic studies were about the pronunciation of Chinese, and if one mastered this subject, he would be able to speak Chinese. Furthermore, there was a specialized course of study for mathematics. This type of education was aimed at educating government officials, but it also resulted in the promotion of people's general education levels, and may have constituted a strong impetus for attracting students in the middle classes or higher to inquiries in spiritual realms. It is hard to ignore this as a reason for the flourishing of Buddhism. For instance, in order to understand **the poetic nuance** of Buddhist scriptures, someone who can speak Chinese is far more advantaged than a person who can read Chinese but cannot speak it. Thus, I can well imagine that the impact on students who studied at the university from listening to monks' chanting was all the more clear and powerful. This sort of background existed in the flourishing of Buddhism.

There were people who performed even more noticeable and remarkable work than

simply too great to be considered a mere product of transplanted art. No doubt its seed is foreign, but the soil and fertilizer are new. At this point, if we were to bring up the issue of "imitation" as a point of contention, then we would have to acknowledge that everything in our time is also a copy of something. Imitation is obviously a natural phenomenon of all human societies, and it is so obvious that it need hardly be pointed out by Tarde's[4] theory of imitation. What is important here is the fact that masterpieces such as this were indeed produced, not whether or not it was a copy of something.

THE EAST TOWER OF YAKUSHIJI

There is another masterpiece in addition to the main image of worship at the Golden Hall. It is the image of Shō Kannon of Tōindō. We all hurried to the Tōindō before darkness set in.

But, on the way from the Golden Hall to the Tōindō, the towering presence of a pagoda called the East Tower commanded our attention. This building is the only extant example of the great architecture of the Hakuhō period. It is such a fine piece of architecture that no one, even in a hurry, can just walk by it. This pagoda features something called *mokoshi* under each of the three roofs; this may be described as a "roofed porch," and gives the building an appearance that six levels of roofs of different sizes are piled on top of each other and, at the same time, makes the building's contours extraordinarily complex. Because of this, the building has a hint of foreign flavor. The strong sense of unification which this boldly undulated contour line helps to create gives the viewer an impression of an odd, striking beauty that is most certainly seldom seen in the architectural style of ordinary stupas in Japan. If, in fact, these additional *mokoshi* roofs were added when the building was moved to the present location during the Yōrō period (717–724), the astonishingly talented architect who designed this building then would have been among the craftsmen who built the capital city of Nara. According to the record that chronicles the history of this temple, it appears that the *mokoshi* were attached not only to this stupa but also to the double roofs of the Golden Hall. We can only imagine the peculiar beauty the Golden Hall must have had, when it sported four "roofs" of different sizes, judging from the impression one gets from the East Tower. We would think that before the top story of the Golden Hall was blown away by strong winds its structure too was bold and unconventional. We have no way of knowing if this sort of building existed only at Yakushiji, but we can be sure that an unusual architect worked at Yakushiji around the time when the capital was moved to Nara. The time was, curiously, when the temple also produced Gyōki, that enthusiastic, evangelical monk. If some sort of cause and effect relationship existed between these two historical facts, this temple naturally takes on a huge, very special meaning (*see fig. 9, photo section*).

We all stood on a grassy area between the Golden Hall and the Tōindō and looked intently at the rooftop spire of the tower. A beautiful flame-patterned metal openwork tops the spire, which I think exquisitely matches the height of this building. This decorative metalwork just sits there, quietly and elegantly as well as importantly, as if it were the center of all the harmony of the building. The celestial beings portrayed in this openwork are indescribably stunning and graceful. The half-naked celestial maidens, turned upside down, are delicate and plump, twisting their bodies pleasingly. The flowing garments wrapping around their round but slender waists and thighs suggestively cling closely to their bodies. But, the metalwork is far away, high off the ground from where we stood, detectable only faintly through binoculars. So if we wanted a closer examination, we had to resort to a plaster reproduction on the first floor of the tower. The delicate decorative patterns of this ornamental piece are an integrated mixture of celestial being motifs and fretwork. It is so exquisitely produced that we are astonished by our own ancestors' brilliant artistry.

We had no time to leisurely savor the artistic genius. We proceeded to the northern side of the Tōindō and took our shoes off to stand on a corridor that was set high off the ground. We walked on our toes on the dark, dusty, unswept floor of the cavernous hall and, with much anticipation, stood before that large altar. The young monk opened the door of the altar slowly. There stood a *kannon*, the greatest *kannon*, incomparable to any in the world.

SHŌ KANNON IN TŌINDŌ

It is impossible to talk or write about the very first impression when one confronts a work like this. Such an experience gives a kind of physical shock. And, this was not the first time that I saw this image. It matters not how many times I see it. This image is always new.

We stood silent and spellbound, interrupted only by occasional words of exclamation. They seemed like meaningful words sometimes and utterly devoid of meaning at other times. When the tension of seeing the image for the first time on this visit subsided, I walked over and sat at a lectern where the monk chant sutras. Then I studied the image for a long time. The *kannon* had a beautiful, magnificent face. It had a strong, majestic body. The grandeur of Buddhist art is expressed here. The indescribable color of old copper that makes one feel an unfathomable depth. The noble chest that bulges slightly from below covered with skin of smooth lustrous copper. The magnificent arms and hands. The immaculate lower body covered with a robe. They are expressions of a dignity that is superhuman, embodied in a human form. And, at the same time, this status is flawless even as a realistic representation of a human body. I was indeed moved completely with admiration by the advanced degree of realism of the Shōrinji Kannon yesterday, but when I stood before this image, the Shōrinji Kannon seemed to pale by comparison. The realism that this *kannon* represents is of course not the same as *shasei* (sketching from life) in the modern period that values individual characteristics. Here an individual being is not portrayed; it portrays the essence of mankind. Here these realistic tendencies aren't a trend of a particular school of art; realism here refers to the realism that constitutes the essence of art. Regardless of which part of the image one may focus on, we find absolutely nothing that even suggests that the artist's eye was somehow flawed. Everything was examined with a penetrating clarity, and what was so carefully observed is expressed by a completely unencumbered skill. Yet, at the same time, the realism is, of course, as it is the case of realism in all, great classical art, no more than a means of expressing something in greater depth. If we assume that a modern masterpiece can portray one human being and embody in it the essence of humanity, then we may say that this sort of classical masterpiece portrays the essence of human beings and embodies the essence of a divine being. Thus, the pronounced undulation of the skin on the *kannon* statue beginning with the shoulders and extending to the chest, the beautiful rotundity of the hands and the arms—all these reveal the mystery of infinite power while using the most typical human shapes (*see fig. 10, photo section*).

Receiving permission from the young monk, I entered the altar and examined the details. When I brought myself so close as to almost touch the *kannon*, I was overtaken by a strange sort of pleasure. It was as if life energy was emanating from this beautiful and ancient copper body. I moved close to the statue's bent right arm and, stroking the ivory-smooth arm, I looked up at the *kannon* from the side. I felt as if a totally new aspect of this statue opened up to me. If someone viewed the *kannon* from the front, illuminated by simple lighting, I don't think he can claim he truly saw the *kannon*. The *kannon* reveals the full spectrum of beauty when its entirety—the beauty of the face, the strength of the back, the perfection of the torso seen when the chest and the back are viewed at the same time, even the arms, lower waist, and the legs—are seen from the side. The modeling of the exposed areas from the shoulders to the arms and from the shoulders to the chest is truly astonishing. It is, frankly speaking, extremely regrettable that we cannot view this statue freely now from any angle, such as from the rear or the side.

The feeble, red light of the setting sun through a latticed window at the front of the building streamed in and shined on the altar. The light reflecting off the altar gave a hint of reddish glow to the statue of Shō Kannon. The setting sun worked upon us and stirred our imagination about the Western Paradise in the most appropriate setting. We were surprised by the fortunate coincidence and held our breath as our eyes dwelled the Shō Kannon. Gradually the light became dim and then was gone. The hall became very dark immediately.

The door of the altar was closed. When we looked back at it, the hall itself looked totally desolate and empty.

Notes

1. The "Other Shore" (Jp. *higan*) in Buddhist terminology refers to a place one reaches when one has finally rid oneself of attachments and achieved enlightenment.
2. There are at least two other differing theories. In another theory, the inscription is interpreted as meaning "Before the land for the temple was bought/determined, the emperor died." A third theory is "Before the temple was completed, the emperor died."
3. Emperor Tenmu presented this poem when he was a prince (Ōama no Mikoto) and had separated from Nukata no Ōkimi, his wife.
4. Gabriel Tarde (1843–1904) was a French social psychologist, who maintained that social phenomena are a result of interactions between individuals and that they are based on imitation and innovation.

Chapter 17

THE PRESENT STATE OF THE ANCIENT CAPITAL OF NARA; THE CREATOR OF THE SHŌ KANNON OF YAKUSHIJI

We left Yakushiji from the back door and boarded our rickshaws. Gently rocking, we passed through the village of Rokujōmura and went straight east, on a road that ran between rice fields in the river basin of the Sahogawa River. The mountains of Yamato, shrouded in evening haze, invited a tinge of sadness, which is truly befitting of the old capital of Nara. When I looked down and gazed over the field of rice paddies, I was suddenly struck with the thought that this area would have been the center of the old capital of Nara. The riverbed of the Sahogawa could have risen over time and the erstwhile dry land turned into wetland. Most of the capital city of Nara, which seems to have been dotted with rice paddies even then, might have been very wet from the beginning. If we find reasonable evidence to back up this speculation, this fact then becomes difficult to overlook, for it may have been the reason for Nara's short life as the capital city. Historians have tried to explain the motivation for changing the seat of the government in terms of politics or some sort of ideology behind the moving of the capital, but the unhealthiness of this wetland could have been the more fundamental reason for the relocation. The epidemic that raged in mid-Tenpyō undoubtedly attacked this very wet area. The illness that befell Empress Kōmyō soon after this epidemic may have been caused indirectly by the influence of this wetland. It is impossible to think that the proposal to move the seat of the government from Nara to Kuni around this time was solely a strategy of a group of nobles to drive away the Fujiwara clan's forces.

What occupied my mind most, while traveling through the rice paddies, was not this issue, however. I spent some enjoyable time daydreaming about the identity of the producer of the Shō Kannon. That producer was undoubtedly a Buddhist monk. In my mind's eye, I could almost see him in a very Chinese robe, not unlike a Greek toga, **draped on** his naked body **loosely** and informally. He stands before the prototype of the statue, which is almost complete. His eyes, clear and penetrating, are beautiful, typical of someone with a mixed lineage of Aryan and Mongolian. As he looks at the *kannon*, his eyes become sharply focused, like those of a falcon. His nose is long but it is not a purely Greek nose. His mouth, fully expressive, is pursed shut. He then exhales a large sigh, unfolds his arms slowly, and tucks up the fabric that drapes down his arms. His arms are strong, but pale.

THE MONK GENJŌ SANZŌ

The production of this *kannon*, according to the *Koryūki*, was commissioned by Empress Hashihito's daughter to memorialize the death of her husband Emperor Kōtoku.[1] If we were to believe this, then the statue must have been produced some thirty years before the three images of Yakushiji were produced. The production date, though, is still twenty-four or twenty-five years after the first Kentōshi mission to Tang China. Four or five years before the production of this *kannon*, Yamaguchi no Atai Ōkuchi, who produced the Four Guardian Kings of Hōryūji and worked in the Suiko style, dedicated an image called Senbutsuzō (One Thousand Images of Buddha) in response to an imperial commission.[2] The time when the Shō Kannon was made is separated by only twenty-odd years from the time when Kuratsukuri no Tori produced the Shaka triad of Hōryūji (623) and I think this Suiko artistic style appeared to be still popular enough to be followed. This was also the time when the civilization of early Tang China flooded into Japan and the time when the Taika Reforms (646) were implemented. So it was possible that in the world of Buddhism, which was at the leading edge of culture, some unexpected bold new trend may have appeared already. In China, Genjō Sanzō (Ch. *Xuanzang*, 602–664) returned to present-day Chang'an (called Xi'an at that time) after eighteen years of an arduous journey to India's western area and brought back an eye-opening culture. That year was Taika 1 (645) in Japan. The first time the Japanese actually experienced this new culture was when the large-scale Kentōshi mission was sent to Tang China eight years later. Those who were members of the first mission returned to Japan in the same year that Emperor Kōtoku passed away. When we put these events together, we find it easier to understand why masterpieces in a new artistic style were produced almost immediately after Emperor Kōtoku's death. The genius that produced the Shō Kannon, I contend, was an artist who was somehow connected to Genjō Sanzō. Perhaps it was someone who followed Genjō Sanzō back to China from the western regions of China. Equally possible is that it was a Japanese who traveled to Tang China as a member of the Kentōshi mission and poured his heart and soul into learning the new culture and artistic style that Genjō Sanzō brought back from India. Whatever the case may have been, we can be sure that he was on a ship led by Kishi no Nagani that returned to a Japanese port from Tang China in the year of Emperor Kōtoku's death.[3]

THE ART OF THE GUPTA DYNASTY AND THE COOPERATION OF THE PEOPLE FROM THE WEST OF CHINA

If the Indian painter Utchibatchina had already arrived at the Sui court by then, it might be a bit presumptuous to assume that Genjō Sanzō was the purveyor of Early Tang artistic style. But even if the new Tang style had already taken root before Genjō's return, we must still give most of the credit to Genjō, who took it to a new height, made it a prevailing style in society, and attracted the attention of Japanese students. The most notable characteristic of Genjō Sanzō's work is that he imported a great deal of culture from India, Persia, and China's west. And this was the first great fruit of Emperor Taizong's military campaign to conquer countries to the west of China, which made it easier to travel between China, western regions of China, and India. But I wonder, why is it that it was in this Genjō's time period that a new-style art first began to flourish? Art that was brought into China was primarily from Gandhara, though it was mixed with some art from the middle part of India. It was certainly the Greek artistic spirit that led the Chinese to a new visual art. In addition, we should note that the art of the Northern Wei dynasty (fl. 386–534) does not seem to have been influenced by Greek art. In this case, except for art that had been sinicized, the art of Northern Wei was either Indian or in the style of the western regions of China and bore no vestige of Gandhara art. Hence, after Genjō brought back the artistic style of the Gupta dynasty (northern India, fl. 320–550), the art scene immediately, or so it seems, took on influences from Gandhara art. This resulted in a type of art in early Tang, which was agreeable, classical, refined, and clearly more religious than the art of the Gupta dynasty. Why did this happen in this way? Was it because that the time was just right for the melding of influences after the Sixteen Kingdoms period (304–439) when a great deal of ethnic mixing took place? Could it be that people were then just beginning to truly understand the art from India and the west of China? This probably was part of the reason. What is particularly important to recognize is that the mature art of the Gupta dynasty was able to transmit the Greek artistic spirit because Guptan art was able to exert strong Indian influences. The art from Gandhara that had arrived earlier did indeed transmit Greek techniques as well as its artistic spirit, but because Gandhara art was weak in plastic art, Greek art only transmitted the tradition of idol worship, that is, the tradition of "unifying art with religion." The Chinese and the Mongolians that ruled parts of China learned from Gandhara no more than how to make idols and how to worship them. Hence, art from the Gupta dynasty stimulated the Chinese with its "beauty." Beauty was not a means with which to promote religion; rather beauty used, as it were, religion as a means with which to express itself. If then we were to compare Gandharan sculpture to medieval Christian art, Gupta dynasty art should be compared to Renaissance art. The Chinese, now awakened to the beauty of art from abroad, reexamined Northern

Wei art. During the Northern Wei, the beauty of the human body that was clarified through a childlike, naïve astonishment of the heart was now achieved through a mature, complex human consciousness. This complete change in the mindset explains all things.

I personally believe that the art of the Gupta dynasty was the largest and fullest blooming of the Greek artistic spirit that had been planted in India. In this sense, India underwent a renaissance more than one thousand years before Europe. Because such unfolding was both natural and orderly, there is no such moment we can call a "rebirth" (renaissance). The Greek seedling planted during the times of Alexander the Great flowered in such places as Sanchi and Bharhut in India. The other seedling remained in Greek culture and was maintained by the Greeks who moved to northern India. Later this early form of art was stimulated by Roman influences and matured as Gandharan art. This style then combined with the art of Sanchi and Bharhut and flowered in the Gupta dynasty. This art was of course Indian, just as Renaissance art was necessarily Italian. Its style and beauty are particular to **India** and not Greece. However, deep within its roots, there is something very much Greek. With this Greek element deeply embedded in the root system, Guptan art gave a violent jolt to China. Thus the Chinese in the early Tang did not warm up quickly to the flavor of this Indian decadence, which was an aspect of Guptan art. Instead, the Chinese absorbed only Grecian grandiosity and sensuous beauty. Then, the Chinese added a typical Han influence to this, that is, a measure of simplification. As a result, a classical art was born, which was fresh, clean, vigorous, and spirited. That, I think, was the artistic style during the early Tang.

In making all these connections, it is necessary to postulate the idea of the people of China's western areas working together. When Genjō was alive, it was the time when these western regions of China were flourishing. There, cultures from India, Persia, Greece, and other places all melted together, and this mixed culture had its own unique flavor. The culture was not as developed as Indian culture, so, naturally, it was not as decadent. If we look at photographs of the excavated items during Sir Aurel Stein's expeditions to Central Asia, we find that nude women from this cultural area, for example, were not depicted with as much a sense of obscenity as their Indian counterparts. Buddhist images, as well, were far purer and holier. This arose because, I think, this area was particularly Buddhist and was not invaded by Indian mythology, in which the believers admired the carnal pleasures of Shiva or Indra.[4] According to Genjō's *Saiikiki* (The Great Tang Records on the Western Regions), non-Buddhist teachings were flourishing more than Buddhism **in India**.[5] But, Genjō also states that non-Buddhist teachings had not yet reached **the regions west of China** and that the Buddhism there was not a type of Buddhism (Esoteric Buddhism) that had incorporated native Indian myths and beliefs. Thus, if we just look at Buddhism, it was **purer and fresher** in China's western regions than in India. We should also note that **these regions to the west of China** connected India and Tang China. If we think about the foreigners that Genjō brought back, it would have been difficult for him to return with many Indians from India but it was far easier to bring back foreigners from the western regions. Genjō returned to Khotan to the north of the Himalayas after traveling for seventeen years. He lived there for some time in order to teach about the Buddhist scriptures. During his stay in this town, he wrote a letter appealing for Emperor Taizong's forgiveness for the crime he committed when he left Tang China without permission and traveled abroad in violation of a ban on travel. The emperor was moved by this passionate plea, whereupon the emperor decided to send an imperial messenger to Genjō along with some men and military horses for his return journey. The kind of travel Genjō did was not the type of travel that just one person could do, for it goes without saying that no small number of people and horses were needed to travel over high mountains and cross deserts carrying a large number of scriptures. Genjō's travel was made possible by the kindness he received from kings and high-ranking officials, not to mention fellow Buddhists, at the various places he visited. Now, with the support of the emperor of the largest and most powerful dynasties in Asia, Genjō would return triumphantly from China's western regions back to Tang China. Under these circumstances, it is quite probable that Genjō would have been able to hire as many people as he needed and take as many articles as he wished on his return trip east from Khotan. If we follow this line of thinking, then, it is easy to imagine that many artists from Khotan would have joined Genjō's return east.

THE MAKER OF THE SHŌ KANNON

The creator of the Shō Kannon that I fantasized was this sort of a man from some place in the west of China. (Coincidentally, I found a description at the end of an entry on Emperor Kōtoku's reign in the *Nihon Shoki* reporting that two men and two women, both from Dvaravati, as well as a woman from Sravasti, drifted to a Japanese shore, something that also titillates my imagination.[6]) In any case, this artist grew up surrounded by Gandharan art and was jolted by the art of the Gupta dynasty. And after nearly ten years of living in Tang China, this man began to love the simplicity, vigor, and strength in Han dynasty art. So we can say that all favorable attributes of Asia now ran through his body. Where would his talent be **crystallized**? Gentle and verdant Yamato, with rivers and mountains, was an ideal location. There, he found nothing that would make him continue to wander aimlessly. Neither did he find temptations that would confuse him or corrupt him. He worked with a focused presence of mind. We do not know how many works he produced. All we know is that he left us with the Shō Kannon.

If we were to find it difficult to believe the story that the Shō Kannon was produced to memorialize Emperor Kōtoku, I may have to reformulate this fantasy. Even in that case, there seems to be no disagreement about the fact that the statue was made before the

Yakushi triad. If that is the case, then, regardless how much we try to push back the date of production, that would be no more than thirty years. That is, there is no huge difference between the times of production.

YAKUSHIJI; RENDERING A DIVINITY IN HUMAN FORM

I recall writing to my friend Kinoshita Mokutarō as follows:[7]

> Among the sculptures you saw, it was perhaps inevitable that you could not see that famous Buddhist statue of the Yumedono Hall, but I do wonder why you did not even mention the Shō Kannon in the Tōindō Hall of Yakushiji. You said that you did not get much artistic impact from seeing the Yakushi Nyorai statue in the Golden Hall, and, if that was your frame of mind on that day, it was the reason why the Shō Kannon did not overwhelm you. You have only yourself to blame for that. It seems that you were feeling just too soft and lyrical on that day, and the tenor of your heart was just as lusterless as the appearance of the Tōshōdaiji was muted to your eyes. I can see you in my mind's eyes trudging alone in the rain. And, when you passed by the pond, with water shields and water chestnut floating on the surface, a quiet rain was falling on the old capital just as it was coming down on your heart. The classical Shō Kannon may have been just too tenuously far off for your lonesome, poetic mood. So that's why you cannot just rush through Nara. I can only hope that you will visit Nara again if not just to see the Shō Kannon and Yakushi Nyorai again.
>
> When I look at the Shō Kannon, I feel that the fluid nature of copper was not utilized to its full potential. I am referring to the technique of rendering the garment on the lower body. In this respect, the maker of the Yakushi Nyorai went as far as he could. Yet, the Shō Kannon possesses an extremely taut tension that comes from trying to reach a climax. I sense that the body, produced with full naturalism, is overflowing with superhuman power and dignity. Look at, for example, the powerful curve like an ocean swell that begins from the chest and reaches the stomach. And the mystical power of the beautiful left hand. And the beautiful face so specific to Asia. As far as I know, there is nothing in Gandhara art that can even approach the **power** of this statue. Granted that among the excavated artifacts in China and China's western regions there are things that could be said to be more **intricate** or beautiful, but I can say unequivocally that no work of **religious art** has impressed me more than Shō Kannon for its **dignified majesty** and **magnificence**. In comparison to the West, I would think that medieval sculptures would not be able to even hold a candle to the Shō Kannon. Religious sculptures during the Renaissance and Greek sculptures of various deities are not, strictly speaking, as religious as the Shō Kannon, so comparing them is a bit problematic, but if we look at Greek sculptures of deities in somewhat similar cultural context, we are surprised by the idea that there seems to be two distinct types of art, rather than the idea of their respective artistic values. That is, one

is art in which a god was created from the human form and the other is art that expressed a god in the shape of the human body. In the first case, artists were also religious figures. In the latter, religious figures were also artists. In the former case, they saw some divine mystery in every inch of the human body. In the latter case, they tried to give material form to mysteries they learned from the universe and life. The first begins from realism to reach the ideal; the other begins with the ideal and uses realism. When we recognize these two distinctive approaches, we realize that our Shō Kannon, despite the rigidity of technique of the lower body, demands straight away that we give it deeply meaningful and significant status in an international context.

I think the inclination to render a divinity in human form, culturally speaking, is analogous to rendering "India" in "Greek" form. And I believe that the Shō Kannon represents nearly the pinnacle of this tendency—perhaps its highest point. If we look at it that way, the Shō Kannon does not stand as the opposite of Greece; rather, it is a new child born with India as the father and Greece as the mother. Christian art is simply Shō Kannon's stepbrother born of the same mother but with a different father. A thought such as this arouses my interest no end.

I was surprised that you found yourself indifferent to the Yakushi Nyorai. At least, I thought, that soft and lustrous feel of the surface would surely be enough to attract your attention. Or, if not that, at least the gentle light glistening off the fingers on the right hand would, I thought. I eagerly wait for your return visit.

Your thought that the murals at Hōryūji could be intimately related to the Yakushiji triad and the Shō Kannon is very much worth considering. Postulating the same producer for all of these works as you did may not be so totally outrageous as to be out of the realm of possibility. I recognize that herein lies the key to understanding the secret of the pinnacle of Asian culture.

STORIES OF MR. S.

Concluding the long day, we all met for dinner. Mr. S., whom we met at Tōshōdaiji, joined us at the table. I had thought that someone like Mr. S., who spends day after day in that stink of lacquer and manipulates, quite literally, the Buddhist images in that old Buddhist hall, would be some unusual superhuman only remotely connected to our present times. It turned out, however, that he commuted to the temple every morning on a bicycle from a central part of the city of Nara. This revelation was as if, all of a sudden, someone in my fantastic imagination turned up as a real flesh and blood human being.

Mr. S. works with ancient makers of Buddhist images, as it were, through their works that are in need of repair. He told us a lot of amusing stories. Particularly interesting was the story about the graffiti drawings some sculptors left on the inside of the statue's base that date from the Tenpyō era. He showed us pictures of some examples. In them, human figures, animals and landscapes were crudely drawn, just like, well, graffiti. Among all the examples he brought, the best one above all was a drawing of a rather plump woman not unlike the design theme for a lady under a tree. In that hall, when the statue was being placed on the base, a man in the construction crew drew this picture of a beauty on the base—the vision of it came to my mind's eye vividly. It made me feel as if I were witnessing makers of statues in real life.

Notes

1. *Koryūki* is a temple record kept at the Katsuōji temple in Osaka. Empress Hashihito (?–665) was also known as Princess Hashihito no Himemiko before ascending to the throne. Emperor Kōtoku lived 597–654 and ruled 645–654.
2. The sculptor is also known as Yamaguchi no Ōguchi Atai or as Aya no Yamaguchi no Atai Ōguchi. He was a skilled sculptor of Buddhist images, who worked during the Asuka period. The *Nihon Shoki* states that in the tenth month of Hakuchi 1 (650), this man produced the sculpture. See the *Nihon Shoki*, in *NKBT* 68: 316–317. The Suiko style refers to an artistic style prevalent during Emperor Suiko's times (554–628, r. 592–628).
3. Kishi no Nagani (a.k.a. Chōtan) led the second Kentōshi mission with 121 students in 653.
4. It is not clear why Watsuji associates Shiva and Indra with sensual pleasures.
5. *Saiikiki* (The Great Tang Records on the Western Regions) is a record of Genjō's (Ch. *Xuanzang*) nineteen-year journey from Chang'an (present-day Xi'an) to India between 626 and 645.
6. I follow the commentators of *Nihon Shoki*, *NKBT* vol. 68 here, who believe that Tokara was the Japanese phonetic transcription of a kingdom called Dvaravati located in the Mekong delta of present-day Thailand. Shae is believed to refer to a large ancient Indian kingdom called Sravasti that flourished during Gautama Siddhartha's lifetime, and was located close to India's border with Nepal. According to other theories, Tokara (also Tochara, Tokhara) may have been a country that existed in present-day northern Afghanistan. As for the name Shae, it could refer to Sogdiana, an ancient country located to the west of China from about 2 c. BCE to 10 c. CE For the record of these foreigners drifting ashore in the *Nihon Shoki*, see the entry for the fourth month of Hakuchi 5 (654) in the *Nihon Shoki*, in *NKBT* 68:322–323. As to the various theories proposed about the identities of these countries, see the entry under "Tokara to Shae" in *Nihon Shoki*, in *NKBT* 68:575–576.
7. Kinoshita Mokutarō (1885–1945) was a highly regarded poet, playwright, novelist, and medical doctor.

Chapter 18

SPECIAL VIEWING AT THE NARA NATIONAL MUSEUM

We started the next day at the Nara National Museum.

Adjacent to the entrance of the museum, there was a small room where guests could be received. In the room there were old-fashioned chairs and a long rectangular table covered with a green tablecloth. The purpose of our visit to this room was to view old paintings. We had made an arrangement that when we asked for certain paintings the museum would bring them out and hang them on the wall for viewing.

When I arrived at the museum entrance with T around 9 AM, we found Mr. Y. standing there with an expression of consternation on his face. He said that the promised appointment time was 8:30 AM, and it did no good for us to be so late. And then he noticed that Z and his wife were not with us. He asked about them, obviously concerned. I said that they might not be able to come because they were so tired from the day before. He quickly became flustered and said that would be very awkward. "You just don't have any idea how much effort the museum, with its extraordinary generosity, has gone in order to agree to show us as many works as we wish. Not coming is out of the question." In the end, greatly disturbed, he volunteered, "I will telephone them." We had been lackadaisical up to this point, but observing how ruffled Mr. Y. became, it finally dawned on us that this special showing was granted on the basis of a delicate interplay of emotion. We stood there dumbfounded, not knowing what to do. As luck would have it, Z and his wife pulled up by rickshaw just then. Relieved, all of us entered the Nara National Museum through the main entrance as if nothing had happened.

A museum clerk greeted us cheerfully. After exchanging greetings and small talk, he asked what we wanted to see first. After hearing our first request, he said, "Ah, yes, there is no question about it, the Hokkeji triad. Yes, I do agree. It must be the first one." Muttering these words to himself, he left the room obsequiously. "What will it be next?" he then asked. "Oh, so you'd like to see the Twelve Celestial Beings paintings from Saidaiji? Did you say you'd like to see just one? Why, let me see, in that case, it ought to be the Suiten (Water Deva, Skt. *Varuna*) painting. And, then, what now? The Kichijōten of Yakushiji? Right, right, it is representative of the period. What's next? *Shigisan Engi*? Splendid choice, leave it to me . . . Do you wish to see any other paintings? That's it? I really don't mind, just tell me which one, and I will fetch it."

We were grateful for his kindness, but he was too solicitous and made us feel uncomfortable. Last year, I remember tagging along on a university field trip to the same museum. We were treated with kid gloves then, and I felt dissatisfied with the fact that ancient art was not shown to the general public. But, today, we were being given even more special treatment, so we could not help but feel all the more strongly that, at least for a few hours, we could monopolize the veritable treasures of the human race. Good art, I believe, should be treated with the goal of making it available for free enjoyment to those who want to enjoy it. Only then will the humanistic nature of the art come to the surface unhindered. In order for that to happen, these paintings must be exhibited at all times. Then, of course, issues of conservation need to be studied more seriously and eagerly. The national government should of course allocate more money to this. Unless a perfect system of preservation, including humidity control and prevention of oxidization, is found, we cannot afford to have these paintings that are designated as national treasures on display for any length of time. I understand that having them rolled up is the best way to preserve them, but it then goes counter to the very idea about how paintings are meant to be viewed. Thus, these paintings are shown in special exhibits only once or twice a year. Otherwise they are shown to a limited number of people who need to view them, knowing full well that unrolling and rolling paintings will damage them. This practice must be remedied as soon as possible.

The museum clerk reappeared loaded with three scrolls of various lengths that were weighing down heavy on his arms. He clearly misjudged the center of balance, so the short one was sliding off. So when he unloaded them on the floor, they fell to the floor with a violent thump. The man then untied the cord, but when he tried to hang a painting on a hook on the wall, the painting turned out to be unwieldy because of its size, so much so that he had to handle it rather roughly. We held our breath as we watched him and became a bit irritated by the sight as well. "This is no way to treat masterpieces of painting that are so easily damaged," I thought. "He has no idea about what it means to treat art with care."

This was the manner in which we as a group first saw the triad of paintings of Amida Buddha from Hokkeji.

THE AMIDA BUDDHA TRIAD OF HOKKEJI

The seated figure of Amida, which is the main image of worship, almost fills the painting. In the background, dark with a mixture of deep, saturated colors, one can see his pale, yellowish skin, with the pigment peeling off in places, and an evocative dark red robe. Below his body, a red lotus base is painted, which seems to receive the weight of the figure well. The dark hair of his head, with a green sheen, seems to hold down the whole composition ever so effortlessly. His obviously enlightened Buddhist eyes were painted with dark, orange pupils. They shine gracefully just below the dark, greenish hair, looking as if they were the center of the painting. The upper torso of the figure is covered lightly with a pleated robe in various shades of red. Just below the chest, one can see the hands held close together with the palms half-open facing the front, in a hand gesture referred to as the *seppōin*. This mudra seems to tactfully give an artistic point of tension to the lower base part of the figure, which spreads out.[1] Lotus flower petals are painted fluttering down around the body and hanging mid-air, silent and immobile, suspended in the painting. It seems as though this painting gives concrete form to a scene of "tranquility" that is all embracing.

The combination of colors is by no means complicated, yet the colors give off an indescribable profound feeling. The composition is also simple yet the shapes suggest some boundless substance. In these, I find an aspect of something eternal, sparkling. No matter, it is a world of the pure and immaculate. I suppose that that desire for living on the "Other Shore," that is, the realm of Buddhist enlightenment (or, to phrase it differently, yearning toward that eternal world by giving concrete form to an idea and adding color to immortal faith), must have produced this Pure Land. If a desire for the Pure Land of Amida Buddha were still alive in our hearts, the colors and shapes would doubtlessly impress us even more profoundly. It is said that great art will capture anyone's heart in any land, but if a masterpiece painting does not move a child, no one questions the child's inabilities. That is, if the viewer is immature like a child, as it were, and does not yet have the heart of a Buddhist, there is no question that such a person would not be able to experience the strong emotions from this painting that a Buddhist would feel. I feel a sort of emotional affinity to this painting but, at the same time, I am aware, though vaguely, that I still have room for a more profound emotional reaction to it (*see fig. 11, photo section*).

When I saw this central painting to the triad for the first time, it was hung inside a glass case, along with another painting on the right, which was of a boy with a flagstaff. On that day, I arrived at the Nara Train Station and straightaway went to the Nara National Museum. I then spent the day looking at sculptures dating from the Suiko to Kamakura periods. And, when the museum was about to close, I rushed to the area where paintings were displayed. This was when I first came across this painting. The gallery was a windowless room and somewhat dark. But the beauty of the boy with the flagstaff immediately caught my attention. And the loveliness of the white face (some of the white pigment had peeled off), the old and elegant flavor coming from the robe painted in light green and blue green which covered the boy, falling lotus petals that contrasted against a dark green background giving a sense of tranquility, the fluttering red flag that gave off a delicate sense of movement—I remained there motionless, transfixed. Noticing it was almost closing time,

I gave only a short glance at the painting of Amida Buddha, the central image of the triad, and left the room. The main impressions I received from this painting were that I thought the body was very flat and the face was uninteresting, though the eyes were striking. I didn't know then that this was the central image of the three paintings and the painting of the boy was just one of them.

That night, I was told by a friend that the painting with which I spent little time was a masterpiece among all Buddhist painting. I felt so ashamed that I didn't have the eye to recognize that. Two days later, I went to the museum determined to reexamine the painting—the central image of the Amida Buddha triad at the Hokkeji. Once I settled myself down in front of it and looked at it carefully, I thought the painting was, indeed, good. The reason why I originally thought the face was strange was because there was a damaged area on either side of the nose. I looked at it a little more carefully. Sure enough, the lines depicting the nose were painted elsewhere. Delicate, thin lines delineated both of the clasped hands in front of the chest. The red of the robe was very pleasing but it would be difficult to use words to describe it. The pleats, with their folds treated somewhat realistically, also had a very effective, agreeable effect. The positions of the falling petals were also just right. The painting, when all is said and done, possesses an extraordinary degree of simplicity and harmony. I stood in front of the painting totally captivated as I sank deep in intoxication.

I will never forget the experience on that day. Now, again, I stood facing this painting without being bothered by the damaged, fallen-out parts. It is not that these damaged parts did not register in my eyes. Even though I could see them, these damaged parts were discarded as my mind judged them alien to the artistic unity of the painting. At the same time, my eyes made an effort to pursue and find something in the painting that belonged to its artistic unity. The contour lines looked just as if they were made of wire, brimming with life, though the lines completely disappeared into the entirety of the painting's timeworn colors and were indistinct to the eye. One tends to focus on the lines and resist the timeworn appearance. The body of the monk was drawn solidly and with majesty but, since many of the colors were gone, the painting appeared insubstantial and hollow. In cases like this, we do our best to supply the more saturated colors by guessing at them from the body covered by the robe. This means that the painting's artistic unification has the power to restore itself to its original state. But this, of course, does not mean that the damaged areas of the painting were somehow repaired. If we don't focus on the latent, original artistic unity of the painting and don't do our best to come as close as possible to the power of recovery, we would no doubt notice the damaged areas more. In other words, it is possible that viewers of this painting, owing to the damage, will be unable to immerse themselves sufficiently.

DIFFERENCE BETWEEN THE MAIN IMAGE AND THE ATTENDANT IMAGES

The Hokkeji triad was reputedly produced at the beginning of the Fujiwara period. But I wondered about these works. First of all, does not the central image of the triad date from a very different time from the other two? Second, I wondered if there wasn't something more to the story, according to the temple record, that these paintings once hung at Empress Kōmyō's bedside.

I have always thought that the left and right paintings must have been produced at different historical times. When all three paintings were placed together as a group and lined up in a room, we could see very clearly that they were unmistakably made at different times. First of all, the contour lines were very different from each other. For instance, take the lines that express clouds. The clouds on which Amida Buddha (the center image) is riding were contoured with lively, rich warm lines to express the cloud's soft, billowy feel. The clouds on which the child (on the right) and a *kannon* and a Seishi Bosatsu (on the left) are riding were painted with rather formulaic, stiff lines. These lines are not as formulaic as the clouds in the painting of *Nijūgo Bosatsu Raigōzu* (Coming of Amida and Twenty-five Attendants) but they are moving in that direction.[2] Then, I looked at the lines for Amida Buddha's robe in the triad. The lines for the Amida look like they're laden with meaningfulness and are faithful to the property of the object being depicted. The line work for the other two images looks as if the brush had too much freedom of movement. Second, their overall tonalities of color are different. The uncomplicated harmony observed in the center painting is not in the other two. The painter's preference for colors looks rather different, too, so that we can almost detect different mental states of the producer. Third, the compositions are different. The right and left paintings depict motion and the center painting is still. These two paintings on either side do not give any support to the idea that, for example, Amida Buddha is about to move to some place on the clouds. That is, the paintings lack a compositional unity. And thus it is difficult to imagine how all these paintings could have been produced by the same painter who was so highly skilled as to paint the main image.

I am certain that some do not share my view about these three paintings, but I am just as certain that some feel the same way I do. Friend T agreed with me about my take on the contour line. The museum clerk, Mr. T., also agreed on the incoherence of the composition. One painter I know told me, in no uncertain terms, that the two paintings on either side of the main painting were added later when Pure Land Buddhism became popular. He was convinced that the Amida used to be the sole object of worship but it then became reinterpreted as Amida Buddha from the Western Paradise descending to welcome the believers. "Look at the mudra," he said. "The mudra is not the one used for welcoming the believers to the Western Paradise." Sure enough, the mudra he pointed out was not the one for welcoming. But then, Amida

Buddha descending over the mountain to take believers to the Western Paradise also showed the *seppō* mudra, not the welcoming mudra. So perhaps the mudra evidence is insufficient. In any case, I thought that this painter's judgment was basically correct.

THE LEGEND OF EMPRESS KŌMYŌ

So the issue then becomes that of the date when the main painting was produced. It is clear the other two paintings in the triad were attached to the main painting in the beginning of the Fujiwara period—and this much is clear from looking at the painting of the boy. Then, what about the main painting? Was it produced around the same time? Could it have been produced even earlier, for instance during the Jōgan period (859–877)? Is there no room for linking this painting to the painting in the legend that graced Empress Kōmyō's bedside? If it turns out that the painting dates from the Tenpyō period, we should expect some resemblance to the three images of Amida Buddha in the murals at the Hōryūji, but there seems to be just too many stylistic discrepancies between this work and the ones at the Hōryūji. If one looks at this painting after viewing Amida Buddha in the murals, for example, one notices a striking difference between them, especially in the way the bodies are treated. For example, just look at how hands in the *seppō* mudra are depicted in these two paintings. The hands of Amida Buddha in the murals are drawn with energy in a very assured manner. This painting, on the other hand, depicts hands, with webbing between the fingers, that are certainly not as vigorous; they appear feeble and vague. If we assume not only that the painting was produced in the Tenpyō period in the same historical period as the murals but also that it was hung at Empress Kōmyō's bedside, the painting in the legend could not have been this painting. Of course, we would expect that paintings that were not murals were also produced during the Tenpyō period, but we would also expect painting to be much more sculptural during this period in which masterpieces of sculpture were produced. Think also about the change of times. The artistic style of the Shō Kannon of Yakushiji developed into the Eleven-headed Kannon of Shōrinji in the Tenpyō period. Knowing this, we would expect that the mural paintings at the Hōryūji would have a successor who can compare favorably to the producer of the Shōrinji Kannon. But this painting of Amida Buddha does not reach that artistic level, although it is not as formulaic and rigid as the painting *Coming of Amida and Twenty-five Attendants*. In comparison to the *Coming of Amida* painting, the painting of Amida Buddha is suffused with a more majestic mood, as well as a fresher life-energy. Judging from these characteristics, this painting of Amida Buddha, I would venture to say, could be dated from the very early Heian period, the period when a delicateness and softness were just beginning to suggest themselves. If that is the case, then, it would have been the period of painter Kudara no Kawanari (782–852) or painter Kose no Kanaoka (?–?) and others, or perhaps some years earlier.[3]

This painting and the seated statue of Amida Buddha in the Lecture Hall of the Kōryūji share some common features. They are both in the exact same **posture**, even their nimbuses are indistinguishable. **Their facial features, except for the atmosphere they project**, are almost identical, including the plump cheeks and narrow and very slightly drooping eyes. Of course, if one looks at the details, there are differences, such as the way the ring fingers are bent—although the hands in both works sign the same mudra—the directions in which the clothing flows, as well as the size of the knees and the way robes depicted on the figures. On the whole, however, I think that the two works are uncannily similar to each other, so much so that the painting could be a sketch of the seated statue. So, I am led to think that this painting was produced in the same time period as the seated statue of Amida Buddha. This statue of Amida Buddha was made at the request of the main consort of Emperor Ninmyō.[4] It was the time when a number of Buddhist monks who had traveled to Tang dynasty China to study were returning to Japan. The statue shows very strong influences of the artistic features of dry-lacquer statues of Buddhist images, rather than Esoteric Buddhist art. In terms of the facial features, it seems that this seated statue served as the model for many Amida Buddha statues that were produced later. In a similar way, most probably, this painting **transmitted the old artistic style of the Tenpyō period** and also heralded a new taste.

If this course of reasoning is followed, one can see that my comments about the Eleven-headed Kannon at Hokkeji also apply to this painting. I would speculate that this painting, no doubt, has some connection to the Tenpyō period. There are some suggestive facts—there was an Amida Hall at Hokkeji. The center of Amida Buddha worship during the Tenpyō period was Hokkeji and it revolved around Empress Kōmyō. Unfortunately, the seated statue of Amida Buddha from this period was lost but, if we assume that some vestiges of it were inherited by the Amida Buddha image of the Kōryūji and that there was an Amida Buddha statue in Hokkeji, it is not outlandish to think that there was indeed another painting of Amida Buddha similar to this painting. In those days, the production of **paintings of Amida Buddha in the Pure Land** was widespread but it is indisputable that painted images of Amida Buddha were also created, as the records of Ganjin's catalogue of items he brought from China showed an item with the description "one painted image of Amida Nyorai." On the basis of this fact, I can be confident in saying that a better, more sculptural painting of Amida Buddha, which **resembled this painting**, could have existed during the last years of Empress Kōmyō's life. It is likewise possible that Empress Kōmyō, who was the period's representative of the yearning for the Pure Land of Amida Buddha, could have wished that a painting like the one I mentioned above be hung next to her deathbed. This painting, then, not only reflects the worship of Amida Buddha during the Fujiwara period but also passes down the vestiges of the painting at Empress Kōmyō's side at her death.

All the above speculations have little to do with the painting's artistic value. On the other hand, we may say that on the basis of the artistic value of this painting our minds are stimulated to love and daydream about the ancient times. Through this painting, we are able to see in our mind's eye a time when any number of paintings that were far superior to this painting existed.

When the people of Japan were producing paintings of Amida Buddha's welcome to the believers because of their aspirations for the Western Paradise, people in the West had visions of the paradise in Heaven and a vision of angels welcoming them. It is an interesting exercise to compare and contrast these two types of visions. To be frank, I think the Western vision lives more vigorously in us. The vision of Dante takes us easily to the life in the world of enlightenment, but the paintings of the Pure Land produced by our ancestors succeeded only in arousing our curiosity. When I was a boy, Rossetti's painting *Blessed Damozel* jolted me violently with both sadness and joy.[5] I also dreamed about the triumphant march and Rossetti's chance encounter with Beatrice in *The Earthly Paradise*.[6] But I must confess that never have I been moved by either the Amida Sutra that described the Pure Land or the images of bodhisattvas on a lotus base! The heart of that boy still lives in my adult heart. This difference in reaction may be explained by the qualities of two distinct visions, East and West. And it is here where we can also see differences as well as similarities between the cultures of the East and the West.

Notes

1. *Seppōin* is a mudra or hand gesture symbolizing the preaching by the Buddha, the mudra of preaching the Dharma.
2. Watsuji is referring to the painting at the Chion'in in Kyoto.
3. Kudara no Kawanari (?–?) was a court painter during the Heian period.
4. This main consort of the emperor was Fujiwara no Nobuko, who lived 808–871.
5. Dante Gabriel Rossetti was an English painter, who lived 1828–1882.
6. Rossetti pursued a romantic liaison with William Morris's wife, Jane Burden, and had an affair with her. He also used her as a model in his paintings. Here Watsuji makes reference to William Morris, *The Earthly Paradise*. 8 vols. (Hammersmith, London: Kelmscott Press, 1896–1897). Rossetti idolized Dante's *Divine Comedy* and Dante's eternal pursuit of Beatrice, Dante's lover. Consequently Rossetti painted a number of paintings with a female subject, paintings of his "Beatrice." There were three lovers / wives but none was named Beatrice; they were Jane Burden (later Jane Morris), Elizabeth Sidal, and Fanny Cornforce.

Chapter 19

PAINTINGS OF THE TWELVE CELESTIAL BEINGS AT SAIDAIJI

Among the paintings of the Twelve Celestial Beings at the Saidaiji, the Water Deva painting gave me a very pleasant impression when I last saw it. So I was looking forward to seeing it again today. When the painting was put up on the wall after much anticipation on my part, I found myself distracted by the chipped paint and brushed-in repairs and it was impossible for me to be quietly drawn into the painting. When I saw the deva painting for the first time, I had looked at it side by side with the *Ryōkai mandara* (Mandala of the Two Worlds), and a painting *Godaison* (Five Wisdom Kings) of the Daigoji.[1] And today we were putting the deva painting next to the Amida Buddha triad, which may have contributed to my disquiet. I am sure this Water Deva painting was a splendid painting when it was produced. Even looking at it now, I felt that the body was painted in such a sculptural way that, in this respect, the Amida Buddha triad is incomparable to it. Some portions of the painting are exquisitely beautiful. These include the faint smiles on the faces, the soft and round arms, and the small figures painted in a lower corner of the painting, just to name a few. The artistic style may be that of the western regions of China or perhaps the Hōryūji mural style. A great deal of shading was used. There is no doubt that this painting was produced in the early Heian period. If we assume that many Buddhist paintings at this time were produced in this style, I can see a glaring, difficult-to-ignore issue of explaining how painting underwent a change gradually from this style to the style seen in the murals of Hōōdō of Byōdōin in Uji, Kyoto. The painter of this painting used lines for an objective depiction of the object and eschewed anything like playful brushwork. If one looks at the colors in this painting, one can tell that the artist also paid close attention to the expression of the plane. If this sort of attention had become more keenly valued and the delicate irregularity of a plane had begun to be modeled with detailed shades of color, I am fairly certain that Japanese painting would have developed along a different path. What the Japanese tried instead was an acute differentiation of their sense of line, not of their sense of plane. While moods that a line could express developed finely in ever so minute, varied, and specialized ways, the representation of planes was disregarded, and any contemplation of the human body as a whole was totally eliminated. This is both a strong point and a weak point of painting of the Fujiwara period, as well as of Japanese painting (*nihonga*) in later periods. Well-known painters of this period, such as Kudara no Kawanari and Kose no Kanaoka, are famous for their tendency toward realism. And I would say that they pursued this realism by means of lines. If this conjecture is tenable, we must also acknowledge that, in addition to crediting Kawanari and Kanaoka as accomplished master painters in the first half of Heian period, they also played a role in setting limits to the destiny of Japanese painting.

THE PAINTING OF KICHIJŌ TENNYO AT YAKUSHIJI

The Suiten (Water Deva) painting was hung on the wall. And on the table, the museum clerk placed a framed painting of **Kichijō Tennyo** (a.k.a. Kichijōten, Kisshō Tennyo) **of Yakushiji**, encased in a glass box. It is a small painting, no larger than about 12 inches by 21 inches, but it is impossible to overlook it as it is **the only extant painting** from the Tenpyō period that was meant to be a stand-alone painting. In this painting, a beautiful plump-cheeked woman is painted in thick paint on linen, which is naturally much coarser than silk. The woman appears slightly bent forward. Fine, intricate lines and highly skilled shading, expressing light and dark, express the gorgeous robe that covers the body. I can say that the artist was able to express the thinness and softness of the garment perfectly, leaving no room for improvement. More specifically, I was drawn to the especially thin, soft garment clinging to the shoulders. It is apparently a gossamer-like thin fabric enveloping the body and it even suggests the flesh of the woman's body underneath. I might say that the round, plump face revealed by the pulled-up hair, as if to make a bun at the back, conveys a carnal beauty rather than a spiritual beauty. The round face, small mouth, thick lips, thick eyebrows that almost connect, and coquettish eyes—all these elements, if I were to exaggerate a little, are just too sensual. The slender hands and an adorable, delicate ear that is half-revealed only add to her sensual charm. In summary I would think that this is an earthly woman, not a heavenly deity. The dignity of beauty expressed in the Roman goddess Venus arouses in us a sense of reverence for perfect beings but, in this figure, unfortunately, no hint of that sort of dignity is detectable. On the other hand, if we regard this simply as a picture of a beautiful woman, it is flawless (*see fig. 12, photo section*).

Earlier in this book, I wrote that I was sorry that we did not have portraits of Tenpyō women, but this painting, though not a portrait, is quite sufficient to help the viewer to get a sense of what the manners and customs of the day may have been like. It is not too farfetched to think, for instance, that the painter of Yakushiji produced this painting modeling it after a noble woman. The woman in this painting possessed the beauty of a simple woman, painted with a melancholic and exaggerated sensitivity, much like women in the *Nihon Ryōiki*.[2]

Hence, I do not think we can say that this painting represents Tenpyō women in every respect. I say this because I think Tenpyō women as woven into the *Man'yōshū* love poems have a more intelligent aspect. What we can tell from this painting is only the external appearance of noble women during the Tenpyō period, who must have worn gently flowing, beautifully patterned garments and their hair up.

Assume for the moment that this painting represents the decadent spirit of the end of the Tenpyō era. Then we are safe to conclude that the decadence is no less advanced than that in the art of the Fujiwara period with regard to delicacy and aestheticism. Moreover, this painting is far superior to Fujiwara period art in terms of artistic energy, freedom, and serenity. Now if we compare the women's attire in picture scrolls dating from the Fujiwara period and the garment on Kichijōten, they are different not simply in terms of clothing taste but also in spiritual disposition. This difference, I say, is recognizable in *waka*, visual art, politics, and religion. In this sense this painting is endlessly fascinating and I never tire of looking at it.

The paint used for this painting is said to be water-based, but I saw some places in the painting that I suspected were not done in watercolor. I asked the museum clerk, Mr. T. He agreed with me. "I never say this to anyone, mind you. To me it looks like the painter used oil-based paint. If it wasn't oil-based, it wouldn't have been possible to paint like this," he said, as he pointed to a shaded area of the figure's clothing. If we are right, then it appears that the idea of painting with oil-based paint on linen was not passed down to the next generation, or at least not to a significant degree. This possibility alone made me feel all the more sorry that only a very few Tenpyō paintings still remain with us to this day.

KICHIJŌ TENNYO (KICHIJŌTEN) OF INDIA

Another issue inherent in this painting is how the main theme was treated. Kichijōten traces it origin to the Mahasri (also known as Laksmi), a female deity of Brahmanism, who is said to bring beauty and wealth. Her husband is Bishamonten (also called Tamonten), which is one of the Four Guardian Kings of Buddhism. The Bishamonten is also known as Kubera in Indian mythology, a deity associated with wealth. These deities were absorbed into Buddhism in ancient times and appear in the *Konkōmyōkyō Sutra* (Golden Light Sutra), so they were apparently worshiped from ancient times in Japan. During the Tenpyō period, in particular, this sutra was used for the welfare of the entire people of Japan and, for this reason, the worship of Kichijōten was also very widespread. So the central government's distribution of paintings of Kichijōten to provincial *kokubunji* temples around the country at the end of the Tenpyō era can be seen as a part of this prevailing trend. The reason why these paintings were produced was, it is thought, because there is a passage in the sutra that reads "Paint a picture of Kichijōten and adorn the canopy for it properly all around." Now the question before us is why this Kichijō Tennyo, who, standing before the Buddha, addressed him in order to obtain a promise that the believer of the Konkōmyōkō Sutra would receive food, clothing, bedding, medicine, and all other material necessities, and who was mainly enshrined to pray for good harvest, was expressed as a woman in that way. Judging from her Tang clothing, it is indisputable that the iconography did not follow the original clothing rules of India. Could it be that some artists in the East read the *Konkōmyōkō Sutra* and conjured up that sort of woman merely from their imagination? If so, to the painter, this female deity of happiness, who "was able to give all manner of pleasure to any number of people," was a voluptuous and graceful woman first, and a deity second. Without this notion, it is not easy to comprehend that this picture of a beautiful woman is in fact Kichijō Tennyo. A female Indian deity is represented here as a mere beautiful woman. This is an extraordinary discrepancy.

After the protocol of ceremonies and various rules were set and became more influential in Esoteric Buddhism, Kichijō Tennyo was no longer to be represented as simply a beautiful woman. Later, Kichijō Tennyo would stand erect, sign the correct mudra, and wear complex decorations from India on her head and chest. Because of the fragrance of the mystery of Esoteric Buddhism emanating from the woman, she makes us feel we are looking at a nonhuman. But the Kichijō Tennyo is, without exception, a plump woman in Tang-style clothing. So it is a stretch to say that she gives the impression of an Indian deity. In this type of representation of Kichijō Tennyo, the sculpture at Jōruriji provides an excellent example, but the reason that statue is outstanding is because it is a statue of a beautiful woman, not of a deity. Since Esoteric Buddhism is a mixture of Indian native beliefs and Buddhism, one might expect that a statue of Mahasri ought to be half-naked in the Indian style, but the fact that it is clothed in Tang clothing must show, it seems to me, that this sort of tradition of representing the figure as a beautiful woman had been well established before Esoteric Buddhism became widespread. In comparison, Suiten (Water Deva) is a deity that became popular with the advent of Esoteric Buddhism, so much so that it preserves much of the flavor of Indian native religions and beliefs. Suiten was originally called Varuna, the water deity, in Brahmanism and serves as the guardian god of the west at the meeting of all Buddhas and Heavens of Esoteric Buddhism, which is represented in a mandala. Suiten, however, never became "a genuine guardian god" of Buddha, unlike the guardian gods of the Tenpyō period. It still retains much of its status as a deity of water.

KICHIJŌ TENNYO OF THE TENPYŌ PERIOD

Now a new question. Can the Kichijō Tennyo of Yakushiji, which is the fountainhead of the very particular tradition described above, be said to represent all Kichijō Tennyo in the Tenpyō period? We cannot answer this question using extant objects, but I would venture a guess and say that other Kichijō Tennyo in that period were probably like this painting. It is difficult to believe that an iconographic rule that "Kichijō Tennyo should be a girl of about fifteen years of age, of light complexion, and appear in heavenly clothing decorated in a delicate manner," was widely known at that time. Since we see that the painting of Kichijō Tennyo in Jōruriji holds a red jewel ball in her left hand, we know that the *Konkōmyōkō Sutra* was not the only source. Could it be that the fact that that sort of figure could be drawn rather freely shows that those cumbersome rules and protocols did not yet exist? If there were iconographic rules for Kichijō Tennyo as a superhuman and that formula were to be followed, it would have been unthinkable to simply change it to a beautiful woman in contemporaneous clothing, even if Tenpyō painters felt that they could express themselves freely.[8]

The *Nihon Ryōiki* tells of an episode about Emperor Shōmu which may shed some interesting light on this point.[3] It is a story about a statue of Kichijō Tennyo at a mountain temple in the area of Chinuyama in the province of Izumi. The story goes as follows. A man from Shinano Province who was residing at this temple in order to seek enlightenment became totally enamored with Kichijō Tennyo and prayed to the deity day in and day out for a chance to meet a beautiful woman like the woman in the statue. Finally, one night he dreamed a dream in which he married this statue of Kichijō Tennyo. The next morning, he visited the statue and discovered that it wasn't merely a dream—they in fact had consummated their marriage. Deeply ashamed, he begged her forgiveness, saying that he only wished to meet a woman like Kichijō Tennyo. I am fairly confident that an episode like this in the *Nihon Ryōiki* appears only in connection with Kichijō Tennyo. This sort of episode makes us think all the more about what sort impression the image of Kichijō Tennyo was likely to give. The harboring of worldly feelings toward a work of art such as the man from Shinano experienced, especially during the era when the image was an object of worship and possessed an anthropomorphic power, cannot be considered to be simply a case of possessing an impure sense of beauty. So the fact that a statue based on a painting that might induce this sort of danger to man was actually and deliberately produced makes me wonder if there wasn't a dark, unknown side.

Well, naturally, one cannot put too much stock in the veracity of an episode such as the one related above. It is possible that monks, after receiving certain impressions from reading the *Konkōmyōkyō Sutra*, made up a parable for teaching purposes. According to the speech made when Kichijō Tennyo was in an audience with the Buddha, she vouched that

---

[8] After this visit, I saw a Kichijō Tennyo statue in the Sangatsudō at Tōdaiji in an altar that had been closed off, which turned out to have outstanding modeling. The statue was damaged considerably but the head, torso, and legs were still solidly intact. It was truly a magnificent statue, on par in quality with the Bonten (*Brahma*) statue (this is described as Nitten [Sun Deva] in the temple records) that stands in the same hall. This one sublimates the statue in the shape of a woman to a female deity. However, it is evident here too that female attributes were emphasized quite a bit, treating this as a "heavenly female being." I think the painting at Yakushiji was produced from this type of statue.

she would appear in the dream of a believer. She said,

> If a believer wishes to see me appear in his dream, he should cleanse the room, or otherwise find a spacious, quiet suitable place. Draw a circle with cow dung and set up an altar. Burn sandalwood and conduct a Buddhist service. He should then set up one main altar, suspend a canopy above it, decorate it properly, and place vases of flowers in this area. Recite the aforementioned prayer and pray for my appearance. I will then think of this person, observe him, and enter his room. I will go to my seat, and receive his prayer and offerings. After having done this, I will let him see me in his dream.[4]

We cannot be sure that this Kichijō Tennyo's pledge wasn't an opportunity that made her believers see her appear in their dreams. If we bring in sleepwalking as an aid to our imagination, then it would be not at all surprising if the story about the man from Shinano were true.

Now let us compare this painting to the painting of a folding panel depicting six beautiful women, each under a tree, in the Shōsōin storehouse at Tōdaiji.[5] It is not certain whether the screen was brought from abroad, but for our purposes, we may be able to judge the standard for beautiful women using this as a guide. According to this yardstick, the woman in the Kichijō Tennyo painting at Yakushiji is unmistakably a beautiful woman. It appears to me that the women on the screen seem to show no small amount of spiritual nuance. Some of them, at least, seem to emit a spiritual disposition from their foreheads that I regard as most suitable for the intense love poems in the *Man'yōshū*. In this respect, our Kichijō Tennyo is much more suggestive of sensuality and it is there, I think, where a special meaning of Kichijō Tennyo is to be found.

THE *SHIGISAN ENGI*

A work called *Shigisan Engi* (The Legend of Mt. Shigi) is one of the most famous of all Heian period painting scrolls. It represents the pinnacle of accomplishment in the tradition of line drawing. It is truly astonishing to witness the skill of a painter who could indeed draw figures and movement with only a few simple lines in such a sure-handed manner. It does give a keen sense of realism, but I am more astounded by the uncanny way of capturing objects. For example, the Great Hall of Buddha is represented by no more than the pillars and doors visible from the front of the building but, at the same time, they are more than enough to faultlessly present to the viewer its grandiosity and beauty. Of course, we must admit the painter somehow had to work with the requirement of fitting the Great Hall into the given width of the scroll, which surely led to abbreviation. If we align our thinking here with the perspective of someone going to the Hall to worship the Buddha, we can say that the capturing of just the essential characteristics of the Hall, the skill to express people's sentiment, and the beauty of the Hall in a unified whole is extraordinary.

This sort of highly deft technical facility of suggesting the whole with very little, I think, is among skills specific to the Japanese. In painting, this skill is applied to **any number of areas,** including picture scrolls in the Heian period, Song-style painting, literati-style painting, *ukiyoe* paintings and prints. This could be extended to include decorative paintings in the *rinpa* style. In literature too, representative examples include *waka* and haiku but also traces are found in scenes in novels as well as plays. If I take this a little further, I might also say that rakugo and Buddhist parables are manifestations of this sort of characteristic. The tendency for contemporary art to put a very high value on technical facility may be a tradition springing from this characteristic of using something small to suggest the whole. But at the same time we mustn't ignore the flaw of putting a premium on technical skill was also responsible for the lack of insufficient development of the subject, for it turns out that such shortcomings have also hindered the development of technical skill in the true sense of the word. This is because the development of a highly vigorous technical skill that naturally became required by the subject development was not possible at this time. This presents us with one fascinating aspect in the history of Japanese art and literature.

Notes

1. The Mandala of the Two Worlds is the most important mandala for Shingon Esoteric Buddhism in Japan. The two worlds are the *Kongōkai Mandara* (Diamond Mandala) and *Taizōkai Mandara* (Womb Mandala).
2. The *Nihon Ryōiki* is a collection of 116 Buddhist stories, compiled around 823, written in Japanese *kanbun*.
3. This story also appears in the *Konjaku Monogatari* (Tales of Days Gone by) in *NKBT* 24:570–571. See also *Nihon Ryōiki,* volume 2 of 3, story 13, *NKBT* 70:214–217. The event is said to have taken place in the area of the present-day Osaka prefecture. Though Watsuji states that the temple was called Chinuyamaji, the *Nihon Ryōiki* simply states that it was a mountain temple in the area of Chinuyama.
4. The quoted passage comes from the Sovereign Kings of the Golden Light Sutra, *TSD* T0665.16.0439c21. There are several passages that are sufficiently similar to the one Watsuji quoted in the Golden Light Sutra that have already been rendered into English. One translation of what one must do to witness the Kichijō Tennyo, referred to as Shri below, is described as follows:

   > Whether in a monastery or forest retreat, they should clean that dwelling, draw a circle of cow dung, offer incense and perfume and provide clean seats. Scattering loose flowers on the ground, they should be seated. Then in that very moment the great goddess Shri will appear and remain in that place. She will ensure there is never poverty in that house, village, city, town, monastery or forest retreat. That place will be replete with all equipment, gold, jewels, wealth and grain.

   The pdf of the Golden Light Sutra is available in digital form from http://kaladarshan.arts.ohio-state.edu. The quoted passage comes from p. 46.

5. This screen is called *Torige ryūjo no zu byōbu,* in six panels, each depicting one beautiful woman in Tang clothing under a tree. The screen is damaged, paint has peeled off, and only the contour drawing in ink is now visible. The screen is recorded in temple records and appears in the record for the first time in 756.

Chapter 20

THE HILLS OF TAIMA

At Mr. Y.'s urging, we hurried to the train station, but the train did not arrive until much later. Mr. Y. had rolled up the *Shigisan Engi* scroll very quickly so that we would not stray from schedule but it now appeared that he did so too proficiently.

We changed to a smaller train at Ōji that would take us toward Wakayama. By this time, the sky had become overcast with clouds, and perhaps our mood reflected it. I did not feel very cheerful. Perhaps because of our dispositions, the rugged mountains of Taima visible from the train window, thick and verdant with foliage, looked rather gloomy and perhaps even a little bit scary. This dark and dreary feeling continued to overcome me even after we got off the train at Takada and made our way toward Taimadera.[9] We walked on a flat path wedging between rice fields and cultivated land. A question then occurred to me. Is it only limited to a child's simple and naïve mind to personify a mountain? The Taima Mountains were many-faced, so much so that they seem to stir up in me the mood of a fairy-tale world. In comparison to other nearby mountains in Yamato, which evoke cheerfulness and tenderness, these rugged mountains, deep and dark with trees, seemed as if they hid some sort of special life energy and held deep secrets. In the past, the temple in Taima became associated with a sorcerer by the name of En no Gyōja and became enmeshed with the legend of Chūjō Hime. This no doubt resulted from this general impression with which the temple is associated.

THE LEGEND OF CHŪJŌ HIME

A single road extends through a field planted with wheat, which was now turning golden. At the end of the road on the far side was Taimadera. The scenery was so perfectly pastoral, and

[9] At the time of this writing, it is most convenient to take a train to the Taima Station on the Ōsaka Tetsudō Line. The temple is located at the distance of half a mile or so from the station. This mountain which I referred to as the Taima Mountains are more properly referred to as the Nijōzan Mountain. The temple itself is on the east side at the foot of a smaller mountain called Marokoyama, which is located due southeast of Nijōzan proper.

it had the effect of taking everyone to a world one thousand years ago. Between lush trees, we caught the glimpse of a tower dating from the Tenpyō period. If I let my thoughts roam, I could feel my mind enveloped by a fantastic, otherworldly mood as if a haze were consuming me.

> In a vast field at the foot of a mountain,
> Wheat grows tall and green.
> Rapeseed flowers scent the field,
> On a path in the middle of the field,
>   She makes her way to the temple of Taima; its pagoda visible from the distance.
>
> Milk vetch and dandelions softly caress her feet,
> She trudges through, flashing white ankles,
> Delicately and sprightly.
> A breeze in the foothills is such a bother,
>   She makes her way to the temple of Taima; its pagoda visible from the distance.
>
> The face of Princess Chūjō, perspiring,
> Gives off the lustrous fragrance of a maiden,
> Voluptuous and round.
> Annoyed by her straggling hair,
>   She makes her way to the temple of Taima; its pagoda visible from the distance.
>
> The Princess raises her head and surveys the tower,
> O how pitiful her mournful eyes!
> Such seductive gloom in the eyes!
> The eyebrows frowning in melancholy,
>   She makes her way to the temple of Taima; its pagoda visible from the distance.
>
> The nursemaid and the lady attendant, silent,
> Follow the Princess, hanging their heads low,
> Walking quietly, stealthily,
> Sighing sighs of sorrow,
>   She makes her way to the temple of Taima, its pagoda visible from the distance.

This princess is Chūjō Hime (747–775), the heroine of a miracle legend.

> She had a resolute nature and she was scornful of man's luxury and extravagance. She preferred to be surrounded by deep, silent woods. Then finally she settled in a quiet place in the temple with a wish only to live in the land of Amida Buddha. On the fifteenth day of the sixth month of Tenpyōhōji 7 (763), she shaved her head and made all preparations to go to the Western Paradise.

This is how she was portrayed in the *Kokon Chomonjū*.[1] It may be that this legend was born not very much before these stories were compiled.

It was this story about this beautiful nun that completely occupied my mind even after we arrived at the temple. Chūjō Hime wished to witness Amida Buddha in the flesh with her own eyes, as she was the most passionate believer in Amida Buddha. Being in Amida Buddha's presence was the most earnest desire burning in this young woman's heart. How could Amida Buddha not show himself to this most devout believer? Suddenly, a Buddhist priestess materialized beside Chūjō Hime. The priestess ordered one hundred bundles of lotus stems to be brought in, and she made thread from the fiber in the stems using her own hands. Another beautiful woman, a celestial being perhaps, began weaving an exquisite mandala with the lotus thread. She worked from eight at night to four in the morning. For light, bundled rice straw soaked in oil was used. When the mandala was completed, the beautiful woman left. The priestess explained the meaning of the mandala to Chūjō Hime. After the priestess' explanation, Chūjō Hime asked, perplexed, "Who are you? And where do you come from?" The priestess answered, "I am Amida Buddha of the Western Paradise. The one who wove this? It was my disciple *kannon* Bodhisattva. We came here to give consolation to your sorrow."

Of course this was all Chūjō Hime's vision, the vision of a dreamer. When Chūjō Hime checked the mandala, she found the tapestry was not woven from lotus thread; it was made from hemp and silk. That is, it was untrue that the fabric was woven from lotus fiber. But wouldn't it have been obvious for everyone, even the ancients, that lotus fiber couldn't be woven into fabric? Why did it have to be lotus fiber? Because Chūjō Hime's vision required it. No matter; even if the fabric were not made of lotus fiber, the power of her vision would not diminish.

THE TAIMADERA MANDALA

In the eerie and spooky semi-darkness of the Golden Hall of the temple, I spent a long time looking at the mandala, which was separated from me by wire netting. To me it looked like a copy of a mandala made during the Higashiyama period.[2] As a tapestry painting, it is by no means outstanding. But the design itself was most interesting. As others in the group were looking at the metalwork on the dais and commenting on the Kamakura period skills in metalworking, I had my binoculars pressed on the wire netting. It is a bit difficult for me to believe that a pictorial representation of Amida's Pure Land in the Tenpyō period would have this composition. On the other hand, however, if the mandala that gave birth to the legend of Chūjō Hime had been of this type, the aspiration for the life on the "Other Shore" as represented by this princess legend would have been none other than an aspiration for a **perfect life of blissfulness** that manifested itself in a very straightforward way. If that was the case, then, would it be possible to say that the mandala represented the entirety of the Princess' state of mind, which was supposed to have been "scornful of man's luxury and extravagance" (*see fig. 13, photo section*)?

On the near side of this mandala, in the lower section, there is a pond with lotus flowers in bloom. Small buddhas sit comfortably atop the flowers. Among the flowers, there appear to be what looks like two treasure boats floating quietly, with small naked men (or children?) poling each boat. Small buddhas sit on intricately designed daises of the boats. In the water around the boat, children appear to be playing, as they are climbing up and down the lotus flowers gesturing with their arms. Two verandas that jut out to the center of the pond from the bottom of the painting appear to be stages drawn (or woven) using the technique of perspective representation. And on these verandas, there is depicted two scenes of dance music being performed. In the larger of the two scenes at the bottom, eight female musicians, in two rows, are seen playing such instruments as flutes, recorders, zithers (*sō*), reed mouth organs (*shō*), cymbals (*dōbatsu*), lutes, etc., and providing accompaniment to two female dancers. The musicians' clothing is all in Indian style, the same as what a *kannon* would wear, that is, neck ornaments and loose garments wrapped over the naked torsos. In the other, smaller scene, musicians also line up in two rows. The musicians (children?) appear to stand with cymbals (*dōbatsu*) and lutes and play accompaniment for two dancers. As for their clothing, they are naked, other than a piece of celestial clothing draped over their shoulders. What type of dance are they dancing? The larger scene of the two appears to portray court dance (*bugaku*) but the smaller image seems very much like foot dance (*butō*). None of the dancers in either scene uses a mask. An exquisitely decorated and balustraded dais extends out near to the center of the pond, which commands a straight-on view of the musicians' verandas. On this dais, a large Amida Buddha sits in the center with thirty-seven attendant buddhas. This Amida Buddha is the center of the picture, and so far as this center of the painting is concerned, all architectural lines converge to the center, somewhat like a representation of perspective. But it is not that individual shapes are portrayed using the correct perspective, so it is safe to say that the designer of the picture was hardly knowledgeable of the laws of perspective. Behind the main image of Amida Buddha, on either side, Chinese-style, multistory buildings appear, in which one can see celestial maidens, who look like ladies-in-waiting, walking to and fro. One can also see tables laden with sumptuous dishes; elsewhere, one can see celestial maidens walking through a corridor holding a tray of epicurean delicacies. In two open-air verandas on either side of the painting, an Amida Buddha sits. In addition, buildings float in mid-air above the central image of Amida Buddha; they look comfortable as they softly hang in the air. Many of the buildings are topped with a tower with a round top, and this apparently reveals an influence from Byzantine architecture. Celestial beings appear to enjoy flying around the rooftops of these buildings, and they are some of the most enjoyable elements of all. The way their clothing flows in the air and their many different shapes make their flights look naturalistic as well as giving a strong impression of empty space.

Every inch of the scenic beauty of this paradise is thoroughly artificial. If a Chinese tyrant were to build buildings or gardens for his own pleasure, I would imagine that they would look like this. There is nothing in this picture that hints at the detachment from worldly desires supposedly attained by Sakyamuni. All decoration is very gaudy, as if to suggest decadence and, in addition, every type of pleasure remains within one's physiological sensitivity. So bad is this that if we were to replace all images of Amida Buddha with those of tyrants and change all images of bodhisattvas into those of beautiful women, no contradiction, I am sure, would be noticed. The eternal aspiration of the people who have this sort of illusion as the life on the "Other Shore" is, after all, no different from an attempt to extend the present world perfectly into infinity. And what's more, the perfection of the present world lies in the same general direction of that which tyrants planned for themselves. In essence, it is materialistic and not spiritual.

THE VISION OF THE PURE LAND

This type of illusion began, indisputably, in India, judging from the fact that it is based on the *Kanmuryōjukyō Sutra* (Infinite Life Sutra), but if I were to venture a guess, what the Indians imagined in their mind's eye would not have been anything like this. I do not know if pictures of the paradise were represented pictorially in India, but the vision that appeared in the sutra was something that embraced the vast universe and is therefore impossible to reduce to a painting. Only music, I would say, comes close to describing the impression it makes. The Pure Land cannot be visualized by a mortal—in each of the eight ponds in the paradise, **6 billion** lotus flowers each made of seven Buddhist jewels are flowering. Each lotus flower is a true circle and is **480 *ri* across**.[3] More than **50 billion jeweled buildings** are built on each of the sections of the land, which itself is covered with jewels. And in each building an innumerable number of celestial beings are playing *gigaku* music. The lotus dais on which Muryōjubutsu (Amida Buddha) sits is made of 84,000 lotus petals, and even the smallest of the petals measures as much as 10,000 *ri* on each side. Every one of these descriptions goes well beyond the human ability of representation. Thus, when this sort of vision came to China and became a pictorial representation of the paradise, it was inevitable that it would become a vision of China-specific palaces in which ascetics were said to live. To the extent that the jeweled towers were rendered in Chinese-style, they also added a mood for *Yūsenkutsu*.[4] Indeed, this painting looks like a picture of Amida Buddha in *Yūsenkutsu*.

But when it was brought onto Japanese soil, the viewer would automatically add a bit of exoticism. The exoticism may compensate for the lack of poetry written in this picture. So, for all we know, it might have given an impression of a pure, clean mood. However, there is no way around the fact that happiness in the Pure Land is represented as an idealization of pleasure in the present world.

I would think that the roots for deep religious requirements are found in the place where an imperfect human existence aspires to live a perfect life. It may very well manifest itself as a heart which desires a **more** complete satisfaction of sensual pleasures. But if Chūjō Hime had been so devout as to become scornful of man's luxury and extravagance and thought nothing of throwing away the conveniences that came with her position as a daughter of a state minister and the privileges of a beautiful woman, it would have been impossible for this woman to be in that simplistic frame of mind. For stimulating her religious exultation, an image of Amida Buddha or an image of a *kannon* would have been far more appropriate than a picture of the Pure Land with full particulars. Being artistically outstanding also means that an artwork would have been an effective inducer of religious ecstasy. Thus, I'd say that the fact that Tenpyō sculptures were more valued than the likes of pictures of the Pure Land was not without good reason.

Chūjō Hime may have in fact had visions of Amida Buddha and a *kannon* related in the *Nihon Ryōiki*. But this event occurred before the mandala was woven, **just as the legend has it**. So, importantly, her vision did not occur because of the mandala.

I think that the pictorial representation of the Western Paradise during the latter half of the Tenpyō period was likely not as cluttered as this one at Taimadera. Judging from the fact that the Amida Pure Land depicted in the mural painting of Hōryūji was incomparably simple in design, I cannot imagine that people in those days would have been blind to this. The pictorial representation of the Pure Land is hardly related to the one described in the sutra, and the three main deities—Amida and two others—are the central theme of the painting. As a painting, this may arguably express the mood of the Pure Land better than the sutra. A painting of the Pure Land, where ponds and tall buildings and such are depicted, is no more than a boneheaded idea of monks and such who do not comprehend what impact a painting can serve. The embroidered tapestry that adorns the wall of the Great Hall of the Buddha at Tōdaiji in Nara, as one might expect, was not anything like this. The tapestry measured 54 feet by 39 feet, and in it only one slender standing image of *kannon* was portrayed. Earlier I hypothesized that a simple image of Amida Buddha, similar to one at Hokkeji, must have graced Empress Kōmyō's bedside, and I would say that a simpler painting like this would have been held in higher esteem in those days.

There were a number of sculptures at Taimadera. We saw most of them. We also did not fail to see architecture there. I will omit all of it here.[10]

I bought some picture postcards. I discovered that the temple holds a Buddhist Ceremony and Reenactment of the Welcoming to the Western Paradise. This reenactment that

[10] I omitted this in the text of the book but the must-see buildings at this temple are the pagodas dating from the Tenpyō period. The East Pagoda is older, and the West Pagoda may have been built as late as the Kōnin period (ca. 700–ca. 800). Both of these are beautiful. As for sculpture, they have all been extensively repaired. The main image of worship, Miroku Bodhisattva in the Golden Hall, and the Four Guardian Kings (Shitennō) date from the Tenpyō period. Many others date from the Jōgan and Fujiwara periods. Also famous at this temple are the library at the Naka no Bō (a small temple in which the founder of the temple is enshrined) and a tearoom.

Eshin Sōzu (a.k.a. Genshin, 942–1017) began during his lifetime is still being practiced.[5]

KUMEDERA AND OKADERA

By the time we arrived at the Takada Station, it had begun to rain lightly. It didn't look like the rain would come down any harder, however. So it was not unthinkable to visit such temples as Kumedera, Okadera, and others of the old capital in Asuka, but by the time we boarded the train and got comfortable, none of us had any courage to get off at Unebi, as we were tired from the hard schedule of the last few days. Mr. Y. did his best to persuade us several times to see the Unebi Shrine, if nothing else, but none of us wanted to get up.

THE CAPITAL CITY OF FUJIWARA

From the train we could see Unebiyama and Kaguyama on the right, and Miminashiyama on the left. The train ran between these lovely low hills. The capital city of Fujiwara in ancient times and the old ruins of the capital in Asuka were within miles of each other. The scenery around here was quite different from that of Nara in that it was much more tranquil, and I thought I could sense the feeling of our ancestors who loved this area. Once upon a time, many temples and pagodas towered high between those hills beyond Kaguyama, where the new cultures of the Suiko and Hakuhō periods (ca. 600–700 CE) spawned. If we go back even further in history, we can say that the human emotions of our ancestors during the times of legends, be it love or hate, is etched deeply into these mountains and rivers. The fact that this was the original place for the **Yamato peopl**e is apparently closely connected to the peculiar characteristics of the Yamato clan. We could see the gloomy-looking Tō no Mine Mountains on the right, then the train changed direction toward the foothills of Miwayama Mountain. This mountain plays an important role in ancient legends, and it is very fitting for the land of Yamato—it is gently sloping with long foothills and shows off superbly its soft roundness that is not unlike *kofun*, ancient burial mounds. The worshiping of mountains, because deities were thought to reside there, was common throughout ancient Japan, but it occurred to me that it was not perhaps rare for a people to admire a mountain like this with its gentle, round curves. I have a hard time imagining how people in those days could feel any **supernatural power** from a mountain in this shape. Instead, doesn't this reflect people's vague admiration for a perfect object or an object in flawless harmony? If I am right, this mountain too is not unlike a book in ancient legends.

MIWAYAMA AND THE CITY OF TANBA

On either side of the train line to the north of Miwayama, any number of small burial mounds could be seen. They were small in comparison to some other giant ones, but they were nonetheless full-scale, old-style burial mounds. There is no other place in Japan where so many of this type of *kofun* are clustered in one place. As Mr. Y. explained all of this to us, he got sidetracked and began talking about stories of excavating *kofun*, searching for ancient art, and the like. Apparently, many of these *kofun* have already been excavated. He told us one particularly interesting story about the grave robbing of a famous *kofun*. This *kofun* had been considered to be a sacred place and no one had set foot into the area, so the grave robbers were able to excavate the site in broad daylight. One day a man found a large stone coffin. With his heart thumping and expecting a large amount of treasure, he plied open the lid. He eyed a fair-complexioned woman lying there as if she were still alive. Completely startled, the man fell backward on his rear. During that infinitesimal moment between the time he saw the woman and the time he fell on his rear, the color of the woman changed and she disintegrated into a pile of ashes. Naturally, no one else witnessed this. The man who saw the woman caught a fever and died a short while later.

Not all excavations ended in success. For example, an extraordinary amount of treasure was rumored to be buried under the foundation stones of a three-story pagoda called Kamo no Tō, now moved to Sankeien architectural park in Yokohama. When it was being moved to Yokohama, a large number of laborers were hired to excavate the site where the pagoda had stood. Everyone was tense with expectations of finding the treasure. The supervisor of the workers was totally consumed by the worry that some worker might do something other than totally honest. The first day, the workers found nothing but rocks. On the second day, more rocks. More of the same on the third day. They dug dozens of feet, but nothing of value was found.

As we listened to Mr. Y. recounting these stories, our train passed the city of Tanba. It is the city in which the new religion of Tenrikyō is headquartered. We see a number of what appear to be large meeting halls all over, so much so that they give off a spooky feeling. A train line that Tenrikyō paid to have laid starts from here to the city of Ōji. Even though we are just passing through on a train, we could still feel the Tenrikyō atmosphere. Then I couldn't help but wonder, "How would I feel if I were to actually set foot in the town?" That the founder, Nakayama Miki (known as Omiki), was born and raised here, not far from Mitsuwa Mountain, titillated my interest considerably and made me think of the tradition of female zealots, who were common in ancient legends. To be sure, Omiki's religion is not something we can ignore when we consider Japan's religious temperament. But what are we to make of the fact that this new religion of Tenrikyō, however powerful it is locally, has little to do with the current mainstream of Japanese culture? My knowledge of Tenrikyō is meager and comes from just a few pamphlets, but according to them, I have little doubt that the founder's faith was genuinely religious. Why then does it not take root and grow vigorously in today's culture? It may have to do with Japan's national disposition, that is, the propensity for degeneration but, even more, I wonder if it is not because the religion is not rooted in a world religion. The religion of Shinran (1173–1262), for example, shares something in common with Christian sentiments, and when this connection is made, it shines with a new brilliance. Likewise, Tenrikyō too will have to metamorphose itself as Japanese culture undergoes transformation. My speculation, which is totally unfounded, is that if the old woman founder Omiki had come from a Christian background, the craze would have been able to produce a far greater movement. Japan would have then produced a saint and would have been able to establish the Christian faith firmly in Japan.

Notes

1. The *Kokon Chomonjū* is a collection of parables and religious stories in twenty volumes, compiled by Tachibana no Narisue and probably completed in 1254. The book contains about 700 stories. For the original version of the story, see *Kokon Chomonjū, NKBT* 84:72–74.
2. The Higashiyama period is a mid-Muromachi period, roughly from 1460 to 1490.
3. Each *ri* in the Japanese measure is about 4 km; in Chinese, a *li*, from which the Japanese *ri* comes, is considerably shorter, now at about 500 m to 600 m. The sutra itself says "12 *yojana*," in which *yojana* refers to the distance a king may travel in one day. Obviously, the precise equivalents to our own measuring units are not important in this context.
4. The *Yūsenkutsu* (Ch. *You Xian Ku*) is a Tang dynasty novel written by Chō Bunsei (Ch. *Zhang Wencheng*, 658?–730). The main character loses his way and finds himself in a cave where ascetics live. He is entertained by two female ascetics and spends a night of pleasure.
5. In this ceremony, held annually on May 14, the hall in which the mandala is displayed is used as the location for the mock Western Paradise. The Shabadō Hall located close to the Niōmon is designated as the world of humans. A long bridge is erected between these two. Twenty-five people dressed as bodhisattvas and their attendants in period clothes walk across to the human world and take Chūjō Hime to the Western Paradise. This reenactment is still being practiced at the time of this translation.

Chapter 21

THE SOUTH GATE OF TŌDAIJI IN THE MOONLIGHT

In the evening, the sky cleared and at night the moon brightly shined. I intended to visit N. and walked leisurely through Nara Park. In the wide expanse of the park, I saw not one soul or one deer; the park was drenched in bright moonlight.

It was this night that I was totally astonished by the sheer size of the South Gate of Tōdaiji. The two roof layers of the gate were silhouetted dark against the moonlit sky, in such sharp contrast that it looked as if the gate had been bitten out of the sky. Underneath, from between the tall pillars of the gate, I could see the hazy moonlit sky, framed by the opening, which made its extraordinary size and grandeur all the more apparent. All this was totally fitting for the gate of all gates. I looked up at the roofs of the gate and thought, although it is hardly necessary to think this, "This is a magnificent gate!" As I thought this, I became more aware that I was here all alone, casting only a small shadow on the ground. When I walked up the stone steps as I approached the gate pillars, I felt as if I were coming out onto the stage to perform, as it were. I began to feel a formal, tense mood.

I stood on the raised base of the gate. When the Great Hall of the Buddha came into view, I was hit by a new surprise. The roof of the Great Hall was the same blue as the sky but was tinged with a bit of rusty color. The roof appeared to float weightlessly as if it were melting into the haze of the sky. The window in the center of the building, that supremely ugly feature, was not visible hidden behind the Second Gate. What I could see was only the top part of the roof which seemed abnormally high. The long roofline, which I always thought was too short, did not look offending tonight.[1] The shoe-shaped *shibi* ornaments at the either end of the ridge line emitted a glimmer of golden reflection ever so faintly, so very faintly indeed, that, in appreciation of this serendipitous beauty, I felt like joining my hands to worship it. The faint gradation of blue and gold colors, which looked almost as if they were melting together and dissolving away, was created by the moonlight. But even if it received help from the moonlight, I could not help but think that the Great Hall of the Buddha, capable of impressing me this much, was indeed great architecture. The root of this grandeur may only come from its sheer size, yet I think that the spatial size of any work of art may be able to provide it with an effective opportunity to be great. At least the huge amount of human power that it symbolizes strongly impressed us with a particular sort of power.

THE ORIGINAL TŌDAIJI COMPLEX

I stood there a moment and imagined what Tōdaiji must have been like in the beginning. The South Gate, first of all, must have had a vast empty lot around it. If it had stood in a small space as it does now, the effect of its great size would have been nullified. If one looks at the gate from a track field located to the right of the gate now (east), one notices an extraordinary life energy that is palpable only when enough distance is allowed between them.

There was a large, level open space between this South Gate and the Second Gate and, on either side of the space, a seven-story pagoda, with a height of about 320 feet, towered over the temple. It is not easy to visualize its height but it is about twice that of the five-story pagoda of Kōfukuji and about three times that of the five-story pagoda of the Hōryūji. The area of the temple complex was accordingly large and had to be at least ten times that of the Hōryūji pagoda. Enclosed corridors were built all around the towers, with four gated entryways, and the floor space of the corridors was apparently larger than the area of the Great Hall of the Buddha. If we think about a sufficient space for these towers and the space around them to bring them out to their best advantage, we can see that the Great Hall of the Buddha, which now stands tall as a single major building, was no more than a small part of the temple complex. Though the Great Hall of the Buddha's height and depth are identical to the original, the width of its front facade had been decreased to a mere two-thirds of the original. So the beauty of it now is no comparison to that of the original, not to mention the size of it. If we draw a rough sketch of the original building and compare it to a drawing of the reconstructed one, we would think the current one looks less than half as big as the original. The front of the original building was longer, so the entire building would have projected a much more stately presence. We can perhaps think of the balance of the roof—the proportion of the length versus the height—as similar to that of the Golden Hall of Tōshōdaiji. The enclosed corridors were double—in two lanes, as it were—not single like today's. In addition, behind the Great Hall, a lecture hall, three living quarters for the monks located to the north, east, and west, a storehouse for sutras, bell towers, a dining hall, and such were located. The lecture hall and the dining hall were large buildings, almost the same in size, erected with seventeen pillars on the wide side, and the buildings had six sides on the exterior.[2]

More than several thousand Buddhist monks and nuns must have lived in the complex. There were professors, students, and priests, as well as seekers of Buddhism. All subjects were taught there, including sculpture, painting, music, dance, theater, poetry, and of course, religion.

I walked passed the pond on the way to the Second Gate and, as I walked uphill on a tree-lined path to the Nigatsudō, I thought about the spiritual undertaking and how it was implemented in actuality. The power of Tōdaiji, as it would unfold later, was symbolized in a group of monk-soldiers called *sōhei*. This great temple complex was burned down as a result of the actions of this secular force. Why did this university not continue to develop as a university? Why was it that this tradition of spiritual undertaking did not sustain a more vigorous life? Then I thought of the conclusion of a friend who studied the *sōhei* system that "the Japanese can easily be corrupted."

THE SANGATSUDŌ IN THE MOONLIGHT

When I climbed the steps to the top to reach the Sangatsudō, my eyes, now accustomed to the darkness of night while walking among trees, were shocked by the bright moonlight again. The Sangatsudō was brightly lit by the moonlight and shined. What brilliance! That serene roof, seemingly weightless, shone silvery in the light. The beauty of eave lines that punctuates the silvery plane of light! The left half of the eave line is Tenpyō and the right hall dates from the Kamakura period, but tonight even that difference made them seem to be in harmonious transition. I could see along the edges of the building's eaves and right underneath the eave line the timeworn and familiar vermillion paint that had faded to gray. It looked whitish but indistinct and fuzzy and faint like a dream. Among these, the white of the walls rang out the sound of silence in clarion brightness as well as forlornness. This is nothing other than art, art that cleanses the soul (*see fig. 14, photo section*).

A CONVERSATION WITH N

The house where N was staying was at a place where the house commanded a splendid view as if it were part of this art all through history. If one were to step out of this house, then the Sangatsudō would be right there as if it were one's own. One can appreciate this building freely at any time of the year: in the moonlight of the crescent moon, in the starlight of a dark night, in the morning light of a dawning sky, in the morning fog, in the evening mist, in the darkest of nights. One can see this building when the rain hits it, when it is blown by winds, without missing any of it.

N sat in the living room, having been entrusted with the house after the people who lived there had gone to see a motion picture. He had a fountain pen, a notebook, and a guidebook out on the table. I told him that I had visited the Taimadera. Then he asked, "What did you think of those wind-bells hanging from the eaves of the tower?" "I didn't pay any attention to them, so I can't very well say," I said. I asked him why he wanted to know. "Well, it just that I wanted to ask you if you liked their shape. I prefer the one at the Hōryūji. The bell strikers that hang inside them are also different in shape. If you look from the underside it looks like a cross." I dropped my head in disbelief, which also had an effect of calming my high spirits.

N had seen almost all the ancient temples in Yamato. The only one he hadn't seen was Murōji. So, naturally, he knew a lot about temples that I had never heard of. He said, "I have decided not to take a single step out of Yamato because, as you know, if I did there would be no end to this quest." "If you have seen them so many times in such detail, don't you want to write a book of your impressions?" I asked. "No, no. I do make notes in my notebook but I treasure my impressions for my own use and cannot very well waste them on a book." He sounded as if the image he got from the old art was now beginning to gel into a work of art. "If you are going to Hōryūji," he continued, "Would you look at the inside of the Yumedono? Carefully? The reason I ask is that since I had made so many requests the last time I was there, I apparently irritated the monk. So it is rather awkward to go there again, and I have suppressing my desire to go back." He then said, "Yes, all I need to know is how the ceiling and the pillars appear at the Yumedono."

On the way back, he walked me to the South Gate. As we walked, he told me how monks lived their daily lives now. He was very knowledgeable about things like that owning to the fact he himself spent a long time at Mt. Hiei. Besides, he had a type of enlightened sense of finding comfort in living a simple life unaffected by his surroundings, not unlike that of someone who had decided to accept the Buddhist precepts. So he showed considerable empathy toward the seekers of Buddhism, and he sounded impassioned when he told me about the plight of a man who left his wife and children behind and accepted the life of a Buddhist. The episode he related about a man living a monastic life who went crazy sounded truly ghastly.

"There is someone like that at this temple, too," he said. "Sometimes he will just jump out from behind a grassy place." He then looked at me and said, "Don't worry about that at night, though. Just like a deer going back to its den at night, he apparently goes back home when the time comes."

We parted on the stone steps of the South Gate. As I walked down the steps, looking back at him, I said, "If I have some free time, will I be able visit you again?" Standing under this gate, bathed in the moonlight, he said, simply, "If we are so destined, we will."

Notes

1. As Watsuji explained earlier, when the Tōdaiji was reconstructed in 1709 for a second time, the Great Hall of the Buddha was considerably reduced in width (from twelve pillars to eight on the south side) but the height was kept identical to the original design, giving the building its current appearance.
2. According to the original drawing, the lecture hall and the dining hall measured 182 feet by 96 feet.

Chapter 22

HŌRYŪJI

The next day, Mr. F. joined us and we set out to visit Hōryūji the first thing in the morning. It was a fine, bright day and we all felt lighthearted. As we walked on the country road leading from the train station to the village, which was no more than a mile and a quarter, my heart began pounding with excitement as we moved ever closer to the five-story tower visible far in the distance. I felt so delighted; it was as if somehow my heart began throbbing in anticipation or as if I was becoming happier by the moment.

When we stood at the South Gate of this temple, I was already steeped in the mood of the ancient temple. I walked on the white sand into the compound. When the ancient Inner Gate came into view, a particular sense, so specific to Hōryūji, again captured me with a tight grip. I began to experience intoxication and felt as if my body was wafting.

IMPRESSIONS OF HŌRYŪJI INSIDE THE INNER GATE

I once wrote about about my impression of Hōryūji to my friend Kinoshita Mokutarō.

> If I might tell you about my personal sensation, it was like this. When I entered past the Inner Gate, at the very moment the Golden Hall, the tower, and the corridors came into view, I felt a very transparent, sound-like sensation sweeping through me. When I visited the temple the second time, I did not feel it as strongly as the first time, but I sensed the same sensation, and the same sort of shock ran through my body. It was not unlike a sensation of numbness. Immediately after that, I felt a sensation of eerie calmness as if "I were in the midst of a forest, a forest of souls." When I first felt this sensation, I thought I was hallucinating. And then I thought about the possibility that the timeworn vermilion paint of the old buildings, half peeled off, could have made me feel its presence in that way. But after reflecting on it later, I found that the memory symbolized by this sort of a transparent, sweeping sound is invariably and tightly connected—and this is unmistakable to me—to the memory symbolized by the faded vermilion color and innumerable window lattices of these old buildings. The sharply shaped latticework, weathered and darkened, seen all around the Golden Hall, the pagoda, and the corridors, all make innumerable neat, vertical parallel lines. One could see, through the windows of the enclosed corridors, the light on the outside as well as the green foliage through this latticework. The parallel

> lines of the latticework and the overall age-worn vermilion color: these two things **in particular** seemed to be linked to that whoosh sound. When I visited this temple the second time, I very carefully studied this awe-inspiring display of vertical lines and savored the very reason for the aesthetic shock I experienced.
>
> But the beauty was not something the latticework alone possessed, independently from all others. To tell the truth, latticework was no more than an accessory to the totality: the beautiful rooflines of the Golden Hall, the uncanny balance between the upper and lower roofs, the bold harmony of energies around the building's eaves. And the tower—the delicate tonality achieved by unifying all five different levels into one singular line, by harmonizing the roof pitches and their balances. There, undoubtedly, lies the main energy that impacts us. That quiet and solemn feel of the entire complex is strengthened, in a strange sort of way, by the latticed windows. And then, it appears to me that the old harmony of blue patina and faded vermilion comes beautifully alive and is enhanced by the dark gray of the latticed windows.
>
> I would suspect that if the temple buildings didn't look so old, they wouldn't be so beautiful. But I suppose this line of speculation is meaningless, because we have only one building in front of us.
>
> I am sorry that I never had a chance to hear your opinions about these buildings. If we suppose that this represents an architectural style that came to Japan through Korea and it is a good example of the architectural style of China's Six Dynasties period, I cannot help but let loose my imagination on the basis of this building. What about the architecture in Khotan during the life of Kumārajīva (344–413 CE), the wooden architecture in northwest India during the time of King Kanishka (r. 127–151 CE)—as I imagine these in my mind, I realize that we don't have a lot to go on. A comparison of the roof of Greek residential buildings and the roof of a building in Chinese-style architecture occurred to me. What about the similarities between the worship hall Stein excavated in Khotan and the wooden structures of China? I have given some thought to that too. I wonder if Japanese-style walls weren't first developed in Central Asia. Or could they have been an invention of the Han people? I have so many questions of this sort, so I look forward to hearing your reports on your trip to the Continent.

This letter is an example of how I tried, perhaps not very successfully, to express my overall impression of Hōryūji as clearly as possible, but I now think that the moments on which my impression are based are probably more complex. Every time I look at the temple, though, the complexity is lessened, as if a knot were being undone slowly. The handrail around the building with the reversed swastika lattice design lends this building a mood of foreignness, and the reason why the building feels so alien is that the handrail is extraordinarily high. Because the roof is considerably curved and its angles sharp, at least in comparison to Tenpyō architecture, the roof also serves as a source of the foreign mood it imparts. The roof of the Lecture Hall, built during the Fujiwara period, has much less curvature, but when we compare it to that of the Golden Hall, the overall feel is quite different, though the angles are probably only very slightly different. This difference is somewhat like the difference between images of Buddha created during the Suiko period and those during the Fujiwara period, and that difference can be clearly sensed here. If we compare this Golden Hall with the Golden Hall of Tōshōdaiji, I am confident that we can find the same sort of architectural differences between them that is very much like the difference between the Suiko and Fujiwara sculptural images of Buddha. If we can describe the Golden Hall of Tōshōdaiji as "integrated," this Golden Hall seems to exude a peculiar sort of beauty—a passionate and sharp sort of beauty. And it seems that this comes from the sharp angles of the building (*see fig. 15, photo section*).

The fact that many of the Hōryūji buildings are topped with half-hipped roofs also has to do with this phenomenon. In comparison to hipped roofs, which are simple and clear, the roof of the Golden Hall gives an impression of complexity, probably from the half-hipped roof. This is perhaps also the reason why this building feels very Chinese. I do not mean to say that all buildings with hipped roofs exude the same feeling. It is those sharp angles and the curvature that contribute to that feel.

ENTASIS AND GREEK INFLUENCE

The fact that a rather prominent entasis has been introduced to the pillars of this building is of particular interest to us since it suggests an influence from Greek architecture. Though we cannot say with any degree of certainty that the Chinese could not have invented this slight convex curvature of the pillars, we can say that this feature has not been seen in Han-style architecture. If we suppose that Buddhism was transmitted along with Greek architectural styles, then it is easy to comprehend that this architectural feature was applied to the element of a building to which it could be applied most straightforwardly. And thus we can agree fully with those scholars who think that this is one example of Greek art that has made its way to the East. If a variety of buildings from the Han dynasty period to the Tang dynasty period remained in China, we would be able to trace unequivocally how art styles of the west of China influenced East Asian architecture due to the transmission of Buddhism. But the architecture that can provide evidence for this line of thought remains only in Japan. If that is the case, the architecture of Hōryūji can be said to be a rare microcosm in the history of Far Eastern architecture. In that microcosm, the convex pillars shine like jewels, as a very prominent architectural phenomenon. If I were to say one more thing, it would be that this architecture tells of its influence from the west of China, evidenced not only in the entasis of the pillars, but also in the entire architectural structure and mood. Before the Six Dynasties period, there was no prominently religious building like this in China. Towers were built, but they were for giving people pleasure. No hall of worship was built there to enshrine heavenly deities, as far as we know. Thus all the great buildings there were palaces and government buildings. So we must acknowledge that the building of halls only for worship by making use of China's architectural style and the building of a pagoda as an object of worship were transformative events in architecture even though they did not result in a great deal of change in style. It was at this time that Indian stupas turned into Chinese-style multi-story pagodas. If we looked at it in another way, we can say that Chinese-style multilevel towers acquired meaning as an appendix, as it were, to the Indian style. But a question may arise—could the Chinese, who did not erect buildings that stimulated their desire for worship, have built this type of majestic tower from their own creative volition? Wasn't there a moment where a new spiritual disposition opened closed eyes? If there was such a moment, it was the artistic spirit arriving from the west of China that used an old style and created a new unification. Thus, the halls of Buddhism in Japan are a product of a molten mixture of Western and Eastern cultures dating from the Six Dynasties period and later. This is no different from the fact that sculptures too were a product of the artistic spirit from the west of China. This cultural blending gradually gained prominence beginning in the Six Dynasties period through the Tang period. The Golden Hall of the Tōshōdaiji, though it lacks entasis, is very Greek in spirit. If we think the high buildings depicted in the Taimadera mandala are Chinese in style, this Golden Hall at Hōryūji is almost not Chinese at all. The early manifestation of non-Chinese style is probably shown in the architecture of Hōryūji.

THE DYNAMIC MOVEMENT OF THE FIVE-STORY TOWER

Another discovery I made on this day was the dynamic beauty of the five-story pagoda. Since towers dating from the Tenpyō period were all but destroyed, if we were to look for a beautiful high tower, then no pagoda compares to this one. Since I have a very soft spot for pagodas, I did my best to savor the beauty of this pagoda from every conceivable angle. I started from the foundation platform of the Inner Gate, to the foundation of the Golden Hall, to a spot next to the stone lantern beside the Lecture Hall, to the foundation of the Lecture Hall, and so on. Then I returned to the spot next to the stone lantern, went around to the right, and walked toward the Inner Gate, moving alongside the corridor. Then I went underneath the eaves of the tower itself, and walked round and round around the tower looking up all the while, until my neck became sore from trying to maintain my head upward. I learned during this stroll how this tower moves in such a beautiful manner (*see fig. 16, photo section*).

The tower is tall. Thus the distances between my eyes and any of the eaves of the five roofs are all different in five ways. The balustrade at each level and the interlocking brackets are likewise different in five different ways. The eaves, balustrade, and brackets are of different distances from each other as well. All the other innumerable and intricate shapes were separated from my eyes at all different distances. When I am still, this fact is not that important. When I am still, for instance, the balance of the five levels is the major issue. What is important, first of all, is when the eaves stick out more, the column that supports the bracket system is set lower and the roof is not pitched as much, and the height of the tower as judged against its ground area shows at least a minimum of balance. Second, the eaves become increasingly smaller as they approach the top story, and the eaves for the second and fourth stories seem to slightly recede; thus, the tower, as it tapers near the top, is given a slight variation, which also makes it more beautiful. These are the important elements. Therefore, when I begin to move, this balance and any number of the shapes that comprise the totality of this tower change their orientation and begin renewing their distances to my eyes. But the speeds in which that can change are not uniform. The ones near my eyes appear to move faster and those farther away, up in the tower, for example, move only slightly. So when I keep moving, some of the eaves move quickly and others slowly. Of course, this is not limited to the eaves; the same applies to the balustrade and the bracket systems. The tower as a whole appears to move in a very complex way, but that complexity is unified into an immobile balance and the towering posture of the tower. In addition, this complex movement of the tower—when, for example, walking around the tower maintaining the same distance from its center, when walking toward the tower, when moving farther out from or approaching the tower at an angle—all comes in different aesthetic flavors. The angle of walking could be large or small and was entirely up to me, thus each aesthetic flavor was distinct from another. Of course, I walked irregularly; thus the tower's movement was likewise ever-changing. The consistent tonality in that ever-changing elusiveness, or perhaps I should say, the fluid, ever-changing tonality, was something that gave no hint whatsoever of ever giving way.

This movement, as may be suspected, was always accompanied with color. The roof tiles of the five roofs were close to weatherworn bluish green and, here and there, above and below the roof, metal fittings were seen in patinated bluish green, that is, I mean the old metal fittings on the ends of the protruding rafters that lined the eaves and those fittings on some parts of the balustrades. The gray of the balustrade, the white plaster walls, the vermillion paint on the supporting pillars and the bracket systems, and the yellow paint on the cloud-shaped bracket arms appeared sandwiched between two roofs. In particular, the vermillion paint was darker and more saturated on parts of the jutting eaves that were closer to the tower and protected from the elements and lighter where it was closer to the tip of the eaves. And, on the parts where the arms of a bracketing system were very complex, the vermillion remained, while the lower on the supporting pillar, the more faded or peeled off the paint became. At the very bottom of the tower, in this party of colors, there were the gray of the *mokoshi* roof fashioned out of wood board, the faintly brown, gray latticework in an infinite variety of delicate lights and darks, right under the *mokoshi*, and a bright white wall that partitioned these two elements uncompromisingly. All these colors moved at different speeds, crisscrossed each other, and ran to and fro, as if all were fluid.

What surprised me particularly was the impression I received when walking around the tower under the eaves as I kept my eyes trained on the roof tips. The apparent speed at which each roof moved was very distinctly different. It looked as if the tower rotated as it danced. Then a thought occurred and I said to myself, "This beauty from movement can't possibly be experienced with Western architecture, because eaves don't protrude as much."

Chapter 23

THE WALL PAINTINGS OF THE GOLDEN HALL

The access into the Golden Hall is located on the east side of the building. As soon as we entered through this door, we took a left in order to go to the front of the main image of worship.

When I came next to the Yakushi Nyorai and the attendants, I looked to the west without really knowing why. And this view took me by surprise. I straightened up, because, from between dark pillars and a line of old statues, I could see the brightly lit Amida Buddha statue, and even the hands, on the west wall. I had never expected to see Amida Buddha so clearly, at such a distance from the east wall. Little did I expect that the beauty of the image that is so sculptural could be so clearly visible at this distance (*see fig. 17, photo section*).

We didn't even take time to look at the Yakushi triad but hurried to the wall painting of Amida Buddha's Pure Land. In my mind, this is the pinnacle of painting in all Asia. The paint has peeled off considerably but even the white spots showing the base, where paint has peeled off, seem to enhance the fresh, vigorous appeal of the painting. A singular thought occurred to me: "I need to think nothing, standing before this painting. It is complete and lacks nothing. All one needs to do is to look at it and be intoxicated."

In the center of this painting, under a beautiful, round canopy, Amida Buddha sits in meditation pose in front of an ornate screen, the design of which is rather unusual. His dark-red robe has large waves of folds and it runs from his shoulders to the arms. It then softly covers the knees and flows down to the lotus dais. The shading on the folds, which appears to depict the play of light and colors, also expresses the ample limbs very effectively. The robe appears rather angular when covering the large shoulders, and soft and intricate when covering the upper arm. It looks taut yet pliable, especially when covering the knees, bringing the soft fleshy feel of the body underneath to life. The material of the robe, appearing to be soft yet not lacking elasticity and heft, is clearly shown in the treatment of it around the edge of sleeves and the folds around the shoulders. The breathtaking beauty of the hands, clasped in the *seppō* mudra—there is something very special here. Judging from the current condition of the painting, it is impossible to tell if there was shading on the hands, but the contour lines remain intact, and these uncontrived lines so irresistibly and perfectly depict the hands. From a modern man's point of view, they could be too rough a sketch, but in this daring boldness and roughness we can feel the power of the ancient painters. Behind the slightly curving and unembellished lines, an infinite amazement and love for the mysterious beauty of human hands seem secretly hidden. Criticizing these lines, someone once said lines expressed **no emotion** and "they are almost all meaningless; they no more than form a shape and serve as the boundaries for coloring." I wonder if it was because of this type of trenchant criticism that line drawing degenerated to the level of artistic play. Now, I argue that this classical, vigorous art must be regarded as the true ancestor of our art. The spirit embodied in these hands must open a new artistic path in the realm of line drawing. The heart that feels deep love toward the hands, the image's **left hand** in particular, is the same heart that is critical of present-day *nihonga*. The beauty of these hands, however, may not simply have come from the beauty of line drawing. The colors that are peeling off in places and the white spots around the painting that show where paint has fallen off are very effective as they make the bald spots appear as if they had been filled with thick paint. This impression of thickness must come from the energetic, linear contouring, but I am sure it owes also to the bald spots in no degree amount. If that is indeed the case, these are divine colors. It is a divine revelation that would serve nihonga painters well.

The face is not as damaged as the hands. The colors of the face must have undergone change, as they appear darkened. It looks like the peeled-off paint has the same effect here but it could be that the face was painted originally with this type of shading. If we look at the nose, which is painted very skillfully to show that it is straight and prominent, I think one will agree that the paint had peeled off just at the right spot that coincidence alone cannot explain. But, in any case, this face is truly majestic. The eyes that open only slightly are deep as if they were staring fixedly at infinity. The tightly pursed lips are strong as if to express the most unyielding willpower. The world of enlightenment achieved through meditation no doubt manifests itself in this figure very concretely. I think that there is no painting of a beautiful human face anywhere that can compare to this painting, which is so completely devoid of human feelings but filled with all-transcendent purity. The loftiness of figures in Western paintings is much more human. Even among the wall paintings of India where Buddhism was born, no painting impresses the viewer with purity as much as this.

The nimbus of this Amida Buddha is also exquisite. I think this painting impeccably expresses the sense that the nimbus radiates from the body and floats around it. It is spiritual light, not the type of light visible to the eye. Thus, this light is nearly transparent, quiet, never obscuring what is behind it, and it envelops the body of Amida Buddha, without obscuring anything behind him. This is how and why this nimbus perfectly embodies the very meaning of a nimbus. I felt a powerful moving emotion from a nimbus for the very first time, from this painting.

Next to the main image of worship are two attendant deities, Kannon Bodhisattva and Seishi Bodhisattva. They both stand with their hips turning toward the main image of worship but their shoulders are pulled back quite noticeably, as if they were drawn by the main image but, at the same time, as if they were maintaining independence. Their heads, too, are tilted slightly and directed toward the main image, just as if they were gazing at a spot in the space just below the space the main image occupies, in the lower part of the painting. If we were to draw a line for each deity's line of sight, from their faces to a point just two feet in front of the main image, it is easy to see that the sight lines converge to this point and the upper body of the main image will appear to be supported by these two crossing lines. The upper bodies of the attendant deities create an impression of supporting the main image from both sides by means of their bent arms on the inside parallel to the sight lines as well as by means of the postures of the deities that respond to the angles of their arms. The postures of the attendant deities perfectly represent their function as "attendants." I am fairly confident that no tighter composition of a painting of Amida Buddha and two attendants exists.

If we examine the attendants individually, they are even more attractive than the main image. The image they project is feminine, while that of the main image is masculine, but the purity projected through their femininity is no less pure than that of Amida Buddha. Someone once said, "I have never seen a painting of the triad that is so very human-like and, at the same time, so superhuman." This comment encapsulates the impression of this painting very well. Their faces are indeed fine-featured female faces, but their majesty and nobility and the expression of samadhi worn on their still faces are not those of earthly mortals.[1] The beauty of the exposed, round arms, the immaculate chests on which neck ornaments hang, the waists and hips wrapped in gorgeous fabric, the sensuality seen through thin, translucent fabric over the thighs all look as if the figures are deep in the same *samadhi* as the main image. To be sure, this is a type of magical beauty. The right arm of the Seishi Bodhisattva, slightly bent, and the right hand of the *kannon* holding a stem of lotus, which is held close to his side—if I look at these two items alone, they are enough for me to feel a type of religious ecstasy.[2] The painter, I think, no doubt felt faint movements of eternal life in the human body. And that feeling is expressed here as a spiritual ray of the body.

Indeed, I contend that this painting is the true picture of the Pure Land. Here we see no pond of jewels, no bejeweled buildings or trees. Nor are there celestial beings flying about in the void.[3] We simply have three images—Amida Buddha, Seishi Bosatsu and Kannon—and some small decorative figures on the top and bottom edges of the painting. Yet, what is represented by way of these beautiful human figures is perfectly fitting to be called the Pure Land of Amida Buddha. It has been advanced strongly that art can bring enlightenment, if only temporarily. A painting like this takes full advantage of this property of art and seems to link it to permanent enlightenment. And the painter appears to have been aware not only of the fact that what would make this endeavor successful is to express perfectly the beauty of spiritual light, but also that the aim of the painting was not to paint the scenery of the Pure Land but to create **meaningful shapes that suggest eternal life**. Therein lies the reason why this work is magnificent as a religious painting.

WALL PAINTINGS IN THE GOLDEN HALL AND THE AJANTA WALL PAINTINGS

Various scholars have pointed out a similarity between this painting and the wall paintings of Ajanta. To make such arguments, the Ajanta paintings of bodhisattvas and this painting of *kannon* were compared. They are indeed "extraordinarily similar in every respect," and these similarities include the posture of the waist twisted in one direction, the clothing on the waist and hip, the transparency of the fabric showing what is underneath, and so forth. The Ajanta paintings of bodhisattvas are indeed closer to this Japanese painting than the heavily clothed, erect posture of bodhisattvas from Gandhara. So it is probably correct that the tradition of this kind of painting is in the line of the Gupta dynasty tradition of painting. This theory can be further corroborated by the neck ornaments and clothing patterns. But being Gupta in style does not mean that it is not in the tradition of Greek art. I would suspect that Gupta art was the sublimation of Gandhara art. Or perhaps we can see it as a renaissance of the Greek spirit in India. The tendency in India for **worshiping idols** is a custom transmitted from Greece. And we can say that Gupta-style art may be thought of as a form of art that developed this Greek art into an Indian style. So it stands to reason that we could conclude that this wall painting is in the tradition of faraway Greek art.

This opinion is given more credibility by the differences between this painting and the Ajanta wall paintings. If one examines the *kannon* carefully, the way the figure's waist is twisted is not the same as is observed in its Indian counterpart. In India, the effect is far more pronounced, so much so that it looks as if the figure were inflicted by a disease. This painting, however, is closer to the ways in which Greek sculptures slightly twist their bodies and yet exert a strong sense of stability. If a smaller amount of twisting had been observed somewhere in the western regions of China, we would be able to assume less influence from Indian style and therefore a **purer** exhibition of Greek style.

THE DIMINISHING INFLUENCE OF INDIAN STYLE

There are other significant differences, the first of which is the marked unification seen in the composition. I think this sort of brilliantly unified design would not be seen in Indian paintings. It is not impossible to attribute this change to the influence from Greek spirit, but it is equally plausible to credit the Chinese. The Chinese had a knack for simplification. Or, if that wasn't the case, it was perhaps that the mood for harmony inherent in the Greek spirit stimulated the Chinese spirit of simplification, which may have resulted in this unification of composition. The next difference is the fact that the mood of the painting was made pure and transparent. In Indian painting one often sees elements of stifling and chronic titillation of the senses. There, regardless of how majestically Buddhas and bodhisattvas were painted, they simply do not express the same superhuman feel, the characteristic of being detached from human emotions. The attendant bodhisattvas in the Hōryūji painting show this distinction quite clearly, but I think the same distinction can be observed in small images of bodhisattvas (?) in the painting. The small half-naked figures painted above Amida Buddha's shoulders are in the same body posture commonly found in similar figures in Ajanta, but these are much more innocent and cheerful looking. There is no evidence for a fixed, persistent, abnormal interest in the breasts and bellies. It is interesting to think about where this change to less interest in these areas of the body might have come from. The Greeks loved sculptures of the female body but never so much that their appreciation exceeded the boundaries of the beauty of life. The Indian taste, by comparison, was clearly much more seductive. When the art in which these two cultural moods were mixed was transmitted to the east, the second was thrown out and the first was retained, which, so far as the tradition of the **worshiping of idols** is concerned, can be seen as a renaissance of the Greek spirit. Who resurrected this Greek spirit?—the people in the west of China, the Chinese, or the Japanese? My guess is that all these peoples did it. And I think it was resurrected more as it went farther and farther east. In that sense, then, this painting represents the Japanese taste, especially Japanese taste that held a special love for the purity of Buddhist images of the Suiko period.

TRACES OF THE JAPANESE PEOPLE

We found traces of the Japanese people in the wall paintings of Hōryūji! People may think this statement is preposterous. But at the moment, we can find no artifact that can support the opinion of those who think that this is preposterous. Even if a monk like Utchi Issō, active in the west of China, may have painted paintings similar to these wall paintings, it is no more than a guess based on written records.[4] Excavations in the west of China have not unearthed anything that imparts the same mood as these paintings. This can be said about every single item excavated by such explorers as Stein or Le Coq.[5] There is something in the mood of these paintings that is so very different from paintings in the west of China. If that is the case, then, do we not feel compelled to connect this painting to the land and wind in which it was painted? The painter could have been a foreigner who worked in Japan. If it was a foreigner, perhaps he was not accepted in Tang China but found in Japan a place of solace and the sense of fitting in. Japanese eyes were opened by this genius, and the people felt that this painter had captured their hearts. The painter of these works, too, respected the simple heart that loved Buddhist images of Suiko and did his best to oblige himself to that desire. If anyone finds that the *kannon* at Chūgūji is different from the stone statues of Buddha in China's Six Dynasties period (ca. 222–589 CE), he will also have to concede that the elegance these paintings is different from that of Tang dynasty paintings, though these paintings were clearly produced in the early Tang style.

The fact that the mood of an Indian wall paintings changed like this in Japan is related to the idea that, although Japan is far to the east of Greece, Japan is more similar to Greece, far more so than Greece is to Persia, India, China's west, or China proper. The vast continent is so different from the Mediterranean peninsula in terms of climate, land, people, and so on, but Japan and Greece are considerably similar. It is not entirely impossible that a person, whose sentiment was never understood by anyone while migrating through the continent, could come to Japan and find life truly agreeable for the first time. In comparison to the creativity in China and India, Japan's creativity was quite meager. But even while the Japanese effaced themselves and strove to copy masterworks of art, their own particular ethnic personality could not be suppressed. If, for the moment, we assume that the land of Japan is characterized as possessing a sweet, luscious, and lyrical mood filled with a sad melancholy, these things can also be thought of as an innate disposition of the Japanese people. The gentleness of the country's legends as recorded in the *Kojiki* and the mercy and the grief expressed in the *kannon* at Chūgūji are probably manifestations of this national character. There, one always finds quietness and tears. So those tears cast a shadow onto the soul to all sorts of earthly pleasures. Therefore, when sensual paintings from India are filtered through these tears, they change into works with transparent beauty. There we witness the aesthetic consciousness of the Greek, which has finally found its soul brother in the faraway land.

No one will dispute that Hōryūji's *kannon* painting has something in common with the Shō Kannon image at Yakushiji. I would think that these two works were made not too far apart in time. Although only a few artifacts from this period are extant, the art of the Hakuhō period is truly astonishing even on a global scale. If Japanese people produced these works by modeling them after originals from overseas, such as the statue of Amida Buddha and two attendants using the *repoussé* relief technique (now at the Nara National Museum) or the embroidered mandala at Kanshūji (now at the Kyoto National Museum), as advanced by some scholars, the artistic energy of the Japanese at this time is quite impressive.

LARGE WALLS AND SMALL WALLS

Up to this point I have only discussed the Pure Land painting on the west wall of the temple. There are other wall paintings, produced on three other large walls and eight smaller walls.[6] They are all distinctively different from one other. At least four painters were involved in producing these wall paintings, according to one theory, and I agree because I sense at least four different artistic hands in these paintings. I hear that they do not all date to the same historical period.

Particularly beautiful examples among the paintings done on the smaller walls are on the east and south walls at the southeast corner of a walkway, which is reached from the main entrance by veering left.[7] They exude a sense that I think is very human and very Greek, and in terms of these features, these paintings are more vivid and immediate than the Seishi Bosatsu and the *kannon* we discussed earlier. On the south wall, the painting of a figure, which stands with a flower in its hand, is so sensual and strong looking that it could be a painting of an Amazon. The next one is on a small wall on the side of a large west wall.[8] The sitting figure on the left stimulates my interest to no end since it has a melancholic, fine-featured face that appears ethnically Aryan. My first impression when I looked at it was that it somehow conjured up Michelangelo's *Vittoria Colonna*.[9] They do not look alike and I cannot imagine why they are connected in my mind.

Among the large walls, the north wall (on the left side of the north side) has almost completely disintegrated, and the large east wall painting (on the right-hand side) is in terrible shape.[10] The large wall on the north side (the one on the right-hand side) is second best after the Pure Land painting.[11] This painting is composed well and the state of preservation is the best of all of them, but the colors have degraded, which hinders the overall impression. If one looks at details, the bodhisattvas on the left and the celestial being pictured to the right of the canopy are very beautifully done. The placement of various figures, too, is considerably skillful.

ON THE PLATFORM IN THE GOLDEN HALL

A number of Buddhist images line up on the platform of the Golden Hall of Hōryūji, over which that famous canopy hangs from the ceiling. But it is very disconcerting that the canopy seems unrelated to the main image and other Buddhist statues. The four Shitennō statues, each guarding a corner, are sculpted simply and impart a tidy taste. They are very nice. When this hall was first erected, with the Shitennō in the corners and all the images of Buddha on the platform unified as a whole, the interior of the Golden Hall must have been splendid.

THE ALTAR OF LADY TACHIBANA

The most noteworthy item on the platform that requires our attention is the altar of Lady Tachibana. I stood in front of it for a long time, but with the support of Mr. Y., I stepped up to the platform and carefully studied the small paintings produced on the altar's base. The overall construction of the altar seems to date from the Suiko period, and its roof, which resembles a canopy, is almost identical to the canopy in the Golden Hall itself. There is a profusion of linear patterns frequently seen in the art of the Han. The paintings on the base of the altar are not nearly as good as the wall paintings but, in terms of the mood they project, they are much more imbued with the feel of the west of China. The stylistic mixture of these two distinct influences in one object feels very odd to us. This is because the two sentiments expressed there are in stark contrast. On the other hand, when we examine the image of Amida Buddha and its two attendants and the screen behind it, which sits in the altar, we find that the Suiko style and the style from the west of China were very ingeniously integrated, and the resultant masterful blend is, as a matter of fact, astonishing. The face of the main image of worship wears a shy or about-to-cry expression, and the light hitting the face from the front should be blamed for this, but if I were to soften that lighting and adjust the dark and light, the strange smile as well as the thick drooping eyelids give an impression of exquisitely beautiful, merciful, and unaffected charm. The facial features were based on a new artistic style, much like the bodhisattva in Indian style with slender legs and large breasts that is drawn on the panel. Despite this, the overall impression of the image is closer to that of the *kannon* at Chūgūji. The softness one senses in the robe's folds is perhaps halfway between the images of Buddha from the Suiko period and the wall paintings. The attendant images resemble the images of Buddha from the Suiko period, but the soft swelling of the breasts and the way the waists are slightly twisted share a feeling present in the paintings on the altar doors. The mood that the faces of the attendant images project, just as in the main image, is specific to this land. The bodhisattvas carved onto the screen behind the three statues are breathtakingly beautiful, especially the soft modeling of the flesh and the free-flowing treatment of the robes, but here too we can sense an indigenization of a newly arrived artistic style. The fact that this sort of art that is filled with this type of sweet, luscious melancholy and mercy was born in Japan by absorbing artistic styles from the western regions of China is profoundly suggestive when we consider the question of the ethnic character of the Japanese people (*see fig. 18, photo section*).

Although it has not been conclusively shown that this altar was that which belonged to Lady Tachibana, it appears that it is not at all impossible that it once belonged to her, considering the date of production. Lady Tachibana was born during the reign of Emperor Tenji, spent her youthful years during the reign of Emperor Tenmu, became the guardian and educator of young Emperor Monmu during Emperor Jitō's reign, and then gave birth to Empress Kōmyō when Emperor Monmu was on the throne.[12] If this altar was indeed produced during the time of Emperors Tenmu or Jitō, it would be when Lady Tachibana lived in the palace and, if that was the case, the altar may be indicative of her taste when she lived in the palace quarters. The extraordinary softness of the decoration, the intricacy, the extreme loveliness of the three statues, and so forth may have given a religious exultation to the aristocratic ladies of the time. If we were to subscribe to the idea that Empress Kōmyō represented an aspect of the Tenpyō period and Lady Tachibana that of the Hakuhō period, the affection of Lady Tachibana still felt for the altar would provide us a glimpse of the life in the Fujiwara palace.

THE KŌFŪZŌ

We left the Golden Hall and entered the Kōfūzō. The Kōfūzō appeared to be a storehouse, and there we found a variety of statues, paintings, and craft items on display.[11] Well-known among these objects is a **nine-headed *kannon***, produced from wood, and the **Yumechigai Kannon** that was produced in copper. The Yumechigai Kannon is comparable in its beauty to the Kōyakushi Nyorai (National Treasure, missing since Shōwa 18 and 2 feet 6 inches high) at Shin Yakushiji. And, there were any number of beautiful statues of Buddha that compare favorably to those mentioned above. There were also a great number of items, such as silk and cotton fabric and wool blankets, in addition to a variety of utensils and implements, which could make us think of the culture of the old days. If we spent some time studying these objects, I am sure the objects would be an inexhaustible spring of interesting findings. Aspects of our ancestor's lives, which may appear now as a void without any details, would surely be filled by means of a close examination of these objects.

I did not have enough patience for this because I was overwhelmed by the multitude of objects that caught my eyes. By this time I was utterly exhausted to the point of losing all my sensitivity. When we returned to the inn to the south of the Yumedono Hall to take lunch, merely removing my shoes once I sat down on the veranda felt like an arduous task.

Notes

1. *Samadhi* (Jp. *sanmai* or *zanmai*) is a Hindu and Buddhist term that usually denotes a mental state achieved through meditation in which the consciousness of the experiencing subject merges with the experienced object and in which the mind becomes still though the person remains conscious.
2. Watsuji seems to have reversed these two figures. The correct orientation is that Kannon Bosatsu is on the viewer's right side, and has the right arm bent. On the viewer's left is Seishi Bosatsu, which holds a lotus stem in the right hand and has a bent left arm.
3. If one studies the reconstructed composition of this wall painting closely, one can clearly see celestial beings flying about as well as numerous other objects and beings.
4. Utchi Issō (Ch. *Yuchi Yiseng*) was a Tang dynasty painter in China.
5. Albert von Le Coq (1860–1930) was a German explorer of Tibet.
6. These paintings, twelve in all, have been numbered for ease of reference, with number 1 starting with the first painting on a long inside wall on the left-hand side as one enters the inner corridor from the east entrance. Proceeding clockwise around the building from painting 1, one finds number 2 on the east wall; paintings 3 and 4 on the south side, paintings 5, 6, and 7 on the west side, paintings 8 through 11 on the north side, and painting 12 on the east side (just to the right of the east entrance). Some of these paintings were damaged in a fire in 1947 after Watsuji saw them in 1918, and they were later restored to the original prewar "deteriorated condition" in 1967.
7. By this phrase, Watsuji is referring to the painting of Nikkō Bosatsu on the east side (painting number 2) and Kannon Bosatsu on the south side (painting number 3).

---

[11] The Treasures of Hōryūji are now displayed in an orderly manner in the newly built Hōmotsuden.

8. Watsuji is referring to painting number 5 of Gakkō Bosatsu.
9. Vittoria Colonna was a poetess and personal friend of Michelangelo during his last years. He drew her likeness in the 1540s. The drawing is now in the British Museum, London.
10. Watsuji is apparently referring to paintings number 9 and number 1, respectively.
11. Watsuji is referring to painting number 10.
12. The basic dates associated with these emperors are Emperor Tenji (626–671, r. 668–671), Emperor Tenmu (?–686, r. 673–686), Emperor Monmu (683–707, r. 697–707), and Emperor Jitō (645–702, r. 690–697).

Chapter 24

THE YUMEDONO HALL

After lunch we went to the Yumedono Hall. When I entered from the western entrance of the temple compound and saw this beautiful octagonal building built in the Tenpyō period, it looked crowded by the other temple elements and did not have enough space around it to show off its beauty. The plan of the Ikaruga no miya palace, which Prince Shōtoku built, seems to indicate a different location for this Yumedono Hall.[1] But the Lecture Hall, which is called Denpōdō, was a residential building that was moved from Lady Tachibana's residence. When I looked at the Yumedono sitting on the veranda of the Eden, where I could also see the Denpōdō, I could barely keep the entire Yumedono building in view—the buildings are that close together. The feel of this architectural piece was somewhat like a comfortable and quiet residential building and less like a building in a temple complex (*see fig. 19, photo section*).

The impression I received from the Yumedono was one of solemnness. Someone opened the north entrance and we walked into the hall, proceeded up two platforms, and approached an altar situated in the center. We felt all the more somber.

THE SHROUDED STATUE IN THE YUMEDONO HALL

We stood on the left side of the altar. The high doors were opened to the left and right. The long drapes were drawn apart quietly. Then a strong scent of fragrant wood hit our senses of smell; at the same time, that very strange, mysterious, indescribable profile of a *kannon* jumped into view.

As if the *kannon*, shrouded in mystery, were pulling us closer, we stepped up to the drapes and looked up at its face. There in the semidarkness of the altar, because our bodies were blocking the light, we saw a head possessing calm and a strange life energy as if floating in the air. Its eyebrows, eyes, cheeks (especially the cheeks), lips—all come together to form a faint yet at the same time piercing smile that has a strange beauty. It is indeed a mysterious smile, but it is not imbued with melancholy. It is full of love but does not have a bewitching

Indian sensuality (*see fig. 20, photo section*).

The surface of the statue is unusual. The almost undetectable gold paint remaining on the dark brown skin glimmers gently, reflecting the ambient light, and exudes a peculiar sort of life energy as if it came simultaneously from a very elastic live body and a pure immaculate skin that was cleansed of human warmth or smell. I felt this not only from his face but also from the beautifully executed hands and chest.

The belly that sticks out a little bit too noticeably is not entirely satisfactory. It is perhaps because the statue was not meant to be viewed from the side. However, the robe that covers the shoulders and flows leisurely albeit straight down is extraordinary.

FENOLLOSA'S POINT OF VIEW

The amazement that Fenollosa felt when he discovered this strangely beautiful image of this *kannon* is worth memorializing for the study of Japanese ancient art, and not to be forgotten.[2] In the summer of 1884, at the instance of the Japanese government, he visited this temple to study ancient art. He tried to persuade the Hōryūji monks to open the altar. The monks did not easily agree to the request, saying that if such a sacrilege were to be committed, the Buddhist punishment would be swiftly carried out, causing a huge earthquake that would cause temple buildings to come down in no time at all. The only knowledge the monk in charge of the temple had about the statue was that it was reputedly a statue from Paekche dated to the Suiko period and that the altar had not been opened for more than two hundred years. Hence, not only was it an understatement that the statue's artistic value had been ignored, but, for several centuries, not one Japanese had ever laid an eye on the statue. Excited with the prospect of finding a rare treasure, Fenollosa and Kuki Ryūichi, who was accompanying him, persistently tried to persuade the monks to come around to their point of view.[3] After a long process of persuasion, Fenollosa and Kuki prevailed. One of the monks finally took the key and climbed to the top of the center platform. The key that had not been used for several centuries now made contact with the rusty lock, and the clanking noise caused these two men to shiver with anticipation. On the altar, a tall statue stood wrapped in cotton cloth. Dust over the centuries lay accumulated on it. It was not easy to remove the wrapping, all the while being almost overwhelmed by the dust. The cloth that wrapped the statue was later measured to be 1500 feet.[4] "But at last, the final folds of the covering fell away," wrote Fenollosa. He continued,

> . . . and this marvelous statue, unique in the world, came forth to the human sight for the first time in centuries. It was a little taller than life, but hollow at the back, carved most carefully from some hard wood, which had been covered with gilding, now stained to the yellow-brown bronze. The head was ornamented with a wonderful crown of Corean [*sic*]

> openwork gilt bronze, from which hung long streamers of the same materials set with jewels.
>
> But it was the aesthetic wonders of this work that attracted us most. From the front the figure is not quite so noble, but seen in profile it seemed to rise to the height of archaic Greek art. The long lines of drapery, sweeping at the two sides from shoulders to feet, were unbroken in single quiet curves approximating straight lines, giving great height and dignity to the figure. The chest was depressed, the abdomen slightly protruding, the action of the hands, holding between them a jewel or casket of medicine, rendered with vigorous modeling. But the finest feature was the profile view of the head, with its sharp Han nose, its straight clear forehead, and its rather large—almost negroid—lips, on which a quiet mysterious smile played, not unlike Da Vinci's Mona Lisa's. Recalling the archaic stiffness of Egyptian Art at its finest, it appeared still finer in the sharpness and individuality of the cutting. In slimness it was like a Gothic statue from Amiens, but far more peaceful and unified in its single system of lines. Its arrangement of draperies seemed to be based upon the bronze statuette type of Go, but suddenly expanded to unexpected beauty by the addition of such slender proportions.[5] We saw at once that it was the supreme masterpiece of Corean [*sic*] creation, and must have proved a most powerful model to the artists of Suiko, especially to Shotoku [sic]; but all that we have to speak of later.[6]

This discovery of Fenollosa's is something for which we Japanese people should be grateful. But I find myself not necessarily agreeing with all the things he said about it. For instance, I don't think we can or should compare this statue's smile to that of Da Vinci's *Mona Lisa*. Admittedly, these two works both express a type of beauty emanating from within that is built on their physical body. They both wear a profound smile. But in *Mona Lisa*'s smile, we see all human glory and hope as well as all human darkness. The smile of this *kannon*, in contrast, is the purest expression of the realm of freedom obtained at the furthest end of meditation. The Venus that I believe lives underneath *Mona Lisa* was forced into a nunnery by the passion of saints, made into the object of spiritual adoration by the knights, and turned into the queen of the underworld, as an act of defiance, caused by her awareness of the totally uninhibited human nature.[7] The Venus hidden within this *kannon* is no more than an obedient maidservant of mercy. That is the reason why this statue of *kannon* disregards all sensuous carnal beauty and draws the viewer only into the beauty of contemplation.

Mona Lisa was born from the mood of spiritual agitation stemming from fear. This was the time when people saw the naked body of a female Satan excavated from the earth; they shook from the fear of sin and of being burned in hell for seeing the shining beauty of her figure, but still could not look away from her.[8] In contrast, the time when this statue of Yumedono Kannon was created was the time when a simple spiritual desire was born and felt strongly in the heart of a natural people, who were unspoiled by civilization. There, people had no knowledge of the bitter conflict between flesh and spirit. The Buddhism that led these people removed itself from the split of spirit and flesh at its birth and recognized its most supreme moment in the harmony of flesh and spirit, or, in other words, in the aesthetic religious ecstasy and idealized mercy. So this *kannon*, crystallized under these circumstances, possesses no hint of darkness in the background. Nor does it have any hint of a deep, sharp shadow of spirit as if it had been dug up from the bottom of human sentiments. It is merely that it is simple and indescribably mysterious. This sort of difference, I think, marks the difference between Mona Lisa's smile and Yumedono Kannon's smile.

Fenollosa's comparison of this statue to those from Egypt is quite interesting, but they are really far apart from each other, not only, for example, in the way the figures display a sharpness of carving and in the creativity they embody, but also in terms of their mysterious moods. The air of mystery that emanates from Egyptian sculpture is intimately connected with the human sentiment that believes in the immortality of spirit and the resurrection of the flesh. The mysterious air of this *kannon* is far more contemplative and nonhuman.

What is particularly interesting is Fenollosa's comparison of this statue to Gothic statues seen at Amiens Cathedral or the Cathedral of Notre-Dame, Reims.[9] In actuality, they are truly, uncannily similar in that they both express a fresh immaculateness. An academic study of the source of this similarity would be, I would think, quite meaningful. I also think that the inquiry would be a question about the religious sentiments of a young ethnic group that had just absorbed a world religion.

It is premature to categorize this as a statue produced in Korea. I would expect some Korean sculptors worked in Japan around the time when this *kannon* was created. But why is it that we recognize much creativity in Korea but not in Japan? If we speak of extant objects, there are fewer pieces left in Korea than in Japan, and consequently we cannot make exact comparisons. So pushing this statue back to Korea just because we cannot ascertain its origin merely means that we are avoiding the issue. In terms of the relationship to China, Korea and Japan are the same. If we assume that things could change after arriving in Korea, the same could have, of course, happened in Japan. So situating this statue stylistically between the Kudara Kannon and Kuratsukuri no Tori-style images of Buddha or comparing it to the relief work in the Longmen grottoes is perhaps not too far off the target in terms of artistic styles. The elongated face and the way the prominent nose was formed may have had its model in China. But all these elements still do not converge to a conclusion that the statue was not produced in Japan. If a Korean sculptor came to Japan, he surely experienced some sort of change in his disposition from living in Japan. And it is equally possible that a Japanese sculptor who studied in Korea could have made additional changes to the prototype. Although some scholars may think of this statue as a result of the Korea-ization of the artistic style of China's Six Dynasties period, I think it might have been a result of the indigenization of it on Japanese soil. I say this because, regardless of how many ancient Korean statues of Buddha we may study, we have not been able to find an indisputable characteristic to conclude that the Yumedono Kannon was in actuality made in Korea.

THE DENPŌDŌ

We walked through the Eden's corridor with its low ceiling and reached the Denpōdō that was just behind the Eden. There we also saw a large number of statues but, after seeing that Yumedono Kannon, my eyes **hardly rested** on these for more than a moment. As we walked on dusty floorboards, I was reminded of the illustration of a pile of broken Buddhist images in Fenollosa's book. Curious, I looked behind the main image of worship, which was in an area that looked like a corridor, and there, just as in the illustration, were quite a few broken pieces of Buddha sculpture. The sight of heads and arms strewn about in the dust gave me a strange sensation.

THE CHŪGŪJI

We left the temple and proceeded toward the adjacent Chūgūji. We walked to a small building that looked more like a retreat than a temple, and it gave me a feeling appropriate for a nunnery. The main hall of worship, which looked more like a small extension of a building rather than an independent building, was being repaired. Thus the *kannon* had been removed from its altar and it temporarily sat in a sitting room of the nuns' quarters. We sat on our knees on cushions in the adjacent room just as any guest would, and someone opened the sliding doors separating our room and the room of the statue. It was very much like we were being "granted an audience" with the *kannon* (*see fig. 21, photo section*).

This familiar holy woman of ours, the statue, was seated on a makeshift stool in the center of a six-mat room. Behind this statue was a *tokonoma*, and in front of it we could see a lectern for the scriptures, a platform for flower vases, a well-stuffed cushion, and some other items. The right side of the statue was bathed in a light that was softened by the *shōji* screen on the right, and the statue sat there wearing a most divine, tender "smile from her soul." It was no longer a "sculpture" or a "Buddhist sculpture dating from the Suiko period." It was the embodiment of a live, noble, and strong mercy, itself worthy of our getting down on our knees to pray, which would actually answer our prayers. All of us individually felt a personal affection toward this Bodhisattva, and we studied it with hearts of pure adoration.

"Move closer to the Bodhisattva." Very politely the nun spoke words to encourage "the scholars of ancient art" to "study" the subject. On this prompt, we moved into the next six-mat room and approached the statue on our knees. We felt nothing but a great joy in coming so close to the image, which was so alien to the sort of scholarly state of mind that the nun had thought we had.

THE *KANNON* AT CHŪGŪJI

That lustrous black surface on the statue is truly mysterious. I would think the mystery arises from this surface. Though the statue is made of wood, the surface imparts a sense of strength like copper. The luster of the wood skillfully brings out the delicate modeling and undulation of the surface. Because of this, the facial expression, for instance, appears delicate and gentle. The eyes that look as if they had closed because of a rapture actually seem to swell and glisten with tears of deep and tender love. And this luster of the skin is probably responsible for the impression we receive, especially around those faintly smiling lips, as if she actually flashed this expression of affection just a moment earlier. The beauty of her ever-so-tender cheeks, the beautifully shaped and enrapturing hand that touches the right cheek, the immaculate tenderness of the upper arms and shoulders—none of these could be achieved without the luster of the surface. If a photographer were to give it a fixed lighting source, not use any lighting at all, or exaggerate it somehow, the photograph still could not possibly transmit the true sense of this statue.

The reason why the luster of the surface can play such a spiritually active role is that the modeling of the statue is superbly executed. In that sense, this statue is very distinct from the Kudara Kannon. Just like a sculpture dating from the Hakuhō period, this statue is in fact modeled very naturalistically. One can sense this most in how the face, arms, and knees were modeled and it is most prominent at the place where the statue is connected to its base. The dais which supports the weight of the statue and the way the garment drapes down both exhibit extraordinary intricacy.

We just sat and studied the statue, enraptured. It was as if my soul at its deepest depth was crying uncontrollably, solemnly, and quietly. It was as if a cup were filled to the brim with mercy and sadness. It was a beauty that was most supreme and a divine beauty to which the word "beautiful" simply could not do justice.

JAPANESE CHARACTER

I do not know whether this statue should properly be classified as a *kannon* bodhisattva or a bodhisattva maitreya (Miroku Bosatsu), but whichever the case, the most pronounced impression one receives from this image is that of a saintly woman. But this is not a saintly mother. True, images of Mary, who is at once a mother and a virgin, seem to sublimate "woman" and make it pure and transparent by crystallizing both a mother's mercy and the purity of a virgin. In Gothic architecture, however, Mary is sometimes depicted as a mother. In Renaissance painting, she is depicted with her feminine characteristics emphasized. Accordingly, the image of Mary sometimes shows her majesty as the mother of the Savior and at other times the sublimated beauty of Venus. But this bosatsu is decidedly not a mother of a human being or of a deity. Its innocent naïveté is that of a virgin, certainly. Yet the face that seems to express such a complex range of emotions cannot be that of a "virgin" who is ignorant of human emotions. But then it is definitely not a "woman" in any sense of the word. Venus, however purified and sublimated, cannot be like this saintly woman. But the bodhisattva still retains a type of femininity. That is, she exhibits tenderness only a feminine shape can express. What is she then? She is the avatar of mercy. The desire for mercy in the recess of every human soul has been crystallized in the form of a human being.

Though I have only meager knowledge on this subject, I think this bodhisattva is a unique, peerless statue as an expression of affection and compassion in world art. Objects with more vigor, more majesty, more depth, more total intoxication, or more passion are probably not rare in the world, but I contend that this symbol of pure compassion and sadness is unique in the world because of its unclouded purity and its thoroughgoing softness. Let us for a moment suppose that a luscious and idyllic sentiment that is also thoroughly steeped in melancholy reflects the disposition of the Japanese; then we can say that this statue is a manifestation of the Japanese disposition. From the poems of the *Kojiki* to the love suicides of *jōruri* from the *bunraku* puppet theater, the art of the Japanese, with *mono no aware* (sadness toward all living things) and a gentle, quiet affection at its core, can be said to be the most supreme and unambiguous representative of the characteristics in this statue. Even if we admit that the gentleness of *ukiyoe* that intoxicates people and the sadness of Japanese music that melts people's hearts both embody a tinge of decadence, the undercurrent of these movements is unequivocally identical to the desire expressed in that *kannon*. From the religious movements of Hōnen and Shinran to the salacious novels produced during the Heian period—all share the same basic tonality that arises from that desire and the tender sentiment that flows from it. What we must reflect on now is how much of this was developed over time. Even if great things were produced as inspirations in the past, they may not have turned into major influential currents. I wonder, therefore, if our culture merely changed, rather than developed, or in other words, if our culture had variations without development. The wholesale lack of effort to make something more profound is quite noticeable among the Japanese people I come across daily. We can also say that this tendency is evident throughout history.Here, we can also detect a weakness inherent in this national disposition.

If we were to regard this statue as evidence of a Japanese disposition, we must also elucidate that of the Koreans. Two masterpieces, useful in examining this idea, now exist in a museum in Seoul. One resembles a slender Miroku Bosatsu now in the Kōryūji in Uzumasa, Kyoto. The other looks very much like Nyoirin Kannon at Kanshinji, Osaka. Both of these are the premier examples among all remaining objects in Korea. They are very similar to their Japanese counterparts, so much so that we cannot but recognize a stylistic similarity. But the feeling they project is distinct. And this distinction is also recognizable in Tenpyō art. Tang influence is already noticeable in these pieces, but I would also like to find the most indisputable example of Tang influence in Tenpyō art that is the greatest and most profound. As I've discussed, we have already recognized Japanese indigenization in the wall paintings of Hōryūji. That case can be said to be evidence of art from the west of China changing to the cultural mood embodied in the *kannon* at Chūgūji. Then is it not possible to say that trace evidence for this sort of change is more prominent at the peak of Tenpyō art? In architecture, I think I can say that the Sangatsudō and the Tōshōdaiji are veiled in that mood, but we cannot be sure of the accuracy of this statement since no Tang counterparts exist. In sculpture, the Eleven-headed Kannon of the Shōrinji and the Bonten (*Brahma*) guardian statue in the Sangatsudō at Tōdaiji both have the grandeur typical of the Tenpyō period as well as a delicacy and softness not seen in comparable Tang objects. I wonder if that characteristic changed its shape and began moving from within and added a different flavor, as it were, to Tang-style art.

The melancholic and noble seated *kannon* at Chūgūji signifies the starting point of our culture, if we look at the cultural context in this way. Poems in the *Kojiki* were not much older than this statue. And it was not even one hundred years later that these poems were actually written down. If Prince Shōtoku's culture congealed to form this statue, then he should be regarded as the first greatest person in Japanese history. The fact is that the Prince died a most beautiful death, a love death, where his wife died with the prince or, in other words, I might say, the death of the prince was closely followed by her death in a most natural way.[10] If we were to make a guess from their deaths, they believed in the unity of souls, realized this unity, and lived a life of quiet mutual affection. And because of the lives they led, their deaths resulted in the Chūgūji *kannon*. It wasn't a mere coincidence that the Constitution for which the Prince is now said to be responsible was very humanistic.

The seedbed that produced these first manifestations of culture was none other than the tender nature of our island country. It is lovely, easy to feel comfortable in, elegant, and yet it possesses an unfathomable mystery just like any other natural environment. This environment, if we were to represent it in human form must be that of a *kannon*—that *kannon* at Chūgūji. The sweet, luscious taste of taking in nature and being intoxicated by it is, I would argue, an undercurrent that runs through Japanese culture. The root of it, just as we saw in the case of the Chūgūji *kannon*, is the natural environment of this country. Take, for example, the delicate love for nature where we are keenly sensitive to the beauty of a drop of dew at the tip of a leaf, the tender embrace of nature where a man communes and becomes one with nature as he travels with nothing but the bare essentials, the intoxication we feel from each and every and very specialized sense, and the religious ecstasy from a playful heart—all these may seem to have nothing in common with this *kannon*. They are, however, very similar; the only minor difference is in where our attention is directed. The objects captured by that attention are varied but, underneath, the sentiments used while capturing them are nearly identical. The mother of this particular beauty of this land of ours gave her offspring the same beauty. That is, any examination of our culture must in the end be based on the examination of our natural environment.

AFTER CHŪGŪJI

When I last visited Chūgūji, I came across a nun who I thought was a perfect steward of this *kannon*. She appeared to be perhaps eighteen or nineteen, with light complexioned skin, and was sensitive, and well mannered. The small child I was with was curious and looking into the altar where the *kannon* sat. The nun studied her for a good while and then said, in a beautiful voice, "The *kannon* is certainly very black, isn't she?" We exchanged smiles, too. I thought then I had never met anyone as pleasant as this young nun. I was hoping by chance that I would come across this nun today, but disappointingly, we never caught a glimpse of her before we took our leave. It was as if the day did not end on a perfect high note.

After we finished with Chūgūji, we then walked to nearby Hōrinji. The pastoral beauty of a quiet farming village, the pond with brasenias flowering, the gently rolling hills in the distance—all was just perfect. The ancient tower of Hōrinji and the image of the Buddha with large eyes were also exquisitely pleasurable to see. I also enjoyed looking at the time-worn temple complex of Hōrinji itself, dilapidated and crumbling in places. I noticed that the bell tower had been appropriated to store a pile of rice straw bales. I also noticed that in the shade of a tree behind the main hall of worship, they'd put out a weaving machine on a straw mat.

Notes

1. This octagonal hall, built in 639, is the only remaining building of the palace. Prince Shōtoku built the palace in 601, but the palace complex was lost to a fire in 643. On this palace site, Hōryūji was built, incorporating the Yumedono Hall into the temple plan.
2. Ernest Fenollosa (1853–1908) was an American philosopher and art historian, who came to Japan as a hired foreigner (*oyatoi gaijin*) at the invitation of the Meiji government.
3. Kuki Ryūichi (1850–1931) was a high-ranking Ministry of Education official who was very influential in art policies, especially as they related to preserving old art.
4. Watsuji's original text describes the cloth as being "one hundred and fifty *jō*" long. As of Meiji 24, 33 *jō* equaled 100 meters, or one *jō* 3.03 m. According to Ernest Fenollosa, ". . . some 500 yards of cloth having been used . . ." Ernest F. Fenollosa, *Epochs of Chinese and Japanese Art* (New York, Tokyo, Osaka, and London: ICG Muse Inc., 2000), 50.
5. In Fenollosa's passage, "Go" refers to the Wu Kingdom (222–280 CE).
6. Fenollosa, *Epochs of Japanese and Japanese Art*, 50–51.
7. Watsuji is referring to the Tannhäuser legend; see Chapter 1, endnote 9. The source of his reference to Venus (Aphrodite) becoming the queen of the underworld is unclear.

8. The female Satan Watsuji refers to is likely an excavated statue of Venus in Greece (e.g., Venus of Milo).
9. The Amiens Cathedral is a thirteenth century Gothic church.
10. According to one account, the wife died a day before the prince.

INDEX

H

L

O

P

R

T

U

V

W

About the Author

Watsuji Tetsurō (1889-1960) was born as a son of a medical doctor in the prefecture of Hyōgo, Japan in 1889. After finishing the First Higher School and the Tokyo Imperial University with a degree in philosophy (under the tutelage of Raphael von Koeber), he taught ethics at the Kyoto Imperial University beginning in 1925. In 1935, he returned to Tokyo to teach at his alma mater until his retirement in 1949. He died in 1960. During his lifetime, Watsuji wrote groundbreaking work on Nietzsche, Kierkegaard, Schopenhauer, as well as a number of important books on Japanese cultural history, religion, and ethics. His prewar work is considered to be very influential in forming the emperor-centric ideology.

Watsuji became Japan's major philosopher and cultural historian. He lived during Japan's maturing years as a nation and contributed to its intellectual growth in a significant way. Watsuji's thought and its intellectual impact on Japan's intellectual development during the Taishō and Shōwa eras (including the postwar years) are often mentioned alongside with those of Nishida Kitarō and Tanabe Hajime, who formed the core of the Kyoto School of philosophers. He was only loosely affiliated with that philosophical school, but Watsuji was nonetheless one of the most influential architects of interwar nationalist ideology. Like other philosophical figures in Japan at this time, Watsuji struggled profoundly with finding a rightful place for Japanese culture in the world, especially with regard to Japanese art, aesthetics, religion, and ethical behavior. Watsuji also sought an intellectually satisfying and justifiable amalgamation of Japanese values and Western thoughts.

About the Translator

Hiroshi Nara is professor and chair of the Department of East Asian Languages and Literatures at the University of Pittsburgh. He works in Japanese linguistics and interwar Japanese intellectual history. His best-known work is *The Structure of Detachment* (Hawaii, 2004), which includes an English translation of *The Structure of 'Iki'*.